Objects and Objections of Ethnography

Objects and Objections of Ethnography

James T. Siegel

FORDHAM UNIVERSITY PRESS

NEW YORK 2011

BRESCIA UNIVERSITY
COLLEGE LIBRARY

A NOTE ON THE COVER

Neil Hertz took the extraordinary photo on the cover of the
paperback edition of this book. The picture leads the viewer from
one point to another, to reflections one does not expect. And this
without an attempt at synthesis—which, however, might occur
anyway. I would like to think it is appropriate to what follows after
it. In any case, the photographer appears in various of these essays
as a writer. I thank him warmly.

Copyright © 2011 Fordham University Press

All rights reserved. No part of this publication may be reproduced,
stored in a retrieval system, or transmitted in any form or by any
means—electronic, mechanical, photocopy, recording, or any
other—except for brief quotations in printed reviews, without the
prior permission of the publisher.

Fordham University Press has no responsibility for the persistence
or accuracy of URLs for external or third-party Internet websites
referred to in this publication and does not guarantee that any
content on such websites is, or will remain, accurate or appropriate.

Fordham University Press also publishes its books in a variety of
electronic formats. Some content that appears in print may not be
available in electronic books.

Library of Congress Cataloging-in-Publication Data

Siegel, James T., 1937–
    Objects and objections of ethnography / James T. Siegel.
      p.   cm.
    Includes bibliographical references.
    ISBN 978-0-8232-3274-1 (cloth : alk. paper)
    ISBN 978-0-8232-3275-8 (pbk. : alk. paper)
    ISBN 978-0-8232-3276-5 (ebook)
      1. Ethnology—Philosophy.   2. Ethnology—Field work.
3. Material culture.   4. Ethnology—Indonesia.   5. Indonesia—
Social life and customs.   I. Title.
GN345.S557   2011
305.8—dc22

                                             2010041134

Printed in the United States of America
13 12 11   5 4 3 2 1
First edition

CONTENTS

Objects and Objections of Ethnography

INVITATION

Undang:: "A call to be present" (Indonesian)
Invite 2. To incite (English)

When I began my first work as an anthropologist, I was lost but I did not know it. Living in Sumatra, I learned the national language and the local language; I established myself and my wife in a beautiful wooden house set on stilts in a shady village in the midst of rice fields. All this far away from everything. At that time, in 1962, this was the best anthropological practice. I had a thesis to write. I thought I was doing what was expected of me. In fact, I was merely waiting for something to happen. In the course of two years, enough did happen for me to write a thesis.. What I learned from that, however, was that my own passivity and bewilderment might, in the end, meet the expectations of others, but precisely in so doing it seemed to me that I had not pursed the aim of anthropology as I understood it vigorously enough. I should have tried harder to find something outside of expectations, as I naively put it to myself. I had not made enough of bewilderment; I had merely let it resolve itself..

The next time I had a chance, I returned to Indonesia, but to Java rather than Sumatra. I had nothing to lose, at that point, by remaining bewildered. I wanted to become actively confused rather than passively so (something easier to do than one might imagine) in order to wander away from what I had been taught. To learn Javanese I had to stop speaking Indonesian, the national language, or I would make no progress. This made me more or less mute. But it left me open to look. There is much to see in Java, and it seemed to be offered to me. I thought I should take advantage of it. There seemed to me to be numerous invitations. Most of them were, in fact, beyond my expectations. I did not know where they might take me. I decided never to refuse an invitation, even when it led me to places I did not like. In fact, I thought to myself, I should learn to like what I dislike. I could, if not decompose myself, at least in that way put "myself" aside. Here, I thought, was the way to find bewilderment. All the more so since initially, at least, it evaded the need to speak. I could be present, fulfill the invitation, but without mobilizing "myself." Who, exactly, was invited by such invitations was never clear.

Liking what I disliked, or what at least I did not like, might be a simple reversal and thus not take me as far away from myself as I had hoped. This way of thinking (or not thinking) seemed to have reached its limit after some years of practice. I was not so sure, however, when, in 2007, I returned to the Indonesian province where I had worked in the 1960s. It was here that the tsunami struck hardest. On a wall in the city of Meulaboh, my two companions and I came across a mural. It showed an arch on which was written "Weel Come to Tsunami Area," in a sort of English. It pictured aid arriving in planes and helicopters and trucks. Lined up on the shore was the welcoming committee, waving to whomever might see the mural. Amongst them, full committee members, it seemed, were hollow figures, mere outlines, apparently representing the victims of the disaster. The dead were amongst those who welcomed us. I thought, "Such an invitation goes further than I imagined." Welcomed by the dead, I could, finally (if I can use that word), be beyond myself.

The essays that follow show the results of this enterprise I have undertaken for some time now. The "objects" of anthropology have revealed themselves through the following of invitations rather than out of the aims and methods of my discipline as they have been codified. But these objects remain within the original aims of anthropology, which developed in Europe out of self-doubt brought on by interest in the other. The objections are not at all to ethnography as such but to the reformulation of the notion of differences on which ethnography depends. I set these out in the last piece. Other essays describe places where I found myself but was without special knowledge of the place. Following these are two essays concerning Aceh, the first of the Indonesian places I have studied, though they derive from recent work there. Neither the last essay nor one of the pieces on Aceh has been previously published. The other essays come either from the journal *Indonesia* or from *Diacritics*. For details, see "Original Publication" at the end of this book.

ONE

Georg Simmel Reappears: "The Aesthetic Significance of the Face"

Michael Landmann, the editor of Georg Simmel's collected works, tells this anecdote about him. Simmel had submitted a piece called "Psychological and Ethnological Studies on Music" as his doctoral dissertation. His examining committee refused to accept it. As the American translator of the piece retells Landmann's anecdote, they

> instead granted the degree for a previously written distinguished study on Kant's monadology. While Zupitza [the committee's chair] would have been willing to accept this study on music, if it were first "cleared of the numerous misspellings and stylistic errors," Helmholtz was more skeptical: "Regardless of my other reservations, Simmel is entirely too confident in his conclusions. And the manner in which he presented the faculty with this piece which is so full of misspellings and stylistic superficialities, which evidently was not proofread, in which sentences which are cited from foreign languages can hardly be deciphered, does not attest to a great deal of reliability. Insofar, however, as he has quite a few illustrious predecessors for what he evidently takes to be the method or lack of

method of scientific study, he may let them serve as some kind of personal excuse. I, however, believe that we will be doing him a greater service if we do not encourage him further in this direction."[1]

It seems it is Simmel's fate to be dismissed yet still to be recognized, if not for the work at hand, for something else. Donald Levine, for instance, notes that in Talcott Parsons's attempt to recuperate German and French sociology for the English-speaking world, there is no mention of Simmel. He says further that his studies of art "are not well known by art historians and critics," just as his work in the philosophy of history is ignored by historians. Simmel died in 1919, but there are still recurrent "discoveries" of Simmel, as witnessed by the sporadic bursts of translations into English. *The Philosophy of Money*, for instance, published in 1900, was not translated into English until 1978, the famous essay "The Stranger" in 1950, and so on.[2] Just as Simmel left no students who worked in the way he did and no school of sociology, the revivals of Simmel, which usually are marked by a sense of anticipation ("now we will not only learn something; we will carry it forward"), tend to die away without leaving important (or at least recognizable) effects.

It is difficult to quote Simmel and to carry on his work through the usual modifications of something already in place. There is, instead, the attempt to present him "nonetheless." Thus Donald Levine, to whom the English-speaking world is much indebted for his translations and presentations of Simmel, says: "The presentation of a coherent account of the whole of Simmel's social thought is complicated by the fact that coherence is generally not considered to be one of the hallmarks of Simmel's writing."[3] Levine writes this sentence in a piece he entitles "The Structure of Simmel's Social Thought." There have indeed been a number of attempts to say what it is that Simmel was trying to do, as though readers had decided that Simmel is unclear but that "nonetheless" we can discern something of great value, just as his thesis committee, in refusing his dissertation, decided "nonetheless" that another piece would do. If Simmel did not deserve a degree for a piece on the ethnology and psychology of music, surely he deserved it for a work on Kant's monadology. It seems to be Simmel's talent to divert interest from whatever he is saying to something else—and always to something of interest and importance. Hence the fact that his influence is much greater than appears from the relative lack of citations to him and the absence not merely of a school of scholarship but of a style of writing traceable to him. His influence disappears at the moment it is most strongly felt. And just when he seems to be out of sight, forgotten, or used up, he reappears.[4]

Max Weber gives us, if not an explanation, perhaps an illustration of the effect of Simmel. He began a critical assessment of him, which he never finished out of fear that it would prevent Simmel from finding an appointment in a German university. It starts this way:

> In evaluating the work of Georg Simmel one's responses prove to be highly contradictory. On the one hand, one is bound to react to Simmel's works from a point of view that is overwhelmingly antagonistic. . . . Crucial aspects of his methodology are unacceptable. His substantive results must with unusual frequency be regarded with reservations, and not seldom they must be rejected outright. In addition, his mode of exposition strikes one at times as strange, and often it is at the very least uncongenial.
>
> On the other hand, one finds oneself absolutely compelled to affirm that this mode of exposition is simply brilliant and, what is more important, attains results that are intrinsic to it and not to be attained by any imitator. Indeed, nearly every one of his works abounds in important new theoretical ideas and the most subtle observations.[5]

It is, of course, a question how work whose methodology is suspect can at the same time be said to be brilliant and to "attain results . . . intrinsic to it." It is not a question of separating out the fallacious and using the remainder. It is rather that Simmel somehow stimulates thinking even when he is wrong. Weber uses the verb *stimulate* several times and insists that it applies to the false as well as the true. Simmel's books, Weber says, belong to a special category, one that includes fallacious arguments that help people to think. "Simmel," according to Weber, "even when he is on the wrong path, fully deserves his reputation as one of the foremost of thinkers, a first rate stimulator of academic youth and academic colleagues."[6]

In my own experience, I turn to Simmel not for explanation but because, when I don't know what to make of something, I think that Simmel must already have thought about it. "Simmel" comes to designate a set of readings one turns to for their capacity to suggest. Once the suggestions have been made, it is difficult to see how one actually uses them. Simmel is the sociologist of modernity (though maybe that is true of all sociologists). Modernity today is not modernity then. "Nonetheless," what Simmel says about a subject has set me thinking, even if he has led me to conclusions that he might well disagree with were he given a chance. How, indeed, one can be misled into a right conclusion, which means led to a conclusion where one disagrees with whomever one has been led by, is the subject of this piece. Perhaps it is just for his capacity to mislead us to a point where we want to go that Simmel drops out of sight—not to say, "is forgotten"—so often.

If the traces of Simmel disappear as his influence is felt, it is unlikely that one could reconstruct them from the final text. I am obliged, therefore, to give an example from my experience and to tell you about rethinking "The Aesthetic Significance of the Face" and how it led me to leave Simmel behind, all the while being heavily in his debt.[7] I read many of Simmel's essays in the 1960s. I often thought about them and occasionally reread them. The translation of *The Philosophy of Money* into English was the occasion for me to give a seminar on the book in the early 1980s, on the first occasion with the critic Richard Klein. Aside from that, Simmel disappeared for me until I arrived in Japan in 1997. Then, lacking Japanese and relying all the more on what I could see, I noticed a discrepancy between the representation of faces in Japan and the appearance of Japanese facial expressions in actual life. I thought of Simmel's essay "The Aesthetic Significance of the Face."

I had seen billboards in the Tokyo subway, ads that announced "Mr. D," with the face of a middle-aged man, apparently Japanese, wearing an expression of confident satisfaction that I had seen in America not only in advertisements but also in life. In my five months in Tokyo, on the contrary, I had never seen a Japanese with this expression on his face. I began to look for other examples both of representations of the face that never appeared in life and of facial expressions that seemed to be imported from elsewhere. I found the first in Japanese art. The second I found while watching television, most notably baseball, but also on variety shows. Broadcasts of baseball games in Japan have a rhetorical form different from those in America. In Japan, after each significant action, the camera turns to the manager. He is calm, assured, waiting with confidence to see what will happen next. It is perhaps the face of a benevolent father, judging but forgiving. But it is quintessentially the face of the American baseball manager, at least in part. The Japanese managers I saw on television did not change their expressions; this is not usually the case in America. Japanese managers had taken one expression from the repertoire of American baseball facial expressions without the others and, holding onto it, impressed on me a sense of dejà vu.

The manager's expression is imported, as indeed are many gestures of the players. This, I thought, was possible because, unless there are serious disruptions of the game—as when, for instance, a pitcher hits a batter with a wild ball—no one in baseball bows. The defining gesture of Japanese hierarchy is absent. The constant return to the face of the manager assures viewers that hierarchical authority is nonetheless present. An expression of benevolent shrewdness is called for, and the American repertoire offers one in the absence of a Japanese version.

However, even if one can say that the usual gestures that govern social interaction do not apply, leaving open the possibility of using expressions that otherwise would have no place, it is still difficult to know how facial expressions can be translated from one culture to another. Ordinarily these are taken as the display of interior states and a means of supplementing the communication that occurs through language. To transfer a facial expression implies that one adds something to the repertory available, a little like borrowing a word from a foreign language. But it also raises the question of whether, as in the case of the word, the expression is given sense. Is it inhabited by its wearer, as it were? Does it, in other words, express the sentiments that I, for one, seemed to think it did or, for that matter, any sentiments at all? And if so, how can one explain the circumstances in which facial expressions might be more than part of a cultural storehouse? How can they become expressions of the individual, as Simmel might well have put it?

We learn our facial expressions through imitation, mainly without the awareness that we are doing so. They are confirmed for us by the response that they elicit. Simmel, in his essay on the face, says, "Aesthetically, there is no other part of the body whose wholeness can as easily be destroyed by the disfigurement of only one of its elements"(276). To take on a new facial expression always risks disrupting the "absolute unity of the meaning" the human face displays. To take on a foreign expression, taken out of the context of the back and forth of the immediate exchange of looks, means one might appear to lack such unity. In effect, one risks appearing deranged. Yet the American expression is worn by a Japanese and given the place of authority.

I turned back to Simmel on the "aesthetic significance of the face." Simmel, typically enough for him, notices something no one else had, something that is, at first, quite ordinary. "The human face is of unique importance in the fine arts" (276). He then asks a question no one else had ever posed, at least to my knowledge: "What is it about the human face that makes this possible?" (276). He adds another question alongside this one: "Does the face have certain intrinsic aesthetic qualities that account for its significance as a subject in art?" (276).

His answer to the latter question is yes. He delineates what one might call the reason that the face is able to signify as no other part of the body can. In asking why the face appears as the preferred subject of the fine arts, Simmel in effect asks why the face is the preeminent human site of signification, because in his essay it is for that reason that it is so often depicted in art. He speaks of the "aesthetics" of the face even apart from painting, in life. The face has a certain unity not only that other parts of the body lack but that cannot be found anywhere else in the "perceptible world": "Within the perceptible world, there is no other structure like the human face which merges such a great variety of shapes and surfaces into an absolute unity of meaning" (277). What connects the parts of the face is, on the one hand, their physical setting, the fact that facial features are manifold and set near one another, and, on the other hand, the "soul" (the word in German is *Seele*, and it is sometimes translated "psyche"): "the soul, lying behind the features of the face and yet visible in them, is the interaction, the reference of one to the other, of these separate features" (277). The soul is "visible" in the face; it furnishes the assumption of the linkage of its features. Simmel furnishes several clues as to why such unity exists and why, then, the face makes soul visible. There is first his assumption of the aesthetic. The face is an aesthetic structure from the beginning. "For aesthetic effect, a form must embrace its parts and hold them together. Any stretching and spreading of its extremities is ugly because it interrupts and weakens their connection with the center of the phenomenon; that is, it weakens the perceivable domination of the mind over the circumference of our being" (277). Simmel's phenomenology ends in the revelation of the mind's control over the boundaries of being. It is an aesthetic problem from the beginning. The ugliness of certain gestures is not a question of taste. It is, rather, that the aesthetic determines whether one thinks that there is or is not control of the face. "The large gestures of baroque figures, whose limbs appear to be in danger of breaking off, are repugnant because they disavow what is properly human—the absolute encompassment of each detail by the power of the central ego" (277). One might read this as thinking that the gestures of the baroque cannot go beyond certain limits. Should they do so, the result is a representation of something inhuman. Simmel slides between art and life throughout the essay. Should one exceed the limits of facial gesture, as when one gapes or stares, there is an "indication" of—"'the loss of senses,' the spiritual paralysis, the momentary absence of spiritual control" (278).

Shifting between artistic representations and actual gestures raises the question of Simmel's aesthetics. We know well that, in certain cultures, gaping and staring are part of the cultural repertoire; they are not indications of loss of control by the ego. Simmel, whose examples refer to Western representation, though he names no particular artists, here imposes a particular aesthetic content.

But his category of the aesthetic is larger and more general. The aesthetics of the face refers to more than painting and sculpture. It governs the use of the face itself. The "properly human," the person-centered control of facial features, is made known aesthetically. The Kantian aesthetic—and Kant, along with Schopenhauer, is the philosopher to whom Simmel is closest—is marked by its divorce from usefulness. It is not that the face, from this perspective, signals particular meanings, but that it is, first of all, merely pleasing. When it is so, when it has an aesthetic character, one assumes there is something that controls the unity that Simmel asserts is at the basis of its aesthetic quality. The "soul" and the "ego" are inferred from the aesthetic, whether in painting or in actuality.

Certain facial gestures, which stretch the "circumference" of being, put one outside the "properly human." But this movement is characteristic of modern life, according to Simmel. In his famous essay "The Conflict in Modern Culture,"[8] he explains how it is that life in modern times continually exceeds its forms. "Life" in that sense is larger than the "properly human" as it is defined in particular times and places.

Simmel's aesthetic analyses indeed often revolve around a notion of symmetry. "In the symmetrical structure, either of the two parts can be inferred from the other and each points toward a higher principle which governs them both. In all situations, rationalism strives for symmetry."[9] Symmetry, the expression of rationality, is "anti-individualistic." On the one hand, the face is inherently symmetrical. The manipulation of its symmetry and, indeed, its unity is at the heart of its capacity to convey impressions. The features of the face are integrated with each other. Only a slight change of position causes "the impression of intense modifications."

These changes are, it seems, largely within the bounds of established form. But the face, as Simmel presents it, impresses one as having a fragile stability. The very sensitivity of the face to slight changes invokes, for Simmel, the "ideal of conservation of energy," which implies that there is much more energy to be used than is normally in use and, further, that one sees in the face an explosive power precisely in the refined quality of facial expressions. The less motion it takes to alter facial expression, the more power is left to break through forms. The breaking of form is inherent in the logic of the face; the very aesthetic character of the face carries with it the implication—and the actuality—of disruption as the behind of the face becomes not only a location of control but a repository of energy.

Up to this point, Simmel explains how the face, considered as an aesthetic object, operates. He gives us something like the rhetorical basis or the technology of the face. The face, as an aesthetic object, is unified and gives the impression of something behind it responsible for its unity. Beyond its unity, however—or, in my estimation, before it—there is another factor, which makes one think that the face is the site "of the veiling and unveiling of the soul." Veiling and unveiling are, above all, an effect of the painted eye. The eye is different from other facial features. It is, says Simmel, important not only because of its relation to the totality of facial characteristics but because of "the importance of the gaze of the persons portrayed in interpreting and structuring the space in the picture itself" (281). What the painted gaze takes in affects the way a viewer interprets the space of a painting. It is, again, a formal characteristic of the eye that allows this structuring. As I understand Simmel's remark, it does not matter, for instance, whose gaze it is in the painting insofar as the gaze affects spatial structure. The eye sees appearances before they are subject to interpretation. The eye, he says:

> accomplishes its finest, purely formal end as the interpreter of mere appearance, which knows no going back to any pure intellectuality behind the appearance. It is precisely this achievement with which the eye, like the face generally, gives us the intimation, indeed the guarantee, that the artistic problems of pure perception and of the pure, sensory image of things—if perfectly solved—would

lead to the solution of those other problems which involve soul and appearance. Appearance would then become the veiling and unveiling of the soul. (281)

It is precisely because the eye sees only appearances and does not refer "behind" itself that appearance, says Simmel, leads to the veiling and unveiling of the soul.

The eye in painting "sees" only appearances. By contrast, our experience of vision in life makes it difficult to separate what we see from a synthesis, if not of interpretation, at least of contextualization and of elementary sense. But the eye in painting has a formal role. It merely sees appearances: "the eye penetrates, it withdraws, it circles a room, it wanders, it reaches as though behind the wanted object and pulls it toward itself" (281). The eye structures painted space by registering what there is to register in the painting. It divorces this registration from interpretation, making no reference beyond or "behind" appearances. Appearances are thus left in a merely formal relation to one another. This, as I read these sentences, at least, forms the painting's space.

In life we cannot see as the painted eye "sees." We imbue what we see with significance. But we see the possibility of such seeing through looking at the painted eye. This eye is not the eye of the other, which sees us, reflects us back to ourselves, and causes us to see in the other something behind his gaze. No matter whose eye it is said to be, it is still the painted eye, and as such it is an element of the painting. The painted eye "sees," but it sees only formally. In painting we see the eye registering what we cannot register simply because it sees purely. It is a formal attribute of painting and a self-reflection of form at the same time.

In life we cannot see pure appearance, but when we are shown it through the structure of painting and the use of the represented gaze, the difference between our seeing and the formal gaze impresses itself on us. To see as the eye in the painting sees, we would have to see only with the retina. We would have to clear our eyes—and our minds—of any attempt to synthesize our impressions. We cannot do this, and so we learn that something does not register with us that nonetheless registers on the painted eye. We see that we see without registering what we have looked at, part of what is seen being lost in synthesis. We are blind, but at the moment of our blindness comes our unveiling.

We cannot see pure form; our capacity to synthesize is a source of blindness. But if we were to see pure form, were we to so perceive, we would live in another world, not human. We could imagine we would be overwhelmed by the number of our impressions. But even if we were not, we would not be in the social world, our impressions never leading us to distinguish humans from tables, for instance. And we would have no control of our eyes as they took in everything there is to see. It is in the rejection of the painted gaze and our own that we appropriate our facial expressions, choosing to be endowed with control of them, endowed with soul, at the expense of a more powerful vision, which in its autonomy is too powerful.

Such a thought leads us to think what the face might be. The hand is the site of signification in certain Japanese art—in sculptures of the Buddha, for instance, who surpassed desire. His face, suggesting this lack of impulse in its perfect symmetry, signifies nothing. His face is complete because he lacks the desire to signify. "I have told you everything," the Buddha said. "There is no secret." When signification is necessary nonetheless, the hands signal, while the symmetry of the face rests undisturbed. The Buddha's wrists are often held at an angle to his arm that is difficult for even the most supple joint. The Buddha's hands nonetheless articulate. But the controlling center of this articulation is in question. His hands are not controlled by the Buddha's personality, located conventionally in the body—the head, the heart, the liver, and so forth. They refer "elsewhere," as the disjunction between head and hands indicates.

In some figures, the Buddha's eyes are mobile. They seem, however, disconnected from any expressive possibility. Because of the immobility of the rest of his face, his eyes are not connected to a center of intelligence marked, imaginatively of course, by the intersection of two lines receding behind the eyes. The Buddha's eyes thus seem separate from his face, as though they were organs added from another creature, which continues to control them in the same manner as his hands. His eyes are incapable of both the structuring function they have in some paintings and the disruption necessary for it to be the site of veiling and unveiling. And when his eyes appear, they do not organize the space of representation.

The face becomes the face, the perimeter of being, once it is the site of veiling and unveiling. Any other part of the body would serve the same function were the eye situated, for instance, on the hand rather than the head. The hand would then be the face. Perhaps the hands of the Buddha are already on the way to becoming his face.

The Buddha's head is a ritual object that has also become an aesthetic object. However, even as aesthetic object, it does not define the human face in modern times, as Simmel suggests happens in painting. Lacking disruption of form, it cannot refer to the life processes located beyond representation except by inversion. It retains the power of some ritual masks to refer beyond itself. There are, for instance, Eskimo masks no more than two inches in length, sometimes attached as apotropaic devices to ropes on boats. They make one ask who wears such a mask. It is clearly not a human. They raise the question that the impassive face of the Buddha does for those who view it from the standpoint of metaphysics: Why is there something rather than nothing? They answer the question, of course, from a nonhumanistic standpoint.

Other masks have a power of reference that is more complicated. Take, for example, the mask of Usofuki from the Muromachi Period in Nikko. The surface is plastic. It is twisted both left and right and it has swellings, for instance, in the area of the cheeks, which cannot, however, result from merely filling the hollow of the mouth with air. It is an autonomous motion of the skin. Such distortions of the face, because they are energized, somehow expressive, and associated with a religious or mythological character, are not taken to be illness. They are expressive, but of what? Instead of "spiritual paralysis, the momentary absence of spiritual control," such masks by their excessiveness indicate a different realm of the spiritual. Of course, their excessiveness can only be measured against a standard, which one takes to be the face at rest, minus its distortions, its symmetries restored. But, though we reach for it, no such representation is given to us. Perhaps as a result, it seems not as though something speaks through the mask but rather that the mask itself speaks out of its surfaces, its plasticity, divorced from any controlling point behind it.

One can compare this mask with certain prints of Kobayashi Kiyochika, one of the artists of the Ukiyo-e. One set is called *32 Physionomic Types: 100 Facial Expressions.* The supplement to these comical prints includes one of a fat woman putting on face powder. The powder marks a tee, the base being her nose and the bar her forehead. There are other marks on her cheeks. The powder is not at all integrated into her expression. The print is amusing not because she is inept but because the putting on of this mask is made to seem inherently impossible. Even when she finishes, there will be a gap between her face and her cosmetically inflected expression. The same gap appears in a portrait of a grimacing man in the same series. His features are twisted in a grotesque and again comical way. But his teeth are shown nearly in their entirety. They are part of an unyielding structure, on which the face is merely motion. This motion indicates nothing. The expressions of these people remain divorced from any point of reference. It is not that there is no interior resonance, but that it is a negative one. What is revealed is merely the physical support of a face that lacks mental unity.

If one follows the gaze of the actors of Kabuki in the woodblocks from the Ukiyo-e, one sees that their eyes are not organs of sight, looking as they do out of the corners of the eyes to some place incomprehensible or being crossed in an apparent expression of ferocity. Eyes in this case are merely signs; they are expressions of characteristic emotions but not sensory organs. They disrupt the space of the engraving rather than organize it. In doing so they refer behind the mask, not to the actor but to the character portrayed. But at the same time, divorcing expression from context, they, like the comic etchings I have mentioned, show that the possibility of delineating the face makes it transferable and that in the delineation of the expression there is already a power of reference, though the question, always, is "to whom" or "to what."

It is a question of technique and even of technology, if one can think of cosmetics and masks as technological. This is the case for the face on the poster I saw in the Tokyo subway, the Japanese with the American expression. Can we locate the control of the man's expression, and if so, where? Is it in America, perhaps, in the studio where the photograph was taken or perhaps in the computer program that possibly generated his image? Or is it in Japan? In the latter case, one needs to know its context to know if the image fits the person wearing it. What, for instance, happened after the photograph was taken? What was the transition between expressions like? Did this expression have to be explained, exemplified; were there instructions about positioning the lips and eyebrows and forming the gaze? One sees here the past before these people as the mask or stereotyped expression is given in advance of wearing it.

The power of the face to cause reference beyond itself and to be the central site of signification is put into question once one interrogates contemporary forms in the wake of Simmel. One then wants to ask not only why the face retains its place but whether it always does so. The Buddha's hands are his face, as it were, both aesthetic objects and instruments of signification. What is the result for the place of the face in cultures where Buddhism is the primary religion? Here, however, there is an obstacle. Simmel, like many people, did not regard Buddhism as a religion. "It is a doctrine of salvation that can be attained by the seeker entirely on his own."[10] The Buddha is outside of social life.

Are there cultures or societies whose members have no face? One can turn to animal societies. There is, we know, communication between animals and between animals and humans; animals, we think today, suffer emotions. Nonetheless, it is difficult to say that the face is central to their expression. The illustrations of animals in Darwin's interesting study *The Expression of the Emotions in Man and Animals* are generally of the whole body of the animal.[11] To show a dog expressing affection, for instance, Darwin reproduces an engraving of the animal rubbing himself against a man's leg. The implication is that for most animal communication the entire body is necessary. The nonhuman animal presumably does not learn his signals; their conventionality is rooted in nature rather than culture. Whatever signals animals might acquire are not passed on from one generation to the next. As a result there may be different cat "languages," one for each animal, but there is no cat culture.

Without the impression of ourselves in the face of the other, one lacks the dialectical setting in which languages evolve. The excited cat swishes its tail. It could see itself doing so if it turns its head, but at that moment, one cannot say which is the front and which the back of the cat. It lacks a face, even if it signals, which means it lacks the orientation to the other that having a face implies.[12] The face, Simmel shows, is an aesthetic object before it is set in opposition to a second face; the dialectical opposition depends on it. Merely putting a cat *en face* with a human or another cat will not by itself establish a necessary orientation, one retained even after the confrontation has ended, because the cat's face is not an aesthetic object in Simmel's sense.[13] One can protest that the cat or dog still has a front and a back. Its eyes, especially, which tell it where to go, are located in front. But the primacy of smell in such animals complicates the question. The dog moves with its nose to the ground, sniffing its way. Its muzzle is in front, of course. But in humans the distance from the ground, the need for balancing on two legs, the specialization of the hands as prototools rather than means of locomotion, and particularly the repression of smell and the dominance of sight all favor a tendency to mark the front, as "facing the world," in a stronger manner than with other animals, all the more so since only with the dominance of sight is there a horizon, a boundary to the world, on the other side of which is something unknown. Many animals have boundaries to their territories marked by scent; the territory of an animal is not its complete world. The dog, like the cat, has a world, but it is not clear whether that world has a horizon. Its orientation to us, its master, is clear. The dog's world centers around us, but until we can say that we form the horizon of that world, we cannot be sure that the dog has a face in the Simmelian sense.

When one is in communication with an animal, it is often not because of the signals it makes with its body, but simply through looking at its eyes. At that moment, one feels that the animal does have a front and a back and a face as well. It is the animal's eyes as one looks at them, combined with the manufacture of signals, that allow one to think it might have an orientation. One sees oneself in the animal's responses and therefore allots the animal a face. If there is a face, hence a front, it is because one senses something "behind" the face that one perceives. And one momentarily, at least, grants the animal the same thought about oneself. But if one looks as a third party at animal communication, one loses such a sense, as one sees the lack of primacy of the head or its parts as the animal signals.

One can ask whether the face could be the center of expression if it were deprived of any reflection of itself either in life or in art. Are there cultures where the face is not the center of expression? Perhaps. In the early 1960s I lived in a remote part of Sumatra, where there were not yet photos except in the city and there were practically no pictures of any kind; the few cameras were owned by professional photographers. When I saw the photos I took there with my own camera of people I knew well, I was uneasy. Light conditions made it difficult to see what the camera could record. At night there was only the dim light of kerosene lanterns or candles. During the day, the intense glare and heat of the tropical sun meant that one saw details only in shadow. When one looked at someone, the lines of his face were usually bleached out in the daytime and only dimly visible at night. In the sunlight one tended to look down, even in the shade, to avoid the pervasive glare. Consequently, my impressions of people depended little on their faces. The camera, however, showed their faces, with their expressions and lines, and introduced them to me as beings I had never adequately seen. The characters etched on their faces were not the ones I had known.

On the other hand, these photos were adequate to my experience in another way. The pictures were black and white. Without color, people blended with their surroundings. The full-length photos in the setting of the village matched my impressions of them. It was a question of their voices, in particular. Their voices were not, in my experience, associated with their mouths or their facial expressions. Words and people were, for me, not conjoined. The people I knew spoke "Acehnese"; for me, they were vehicles of that language, points where the language emerged into the world. Though of course I knew and appreciated them individually, nonetheless, language and face were not fully conjoined. In their full-length photographs, with their faces unimportant, I seemed to be able to hear the names of the people and the Acehnese words for the objects with which they were pictured. The surroundings spoke as much as the people themselves.

That is a little like Robert Musil's *Young Törless*.[14] In this philosophical novel, descriptions of negative numbers and the openings of sexuality and imagination aroused by the idea of them cannot be precisely situated within the heads of particular characters or narrators. Photography, however, locates speech within the head. In Volker Schlöndorff's film of the novel, heads speak, and the philosophical discourses of the novel, which perhaps by definition lack spontaneity, are necessarily truncated, as the film presents people at certain moments in time.[15] The exteriorized quality of thought, its arrival to us from outside of ourselves rather than as the products of particular subjectivities, impresses itself on us in the novel but not in the film. It is exactly this disjunction of exterior and interior that Simmel points to as a leading characteristic of modernity and that is, today, technologically modified.

When photos—and cameras—became easily available in Indonesia, Indonesians were eager to have them and to use them. Today one sees Indonesian tourists marching up the Borobodur, scarcely looking left or right, taking each other's pictures at the top, and directly afterwards descending. They are not memorializing their visit, if that means saving up an experience, because there is at that point not yet an experience. That comes later, when they look at the pictures and see themselves next to the great aesthetic (and formerly ritual) objects of their nation. They recognize themselves then and see that they are part of their nation, associated with one of its major emblems. They link themselves with the Borobodur as I associated

Acehnese with their surroundings. They use the camera not to see the possibilities of their faces, not to reveal unexpected turns in their characters, but to discover themselves with the objects that symbolize their nation for them. They become nationalists of today not by their subjective beliefs but by the possibility of being themselves objectified.

Before the camera, one might argue that they did not yet have faces, or that their faces were not the front part of their skulls. The eagerness to have the camera from the moment it became available, however, shows that the possibility of the face was already present within them. They knew, somehow, that the contemporary form of representation of themselves was inherent in themselves. They needed only to make this state objective. But if they "knew" this, it is because they had seen photographs and wanted themselves to be part of the picture, which is to say that the possibility of the face as the center of expressiveness, even when it may not (yet) be realized, seems in retrospect to be already present after the photograph appears on the scene. What is needed is a means to show one one's own face in an authoritative way so that, seeing it, one is sure that one recognizes "oneself." What one expects to be necessarily primary to what is represented, the face as site of expressiveness, is really secondary to its representation, as Simmel suggested.

Face to the camera, Indonesians transmit themselves to themselves. "I recognize myself" is the response I assume these photographs in effect provoke. It is a recognition whose authority comes not from previous knowledge of how one looks but from the constitution of the face as it passes through the camera onto the film, to appear alongside objects of undoubted aesthetic value. Face simply to the mirror, one's recognition would lack certainty. It is the (aesthetic) representation of the face that matters in giving themselves a face. But this is far from assured by its technological transmission. The photograph reveals what no one can see. Or, rather, what one has seen, perhaps in the mirror, but not registered. To recognize that one has not registered (Simmel would say not "synthesized") what one saw and that it is "oneself" one has missed is to find a face for oneself. There is more to oneself than one thought, and one cannot quite grasp it.

The aesthetic in my story of the present is no longer to be found in the fine arts. It is discovered on television and on posters in the subway. If the Japanese baseball manager appears with an American expression, it may not be because baseball originated in America or because the manager simply adopted his expression through habituation to his job. Habit is one form of accommodation, to be sure. It may have begun that way. But the manager's ability to inhabit his expression could also have come when he saw himself on the replays. It would then be the result of wanting to be the point of reference of the televised version of his face as he becomes its addressee. He is already, as I have said, the formal point of reference of the televised game. His eye, shown on tape, penetrates, circles, pulls in what it sees toward himself. He is the formal representation of himself in relation to all other televised forms. As such, he sees what the manager in person could never have seen. His authority comes from his omniscience. And he borrows his omniscience from the camera, from the difference between his eye and its lens. But this omniscience is defective; it comprises only appearances, because the camera sees only appearances. There is something more behind the eyes, which is not in the camera. It is not merely when the manager, seeing himself on film, imagines he can indeed see everything that he adopts his expression as his own. In that moment he sees also that, on television, he sees without comprehension. His photographic image reveals a disability. It is only when he takes on his image for his own that he adds what is lacking in the image. He obscures how it is that he becomes omniscient in order to be "the manager" and not merely the camera.

The televised face of the manager does not indicate a place behind it from which facial features are synthesized. It does, however, indicate a place of manufacture: it is the camera and its related pieces of apparatus. The manager's face gains an aesthetic quality; it appeals to the senses and becomes "pleasing" and "useless" when, confronted with the possibility of the disfigurement that comes with the reception of mere appearances technologically communicated, it is not equated with a camera. The manager evades the power of the camera to take in "everything," even while that possibility is acknowledged. The photographic image thus develops into "his" face, as it were, even when it wears an expression from across the ocean, which, till the moment he makes it his own, is senseless. Which is to say that the unveiling of the power of the camera as it produces images, appearances, as it governs the face unaesthetically, is veiled again; it becomes "aesthetic" and is humanized. At that point it is, after all, himself that the manager sees.

Veiling and unveiling here reveal and obscure the power of the eye as lens. Simmel's notion, extended to the conditions that prevail today, is close to Walter Benjamin's idea of the "optical unconscious": the power of the camera to reveal what the eye sees but we do not register. As such, Simmel's Kantianism is surpassed. The camera, like the painted eye, sees mere appearance. The "unveiling of the soul" that results from the consideration of pure appearance does not open onto intimations of noumena or the mental structures in which appearances are embedded. It is, rather, an effect of knowing that we see more than we take in. It is a falling back onto human-centered notions necessary to have a face: "I am not a camera" is the response when "appearance become[s] the veiling and unveiling of the soul." One might instead conflate the viewpoints of the person and the camera, as Benjamin also suggests in another place. But this formulation reduces what the camera sees to what the eye sees and so ends up in the same place. Appearances that escape human registration have the indefinite reference of some of the masks I have discussed. The human face is founded on the refusal to consider appearances that cannot be taken in.

The power of the camera avoided, Simmel's humanistic version of modernity endures in this story of mine. But it does so, I am afraid, at the expense of the disappearance of the traces of his thinking. By thinking out loud, as it were, as I have tried to do here, one sees that he survives even as he vanishes, only, I am sure, to reappear later, when once again I am certain he saw something I have missed.[16]

Academic Work: The View from Cornell

Many American universities were founded outside cities, often in places that evoke the admiration of European visitors for their beauty and sometimes evoke surprise that one would think of having a university in such an environment. The attempt to separate the university from the rest of society continues even where the city has caught up to the university, as, for instance, in the case of Harvard. Every attempt is made to keep the boundaries of the American university clear; what belongs to it and what is excluded from it are a matter of concern, as they are not in European academic institutions.

I hope to show that the question of the setting of universities is connected to notions of academic work and thus affects the imaginative scenario of being a student or faculty member. I will study a particular institution, Cornell, in order to do so. Settings vary from place to place; what is true of the particulars of Cornell need not hold anywhere else. But it may be that there is a relation between the settings of other universities and the conception of work there.

The View and the Place

The condition Ezra Cornell made for his contribution to the establishment of a university was that it be located on a site "overlooking the village of Ithaca and Cayuga Lake."[1] He had a particular site in mind, which he donated to the university, the crest of a hill "overlooking" the town and lake and offering a view of a range of hills to the west. He needed to convince even those who thought the university should be situated in Ithaca that it belonged so far up the hill. Cornell felt that only his location offered the necessary space. Those who disagreed with him he accused of lack of vision. He would take visitors to the hilltop and, to their objections to the site, say, "You appear to be considering . . . half a dozen buildings . . . whereas you will live to see our campus occupied by fifty buildings and swarming with thousands of students."[2] The trustees all wanted a site closer to the town. Cornell, however, brought them up the hill. "Then," according to A. D. White, the university's first president, "we viewed the landscape. It was a beautiful day and the panorama was magnificent. Mr. Cornell urged reasons on behalf of the upper site, the main one being that there was so much more room for expansion," and the board agreed.[3] One can understand that a view could provide a pleasant context for a university and that the board would find Ezra Cornell's site appropriate for that reason. But Cornell's choice of a site made it difficult to reach the university from the town. Considering the difficulties his choice would entail—the need for new housing on the hillside and the distance created between the school and the library Cornell had earlier founded in Ithaca—the pleasantness of the view seems too casual a consideration to make a difference in deciding the location of the university. Nonetheless, the view seems to have figured prominently in the decision to locate the university where it is today.

Kermit Parsons has pointed out that, before Ezra Cornell, others may, upon seeing the view, have thought of a university. De Witt Clinton, for instance, found the view "alternately picturesque, beautiful and sublime" and added that "before the revolution of this century, this country [Ithaca] will become consecrated to classical inspiration." Parsons also notes that, for Ezra Cornell, the association of the view with the university had something to do with death. Indeed, Cornell's plan seems to have been shaped by the thematics of the Romantic sublime, which practically guaranteed that in the presence of certain landscapes a cultivated man would find his thoughts drifting metonymically through a series of topics—solitude, ambition, melancholy, death, spirituality, "classical inspiration"—which could lead, by an easy extension, to questions of culture and pedagogy. A book published locally earlier in the century, thirty-one years before the founding of the university, can provide us with some telling instances of the particular inflection sublime motifs took in upstate New York. It is Solomon Southwick's *Views of Ithaca and Its Environs*,[4] a typical combination of locodescriptive prose and interspersed poetry. Here, for instance, are some lines from Southwick's concluding ode:

> Farewell, lov'd Ithaca!—from thee I part.
> But not without a sigh that rends my heart:
> For still, whene'r remembrance shall renew
> The smiling landscape, the romantic view:
> The rushing cataract, that ever fills
> With nature's melody thy vales and hills;
> The gulf profound: the eminence sublime:
> Those everlasting solitudes of Time! . . .
> Ithaca shall prove
> Through time, the seat of science and of love.

Earlier, Southwick had stationed himself at the Ithaca cemetery, "delightfully situated, on a lofty eminence, as all graveyards ought to be, and surrounded very nearly by beautiful prospects" (12). It is while he speaks of this view that Southwick comes to think about learning and particularly about writing. He begins with some general remarks: "These communings with the dead, and the dust that covers them, and the grass and wild flowers that wave over their tombs, are refreshing to the soul; and cannot be too often repeated, whenever a temporary release from the cares and duties of life will admit of them. Though the grave be dark and silent, and the clods that cover it be dumb; yet do they hold most eloquent discourse, and speak in a voice which reaches both the head and the heart" (11). The "silent" dead "speak" to Southwick when he is aware of their presence, that is, when the grass and wildflowers that grow over the tombs cause him to remember that the dead are unaware of them. But Southwick's thought takes a curious and interesting turn shortly after this, when he begins to describe the cemetery itself:

But the careless manner, in which it has been left open to the inroads of cattle—the prostrate and broken grave-stones—and quaint rhyming inscriptions, on many of the monuments which are left standing, made an impression upon me, blending so much of the ludicrous with the serious, that I wished myself out of the place, lest I should profane it by the indulgence of improper feelings. As a specimen of the Inscriptions take the following: But stay my pen; for it would not be right to ridicule inscriptions, which, however, quaint, or inane, or ludicrous in themselves, are the offspring of a feeling which ever is, and ever ought to be, held sacred by all mankind. (12)

For Southwick, "quaint, rhyming inscriptions" and broken tombstones lead to "improper feelings," that is, feelings about the inscriptions themselves and what they are written on. The ridicule these inspire is deserved. It is, nonetheless, out of place, "improper," because it does not take cognizance of the presence of the dead. The situation at this point is reversed from the time of Southwick's first musings on death. When he said that the graves, "though dark and silent . . . speak," he meant that, looking at them, he had death in mind. When, however, Southwick sees the "prostrate" tombstones and reads their inscriptions, he is no longer thinking of the dead, while nonetheless remaining aware that he is in a cemetery and should be thinking of them. His thoughts are "improper" because there is something in the world—death—which is also on his mind but he feels is not given expression.

To have death in mind when it ought to be in mind means being aware of its presence in the world. Awareness of the presence of the dead comes for Southwick only when the language of the tombstones does not divert him from its intended reference. When language functions as it ought to, the dead are locatable in the world—in the grave, to be precise. To be distracted by inept inscriptions means, for Southwick, feeling the presence of the dead in an uncomfortable way. It results in an undesirable mixture of things that should be kept separate: the "ludicrous" and the "serious"; the "quaint" or "inane," which nonetheless is "the offspring of a feeling which ever is . . . held sacred by mankind." When, however, the inscriptions are as they ought to be, boundaries are drawn between different kinds of thoughts, keeping each in its place. When the dead are thought of "properly," they are thought of in their tombs, where they belong ("these communings with the dead . . . and the wild flowers that wave over their tombs").

When Southwick felt that the tombstone inscriptions were inadequate and that his thoughts were thereby infected with notions he found to be out of place, he proposed to write an "Essay on grave-yards and tombstones" (12). With such a manual at hand, people would know how to write epitaphs, and Southwick would, thus, no longer have to fear finding himself in the uncomfortable situation he experienced in the Ithaca cemetery. Thoughts about death not fully brought to mind but nonetheless seeming to mix with other thoughts thus impel Southwick to tell of his experience in his account and to propose to consolidate what he knew in writing his "Essay." It is this recourse to language that keeps thoughts of the dead pure, in effect keeping the dead in their tombs rather than having them haunt the living. Ezra Cornell's thinking was something like Southwick's; it was mediated by the same tradition. (Today we know his thinking on the subject only through the stories recorded by W. T. Hewett and others some time after the fact. These stories may be inaccurate, but if so it is in the interest of mythologizing the view, which is precisely our topic.) Here is Hewett's account:

> In the summer of 1863 [Ezra Cornell] was seriously ill for several months. As he recovered he said to his physician, "When I am able to go out, I want you to bring your carriage and take me upon the hill. Since I have been upon this sick bed, I have realized, as never before, by what a feeble tenure man holds on to life. I have accumulated money, and I am going to spend it while I live." They drove subsequently to the hill, which constitutes the present site of the university, to what was then Mr. Cornell's farm. He spoke with the greatest enthusiasm of his determination to build an institution for poor young men. Mr. Cornell described the buildings which should crown the hillside, and pointed out where they should stand.[5]

The university, coming to mind when Cornell "realized as never before by what a feeble tenure man holds onto life," was to be his project "while I live." Cornell's house was just above the graveyard Southwick described. It was in this house that Cornell came to think about the imminence of his own death. His statement shows that, when he thought of the university, he thought also of leaving the house and going to the top of the hill. The house and the cemetery would have been visible from the top of the hill. Usually, however, it is assumed that the view referred to was the sight of the lake northwest of the university, whereas the cemetery and house were to the southeast. To see the lake would have meant turning one's back to Cornell's house and the graveyard. The trustees' inclination was to build the university in the vicinity of Cornell's house and the cemetery. In countering the trustees' opinion by arguing that the university should be at the top of the hill, Cornell also removed the university from reminders of death.

Cornell's argument, we know, was not that the view itself was essential but that only at the top of the hill, where the panorama was available, was there room for future expansion. The university today, however, extends down the hill and occupies the land Cornell rejected as its original site. I know of no reason why it could not have begun lower on the hill and expanded upwards if room for expansion really was what Cornell had in mind. The advantage of the site to Cornell seems, rather, to have been its separation from death.

It is not that Cornell, any more than Southwick, wanted to deny death. Rather, he wanted to place his efforts in the proper relation to it. The university was to be the embodiment of his efforts "while I still live." In that sense, thoughts of death would not be out of place in regard to the university; on the contrary, Cornell may have thought of the university as a tribute to himself that would extend beyond his lifetime. But the question of room for expansion suggests more than merely the building of a useful institution within the compass of the abilities left to Cornell in his lifetime. It is, rather, an insistence on his continued vitality just when that vitality had been severely threatened. When Cornell said, "you will live to see [not half a dozen buildings but] our campus occupied by fifty buildings and swarming with thousands of students," he was insisting on his continued power. Putting his efforts in relation to death thus meant expelling thoughts of death, giving himself time and energy enough to ensure the building of a university equal in size to his aspirations.

Cornell seemed to feel he saw what no one else did: "you appear to be considering half a dozen buildings [whereas I]." The trustees, in any case, saw him as speaking with "inspiration." His son Alonzo Cornell, who was present when the site was chosen, reported that "his remarks were astounding to his hearers who remained in silence for many minutes."[6] Cornell was not ordinarily an eloquent man. The university's first president characterized him as "saying little and that little dryly."[7] His unwonted eloquence in the face of the view may have had nothing to do with anything inherent in

the view itself. It may, rather, be that on the top of the hill he felt as Southwick did when the latter proposed to write an essay on the proper composi-
tion of epitaphs. Placing the university away from the graveyard meant it
would embody his living energies, freed from any threat of imminent death.
That Southwick wanted to recover thoughts of death and Cornell wanted
to put them behind him does not matter; both wanted to keep ideas of death
and life uninfected by each other. It may have been his sensing of death and
the attempt to push it away that impelled Cornell to his unusual recourse
to rhetoric. In any case, Alonzo Cornell's report shows him turning his back
to the view, but more explicitly turning his back on the proposed sites near
the graveyard at the moment he made his decisions. Alonzo Cornell reports
that, at the top of the hill, directly above the cemetery, he listened to the
trustees' proposals to have the university further down the hill. "Finally he
was asked where he thought the location should be made. Turning upon his
heel and facing the east [thus away from the view and with his back to house
and cemetery] he swung his arms north and south, saying, 'here on this line
extending from Cascadilla to Fall Creek [the names of the two gorges], with
their rugged banks to protect us from uncongenial neighbors, we shall need
every acre for the future necessary purposes of the University.'"[8]

Cornell's wish, later inscribed on the university seal, was to "found an
institution where any person can find instruction in any study," the condition being that it could not be founded just anywhere, but in a particular
location.[9] His hope seems to have been that, in the face of the view, the
university would stand removed from the site of his awareness of his death
and thus, in a sense, in opposition to it.

Today the opposition between the university and life on the one side and
death on the other still stands, as we shall see. It is, however, no longer the
cemetery and Cornell's house (no longer extant) but the view itself that has
come to suggest death. The view is now accessible to most people from the
bridges that span the gorges running through Cornell to the north and
south. Looking west from them, or downstream, one looks over the gorges,
some more than two hundred feet in depth, with streams running west to
empty into the lake. These bridges are approximately four hundred feet
above the town, about a mile distant, with the lake somewhat further on.
About five miles west there is a line of hills, which rise a thousand feet above
the town to mark the horizon. The lake runs roughly north and south, but
at its northern end it bends west, so that its furthest western rim is not

visible. The lake and the hills together thus delineate the western, or down-stream, horizon.

In order to look into the question of the view, for three years I had students in my class on ethnographic description interview pedestrians as they looked downstream and then upstream from the bridges (the order is sometimes reversed).[10]

Two such interviews follow.

1. Downstream

I want to jump.

How come?

Oh, not because right now it makes me want to jump so much as because it's just such a thing about these gorges.

What do you mean? Because you have passed by so many times and thought things and that's what you think now?

No, no. It's the gorges and what there is about them.

You mean the history and that you know that people jump?

Yes, the history but also just because of what I think added to it. I always want to jump.

Well, what is it? Just look at it and say what it is.

Well, it's so far down. And it's water you know and somehow it seems a beautiful way to die.

To go out with it.

1. Upstream

I don't want to jump here.

Why not?

It goes the wrong way. The other way you get the feeling it will take you away when you're feeling you don't want to be here. This one won't. It's desolate.

It's kind of like if you were going to kill yourself with a knife. You could throw yourself on it. But to drive it into yourself would be so hard.

(She displays these movements by the stone wall of the bridge and mimes a look of quick horror when she thinks of putting the knife in herself.)

2. DOWNSTREAM

This makes me very self-conscious. I could take it from so many different levels. I could take any of the paths.

Take whichever of the ones you can find the words for most easily.

I guess, well, what it makes me think about the most is time. Because of geology class, you know, the field trips we had to take walking up this gorge. I could talk about all the details. I was a real pain in the ass that day. I asked the TA so many questions. I mean, I couldn't ask enough. I wanted to know what was there, what had happened when to put things the way they were. I was just amazed by the amount of time that the earth has changed in. And I wanted to get it down to the details, as far as the TA knew about, as much as he knew, the salt layer and further down. It wasn't enough. (Pause)

But about time. I really got into thinking about that, the vastness of earth's time. When I was little I'd think about the huge dragonflies and brontosauruses, but it didn't seem like this world. I couldn't imagine the world having really changed so much as to accommodate this. But I was getting into it last year, I wanted to know every particular. (Pause)

I guess in some ways the intellectualness of it takes away from the wholeness somehow. Somehow it wasn't so good for my ideas of time to study the sciences so closely. I was studying things like astronomy to just see if I could feel the hugeness of the numbers. But in some ways it seems to take away from it.

Also, I guess I just thought of something else. I was working in a pizza parlor. I think about the cracked heads down there, you know, when people jump. These people I worked with also worked for the fire department picking up the bodies afterwards. They're split right open, they said. (Pause)

Like ripe fruits?

Well, no, maybe. But they said it was just like they weren't people, bones and mangled. They talked about how the friends would come in and be so disgusted.

But this gorge is really young compared to, like, Fall Creek. Only ten thousand years, and that's short geologically, but it's such a scarring of the earth.

In both of these interviews, as in most others, only the western or downstream view promotes thoughts of death (usually suicide). This association, we see in the first interview, has to do with the distance ("it's so far down") and with being carried away ("to go out with it"). The second interview spells out the meaning of "distance." The speaker is confused about the number of ways she could explain her thoughts ("I could take it from so many different levels. I could take any of the paths"). The distance down from the bridge is translated into time, geological and then astronomical, the two idioms containing the longest spans of time. The interest in quantity is expressed also by the number of questions she reports asking ("I asked the TA so many questions, I mean I couldn't ask enough") and the amount that the TA knew ("as much as he knew.") The exhaustiveness of her questioning ("I wanted to get down to the details") leads her to think of the sheer "hugeness of the numbers." This quantity is more than she can conceptualize ("I guess in some ways the intellectualness of it takes away from its wholeness somehow. Somehow maybe it wasn't so good for my ideas of time to study the sciences so closely"). And this failure to image or to conceptualize leads her ("I just thought of something else") to substitute strong images for what she can no longer think. These are the images of "cracked heads" and, by association, of the look of a pizza, a splattering of whites and reds.[11]

When one faces downstream, the horizon is in front of one. Measurable distance gives way to the space of the horizon. The effect is compounded by the movement of the water, which seems to pull one away or to evacuate one, doubling the sense of the vacuity of one's thoughts. The view upstream works differently. There the bottom of the gorge seems nearer. It is so, in fact, but the difference in distance does not seem great enough to account for the difference in feeling. When one looks upstream, since one is on a hillside, the earth and not the horizon is in front of one. The difference between looking downstream and looking upstream is that between seeing into a void and having "something" come rushing at one, as the following interview shows:

3. DOWNSTREAM

I think of its vastness. I like heights. I like to work at heights, I think, because of the feeling of danger and its bigness. . . . I respect it. It doesn't scare me. I don't feel out of control, but sometimes I like to have to walk on a narrow line.

What work have you done at heights?

Well, I've worked on boats where I had to go aloft a lot, And I like to rock climb.

With ropes and everything?

Yes.

3. UPSTREAM

It's not as far down. That's the first thing I can think to say. You know, what it reminds me of in comparison to distance is, you know, on a ski lift, when you are going up and the ground is coming up towards you from between your skis, it doesn't look steep at all.

But all you have to do is turn around and look down and it's very steep.

You know, what I like to do sometimes is look at the water rushing over the rocks. I like to do this really more from the side than straight on like this. But there's two ways you can look. You can either watch one rock and the water blur over it as it passes. Or else you can keep your eyes on a single drop of water and follow along so that the rocks blur under it.

To describe looking upstream, it is necessary to resort to metaphor, just as when looking downstream. But metaphor here does not pertain to a quantity that is too great to be described and that is therefore "nothing," but to the constant filling up of space. When the person speaks of "blurring," it is not because something is blanked out but because space is over-crowded to the extent that he must attend to one impression at a time, something he feels competent to do.

The frequent mention of death and particularly of suicide in these interviews is often a function of the logic of sublimity. The mind, set in motion by all that is seen, is not able to match what is seen with a stable image. One seems to be in the presence of more than one can think about. To imagine death by leaping is to expel the felt absence in one's mind into the scene one is viewing. The fear of losing oneself in the abyss expresses nothing about the abyss itself, but something about the inability of the mind to think all that it feels it is trying to think. The thought of suicide in the circumstances is comforting; even if it is frightening, it is better than the panic that comes with rushing after images always beyond one's control.

The person in the second interview speaks of geological details that, added up, express the profusion of things that she can not grasp. What she hopes for, however, is a set of details that express the whole in a compass compact enough for her to understand. She finds this, finally, not in geological detail but in the image of cracked heads, the result of suicidal leaps. When the person interviewed on the bridge thinks of suicide, it is as though the image of the body were a body part, a detail that has separated from the whole. Though the thought of suicide may be horrifying, it is, again, basically comforting because it establishes death as "there," whereas the speaker is on the bridge "here."

The logic of "here" and "there" encountered in mental representations of suicide may explain the strange association of suicide and food. In one interview, suicide is brought up in conjunction with pizza. In another interview it takes this form: "If one jumped and committed suicide, it would probably really hurt to fly down all those rocks. Jesus, you could end up in some restaurant down in Ithaca, and that would really be tacky." After the idea of suicide has established the distance between the speaker and the image of his demise, food is pictured as something that can be retrieved and reincorporated. What is lost is thereby reconjoined.

In addition to thoughts about suicide, the bridges prompt a sort of self-consciousness about thinking, as in this example: "It's a place to think. If you're really thoughtful, you really need to just think, this is the place to go. I guess that's why people jump here. Like, you know, you could jump off a scaffold, you really could, but you just can't think on a scaffold." The thoughts about thinking in this excerpt are a way of conceptualizing the person's own thoughts. It is a means for the respondent to bring herself into the picture, to find something of interest equal to the view but opposed to it; once she has a picture of her thoughts, she is "here," thinking, while the view is "out there." The distance between the two is thus stabilized.

The oscillation between thoughts of suicide and thoughts of thinking and particularly of language occurs again in the following excerpt: "Yeah, the library is right next to the gorge. (Pause, looking over the edge.) I guess the other thing you think about up here is suicide—not that I'd ever do it myself or anything—but it's always talked about and written about and everything—they make a big thing out of it up here."

The library is not part of the view; it is not visible from where the respondent stood on the bridge, and it is not on the edge of the gorge. Suicide is here sandwiched between the library and talk and writing, thus embedded in an ideality that stands opposed to the view.

Looking downstream, many people spoke of feeling a "pull." We have seen this already in earlier quotations. Here is another excerpt: "I'm sort of attracted to the bottom of this side; I think it's because I feel with the flow and not against it. I wonder which side of the bridges most people jump off of?"

Compare this thought, looking upstream: "I feel a good sense of order and place looking up there, it makes me feel introverted, closed, nice and compact." The pull is the sense of collapse of the distance between oneself and the horizon or the bottom of the gorge: more accurately, it is the feeling that accompanies the sense that one's mind is not adequate to the view and that therefore the opposition of viewer and view has collapsed. This feeling has another aspect, as well, which is most vivid in this excerpt:

How do you feel about the other side? Upstream?

It's easier there because it's not so far down. I feel more pulled, downstream. Over there I don't feel so pulled.

When you look, where do you look?

Straight down. I look down, and that pulls me out. It draws me downstream. Like, against my will it could pull me over the railing. If I looked down too hard, it'd really do it, like in the cartoons, when someone's body is just—zooooot—pulled over. (Pause) I really, let's get off now.

What is interesting about this excerpt and the one above is that the bridge appears in the respondent's replies only in connection with the feeling of being attracted or pulled by the view. When the speaker is looking up-stream, it is not mentioned. When she is looking downstream, the bridge, in particular the railing, is erected in imagination in response to sensing the collapse of self into the distance. One thinks of Southwick's disturbance at the sight of prostrate and broken tombstones with their inadequate inscrip-tions or of Ezra Cornell pointing out where the first buildings, which cut off the view, were to be erected. In each case it is a matter of a line drawn, across which the sense of absence in the mind is transferred to the world and thus conceptualized and stabilized.

In upstate New York there are many places with gorges and bridges over them. Only Cornell (and not even Ithaca), however, so far as I am aware, is known as the "suicide capital," with its own term for suicide, "gorging out." It appears to be the case that Cornell has no more suicides than most uni-versities; of the suicides at Cornell, a majority are not from the bridges.[12] The myth of suicide at Cornell—the idea that Cornell has an exceptionally great number of suicides and the association of suicides with the bridges—comes about not only because the logic of the sublime confronts students and faculty as they cross the bridges to the university but because there is an interest in putting suicide, suggested by the view, in relation to work.

Suicide became an issue at Cornell, along with the question of work, in the fall of 1977, when there were three suicides. Students demonstrated for a fall-term recess, claiming that the pressure of work was too great. The pressure of work and suicide were so closely linked in the minds of most people that it was necessary, according to the *Ithaca Journal* of December 13, 1977, for "those who work with troubled students to downplay the idea that academic pressure is the major culprit."[13] The connection between work and suicide in this assumption is not that work causes death but that not being able to work does so. Not standing up to pressure, one is over-whelmed. But so long as one does work, one stands up to it, one lives. As one faculty member put it, "for some students the high suicide rate provides confirmation that they go to a tough school and are tough enough to survive it."[14] The line that sets a boundary to the view also establishes something on this side of the line. If the view downstream is associated with sublimity, absence, and death, the other side is associated with presence, the positive, the university, and work.

When suicide and the pressure of work became issues at Cornell, the view became an issue too. Barriers on the College Town bridge were pro-posed to hinder suicidal leaps. The opponents to these barriers, the vast majority of those who spoke up, did not say that the view was innocuous or merely pleasant but rather that the view was worth preserving because it was more than pleasant.[15] As one faculty member wrote, "being able to 'commute' across the suspension bridge was worth at least a thousand dol-lars a year in salary."[16] His fear was not that barriers would make the bridge impassable but that they would block the view. The arguments against the barriers were in part that they would be ineffective or even counterproduc-tive, that the depression caused by loss of the view (and the thoughts of suicide on seeing the barriers instead of the view) would promote suicide.[17] In part they were that, even if the barriers would be effective, the loss of the view would still not be justified. In all cases, the motivating factor in the opposition to the barriers was the desire to preserve the view. One faculty member claimed that blocking the view would mean "destroying the es-sence of the university."[18] No one in the controversy over the suicide barri-ers spoke in favor of death. Those who spoke in favor of the view assumed it was in some way "life enhancing," in a phrase often used. One thinks of the mournful tone when talking about being deprived of the view, as in this letter about the suspension bridge, on which suicide barriers had already been raised, included in a deposition to the Cornell Campus Council hear-ings on suicide barriers:

I wonder how many other people felt like weeping when they saw what has been done to our once beautiful suspension bridge. A few weeks ago one lingered across its light airy openness as an intimate part of the beauty of Fall Creek gorge. Now the serried ranks of close-spaced bars make a prison corridor. A few weeks ago the bridge blended into the green of its surroundings. Now it glares at the transient hurrying through its claustrophic channel with a honky-tonk garishness worthy of Las Vegas. A few weeks ago the hand of man was unobtrusive. Now silver paint coats not only the bridges, but grass, ground, bushes and trees; weary smears reminiscent of New York subway cars mess the still unrepaired walkway.[19]

Someone had responded to the letter, originally published in the *Cornell Chronicle*; the letter writer included the response in his deposition:

I received a letter in response expressing the view that "saving even one young life is so much more important than saving the bridges as they have existed for so many years." My reply to which I still adhere two years later: ". . . I do not believe life can ever be so protected as to achieve the goal you suggest, nor should it be; a society in which suicide is impossible would be an intolerable physical and psychic prison. Moreover, efforts to create such a society are almost sure to be self-defeating. Many people were and are truly depressed by the prison-like atmosphere created by the "cure" applied to the suspension bridge. Simple survival is not the absolute value in this or any other society. Safety is, and always will be one of our values. Freedom fostering self-responsibility and aesthetics have their place, and they are by no means always consistent with maximum safety. Thus I do not take it as a given truth that saving one young (or old) life from self-destruction is to be weighed more heavily than the rare opportunity the suspension bridge once offered thousands of people every year to be immersed very closely in God's beauty.

In saying that the view from the bridge is worth the possibility of suicide, the writer acknowledges the association of the bridges with death. The bridge, with its "light airy openness" an "intimate part of Fall Creek gorge," offered the "rare opportunity" to be "immersed very closely in God's beauty." "Very closely," but not totally. To be totally immersed in the view would be to expend all one's thought in it, to have nothing left for "oneself." To be only "very closely immersed" in the view is not to lose oneself in it totally, not to be suicidal. In that distinction rests the connection between "self-responsibility and aesthetics." Without "absolute safety" one risks immersion in "beauty," from which "self-responsibility" holds back.

The "depression" that goes with the suicide barriers has two causes. The first is being deprived of nature ("a few weeks ago the hand of man was unobtrusive"). The second is being imprisoned (the writer goes on to say, "one would as soon linger in a jail") with "garishness," associated with Las Vegas, thus with gambling and risks taken imprudently and, since the chief cause of Las Vegas "garishness" is its enormous signs, with writing. The "silver paint" that smears the gorge reminds the writer of "New York subway cars" and thereby recalls graffiti. The suffering that comes with being deprived of the view thus comes from being shut up with writing. To be deprived of the opposition of writing and view (which is that of work and view) is to become depressed, to think of death, and even, in an extreme case, to become suicidal ("who knows whether that added sense of oppression will tip the scales in a particular case").

When one has risked total immersion in the view and won, that is, held back, the view is established as the place of death. The view is valuable precisely for being the place of death, the site where death may be safely located, because that place is not "here," not the university. The particular myth of suicide at Cornell, however, indicates that, though the view itself suggests death, to become mythologized something more is needed. One also needs a notion of "academic pressure" or some equivalent. The availability of suicide, the bridges, and Cornell for mythologizing depends on looking at the view from the standpoint of work. From there, the interest in the view is an interest in creating a place to which notions of absence arising within work can be expelled, as we shall see.

Work and the View

The relation of work and view is one of mutual support but also mutual exclusion. One suggests the other as its replacement. This can be seen in the way the view is accessible at Cornell. The gorges were designated by Ezra Cornell as the boundaries of the university. Today the university extends over both sides of the gorges. There are no markers indicating that one enters Cornell when one crosses the bridges, but the gorges are still felt to be the limits of the university. Most people insist on thinking that the gorges mark the university boundaries, even when they know it not to be the case: "I think the boundaries of Cornell (pause), well, I don't know (pause), mostly between the gorges—it's natural. The boundaries are not literally between the gorges—but in a sense."

Once one has crossed the bridges into Cornell, the view disappears from sight, to be glimpsed again only from certain locations. The university buildings themselves are what shut out the view. Indeed, the history of the construction of the university's first quadrangle reveals an interesting tension between the wish to integrate the view to the west and the wish to shut it out, practice always favoring the latter. The first buildings constructed— Morrill Hall (1866), White Hall (1867), and McGraw Hall (1869)—were placed in a line running north-south of the western edge of what was to become the Arts Quadrangle. Originally the plan was to locate the eastern edge of the quadrangle on higher ground, thus preserving the westward view over the rooftops of Morrill, McGraw, and White. But this plan was abandoned: the line of buildings that now forms the eastern edge of the quadrangle is level with the original structures. Again, in the original plan, Morrill, White, and McGraw halls were separated from each other in order to prevent the spread of fire; this had the effect of allowing the view to be glimpsed from almost anywhere in the quadrangle. But A. D. White planned to fill up the gaps between the original structures with fire-proof buildings; although this did not materialize, the area was subsequently land-scaped and a statue of Ezra Cornell placed in such a way as to block the view. Looking west across the quadrangle today, one sees the form of the Founder outlined against the sky. Another plan—this was the suggestion of Frederick Law Olmstead—was to place a terrace on the west side of the original buildings, thus orienting them toward the view. Their main en-trances were intended to face west, opening onto the terrace. Now, how-ever, they face east, into the quadrangle: the terrace, discussed off and on for over ninety years, was never built.

Nowadays, from inside the Arts Quadrangle, the view to the west is blocked by the strong line of the three earliest—and architecturally simi-lar—structures. Through what space remains between these buildings, one can catch sight only of the tops of the hills across the valley and thus, once again, of the horizon. The ridge of hills to the west, about five miles distant, however, brings the horizon considerably closer than a continuously open perspective would allow. An effect similar to that connected with the gorges is noticeable, nevertheless, although in this case the view of the distance is transformed not into thoughts of suicide but into assumptions about the age of the buildings that form the line barring the view. Asked to estimate the dates of construction of the buildings surrounding the quadrangle, students invariably overestimate the age of the original three in relation to their only slightly younger neighbors. This would seem to be a way of conferring a special authenticity on the western wall of the quadrangle, as though one were reading the age of the buildings as a sign not of their dilapidation but of their archaic strength. It is as if the buildings were petrified or immoveable natural outcroppings, incapable of being overturned or demolished. By a trick of the mind, the infinite distance associated *with* the view to the west is converted into a depth in time, and this monumental quality is transferred to the structures that serve as a protective barrier *against* the view.

The place of the view with respect to the Arts Quadrangle becomes still clearer when thought of in connection with the main library. Though the library is on the south side of the Quad, its height, making possible views over and between Morrill, McGraw, and White, allows it to be oriented to the horizon. The windows of the library open out to the view, but they stand in a certain relation to the books as well. The pattern of the windows is such that there are no long views wherever there are books. In the stacks, windows are small and offer, therefore, only framed views, mostly of familiar sights, to anyone not directly next to them. They function more to let in light than to allow one to see out, especially since the stacks are located directly in front of the windows. The west side of the library, however, does have uninterrupted views from large windows. These views, however, are from either seminar or study rooms, where the books are limited to furnishing specific needs. What one can see from the stacks is familiar, controllable, and thus, put in conjunction with the books, reassuring.

On the seventh or top level, however, there are views of the horizon that stretch from one end of the stacks to the other along the north and south sides. The peculiarity of these windows is that they are set back about five feet from the edge of the top of the sixth floor. A single railing runs around the rim of the building. There thus appears to be a walkway between the glass wall of the seventh floor and the edge of the roof. The railing marks off the rim and thus the view. There are really two scenes. One is down from the seventh floor to the Arts Quad or the university directly south of the library, and the other is out beyond the university to the hills, lake, and sky.

The salient feature of both of these scenes is that viewers describe them not simply by remarking upon the landscape but as though the view were itself a representation. Here are three responses.

> It's like a giant mural of "Cornell, an Ivy League School."

> I could be looking at a very intricate Breughel picture, where hundreds of little things are happening at once.

> I am reminded of looking out into a visualization, a visualization of a vivid scene in a book.

People looking at the view from the seventh floor do not seem to notice the railing until it is called to their attention. After describing the view, for instance, one person asked about the railing said: "I had a carrel up there for two years and never noticed it. Wait a minute; I used to watch the rain drip off it. I used to have a carrel on the seventh floor. The view was relaxing. It wasn't distracting. I don't know why the railing is there, but it doesn't really obstruct the view.' As we see in the following excerpts, when the railing is mentioned, the idea of falling or of death comes to mind.

> It's stupid, useless. You can't go out there anyway. It definitely destroys part of the view. It's straight and everything down there is not straight. It's not solid, it's weak, an unsafe railing. Ridiculous. Railings usually protect you from falling off, but since no one's allowed out there anyway, I've no idea what this one's for. Maybe to make you feel safer in here. (Pause) Even if you were allowed outside, you couldn't fall.

The following respondent, asked "What is the railing for?" had a precise idea of its role: "It's to keep you from falling off in your mind. It directs your vision above the railing when what your vision wants to do is just drop off."

These interviews suggest that the view from the library, when it excludes the railing, appears as a representation. When it does so, it establishes the viewer safely at a distance from what he sees. When the railing is called to mind, however, the distance between viewer and viewed collapses as the viewer thinks of crossing over the railing or falling.

To see the importance of this, it is necessary to consider the view within the library itself—the view of the books. The following excerpts from interviews indicate that the books furnish another version of the sublime:

My first impression as I stroll around the fourth-floor stacks of Olin is the incredible amount of words, sentences, and thoughts that are all bound in this small area.

I get a feeling of futility, of chaos . . . the mass of the books, number of them. (Pause) If you imagine that every word printed has been vocalized by someone, and if all those words were vocalized at the same time, what a terrific chaos it would be.

In the face of such a profusion of impressions, there arises a feeling of incomprehension: "Because the windows are so thin [that is, narrow] and the rows of books block them, I feel like I'm penned in by the books. The books look very dark and foreboding. Most of them are in foreign languages, or so it seems, so I feel like they're inaccessible. The books are like corridors that stretch on and on." The feeling of incomprehension is sometimes expressed as a sense that there is something hidden:

I see straight corridors, channeling my thoughts, directing me. I see layers and layers of shelves, horizontal, ordered knowledge, then, books and books of recorded thought. I look down the straight aisles and contrast them with the winding paths, wandering people, partial buildings, and disorder down below. I feel trapped between the catalogue of books and the building right in front of me. Something feels hidden. There is an urge to be directed and an urge to figure out the mysteries of the obscured view.

In this interview, as in others, the straight lines of the corridors are contrasted to the curves in the views from the windows. From the perspective of the books, the curves outdoors seem to be linked to the features of the landscape they designate, whereas the straight lines of the rows of books repeat themselves regardless of the particular books they stand for. In the passage above, this repetition immediately precedes the sense that something is "hidden" and the urge to figure out the "mysteries" of what is felt to be obscured. It would be by interpretation, by reading the books, that this woman would be freed of the sense of being "trapped" or of having repetition "channel [her] thoughts." The choice is either to be controlled by repetition or to sense that something is hidden by it, thus allowing her to be free of it by finding out that which is hidden. ("There is an urge to be directed and an urge to figure out the mysteries of the obscured view.") Another version of this logic appears in the next excerpt:

In the central corridor, looking at all the books, I have a feeling of not recognizing them as books qua books en masse. A feeling that I need to personalize my relationship to a particular book; by reading a title, by opening a book and reading something. A feeling of blocklike stolidity and of immovability. The way the stacks are arranged in the attempt to be symmetrically parallel reminds me of "op" art, of optical illusions done with parallel lines in order to deceive one about the distance or space between certain lines.

Here the books have lost their identity because of their great number. The view of the stacks as a series of parallel lines expresses the multiplication of the books in another form. If the parallel lines can be said to form an optical illusion, it is only necessary to expose that illusion to restore intelligibility.

In nearly all fifteen interviews in the library, there is a sense of being "caged in," as one person put it, or "trapped," as we have seen in the excerpts quoted. This sense of being in forced proximity to the books is an expression of being in the grip of language, over which one has no hold. The view from the windows, either the small framed views of similar sights from the lower stack levels or the view as stable representation from the seventh floor, offers the reassurance of an outside to which one can always turn for escape. The condition for academic work, however, is that one remain turned toward the books. It is then that we see "academic pressure" rising. It is possible, in the library, to turn to the view for relief. But when one feels unable to stand up to one's work, thoughts of suicide arise. Associated with the boundaries of the university, in particular the downstream side of the bridge, these are thoughts of breaking out after having been "caged in" or turned toward the books. It is then that the view becomes thought of as a place of danger. But by the same mythologizing thinking, ability to do one's work is taken as an indication of one's own safety. The sequence is as follows. First the view appears as a stable representation, establishing the viewer apart from it and thus in confrontation with his work. Then, as one feels the pressure of work and feels inadequate to its demands, the distance between viewer and viewed seems to collapse. This collapse calls to mind boundary markers, such as the railings on the seventh floor of the library. More pertinently, it is the bridges, the boundaries of the university, that come to mind when "academic pressure" is associated with suicide. The summing up of these boundaries reestablishes them with a reversal of signs. Once suicide is the result of academic pressure, the ability to do one's work is associated with life, while death has been expelled from within the confines of the university.

THREE

Kiblat and the Mediatic Jew

> *kiblat*: 1. direction of Mecca (at the time of prayer); 2. direction; aim; compass point, esp. one from which the wind arises; *berkiblat*: directed toward . . . ; e.g., politics directed toward the interests of international communism.[1]

Practically speaking, there are no Jews in Indonesia. Nor do Indonesians usually claim that there are. But it is now said that strong Jewish influence is corrupting Islam, sometimes disguised as orthodox Islamic truth and producing political unrest. There has long been anti-Semitism in Indonesia, but the amount of anti-Semitic material increased greatly during the regime of President Suharto. The Protocols of the Elders of Zion has been republished several times, as well as other anti-Semitic literature.[2] Nor is it unusual to hear Jews referred to as the cause of Indonesia's present economic crisis.

In Europe and America Jews are thought to be knowable by their names. But in my experience, even Indonesians who have spent long periods in America or Europe often do not recognize "Cohen" or "Siegel" as indicators of Jewish origins. Nor do faces provide a clue. I was told several times by Indonesians, for instance, that my nose, long and pointed by Indonesian standards, is admirable. It was admired in particular because it resembled the noses of Arabs. A Jew arriving in Indonesia, then, is likely to go unrecognized unless he says he is Jewish. But even this is not definitive. Once in Sumatra I told some Muslim friends I was of Jewish origin. They offered to take me to a co-religionist. Arriving at a house, I saw through the window a large Orthodox cross. The religious identity of the Jew, if this anecdotal evidence is worth anything, merges into that of the Christian, while the face of the Jew dissolves into the face of the Arab, the latter admired, the former feared. A Jew, even when he is present in the country, is without a face or an identity of his own. Even as he announces himself to Indonesians, within Indonesia he seems to disappear.

Translating Allah

It may be useful to look at some examples of current anti-Semitic usage. The first was stimulated by a proposal for a new foundation for tolerance among religions. Nurcholish Madjid was the leader of the Indonesian Muslim Students Association (HMI) during a critical moment in the establishment of the New Order, the term Suharto gave his regime to distinguish it from that of Indonesia's first president, Sukarno. Nurcholish is well known among the figures who speak for Islam on the Indonesian national stage. In December 1992, he gave a talk about tolerance that aroused a furor among many Muslims and led to his being called a Zionist agent and a member of the International Jewish Conspiracy.[3]

Nurcholish provoked his audience in the first place by claiming that religion (*agama*) is a danger. It stimulates intolerance and violence. He had recently returned from America, and he relied on the self-designated "futurologists" of the moment, people such as Alvin Toffler, to warn against certain dangers. Religion, as he saw it, needs to be saved from itself. He repeated something he had said twenty years earlier, when he had recently arrived in Indonesia from the United States, where he studied at the University of Chicago. Then he coined the slogan "Islam, yes; Partai Islam, no [Islam, yes; Islamic Party, no]." In sum, the problem with religion is its organized element. The religious spirit is valuable, but the institutionalization of religion provokes conflict and other difficulties. In 1992, he thought the danger was cults. Cults—meaning the bands of sometimes violent devout then a concern in America—are the result of a perverted religious impulse. They are an effect of the "alienation" (a term he borrowed from Erich

BRESCIA UNIVERSITY
COLLEGE LIBRARY

Fromm) caused by industrial society. They produce intolerance and even violence. Cults, said Nurcholish, represent the flight of the spiritual, for the spiritual has been driven out of industrial society by its characteristic confusion and loneliness. Organized religion cannot assuage this condition.

No one, Nurcholish added, claims that cults exist in Indonesia. Rather, Nurcholish fears that, given the nature of religion and given also Indonesian social conditions, cults could arise: "But in Indonesia up till now, precisely the uneven distribution [of wealth] and inequality are characteristic; this emerges clearly in the distribution of information, opinion, and opportunity. Thus the crisis [*krisis*] here would be in fact much worse than in America, were it not for other factors which work to contain it. This crisis can take different forms of expression. One in particular could threaten and at the very least disturb stability [*stabilitas*] and national security. In other forms, it can be the emergence of cults and fundamentalism."[4] There could be cults. They would arise just at the point where another danger threatens. In speaking of threats and disturbances in Indonesia, Nurcholish echoes conventional phrases employed by the New Order, which repeatedly warned the nation about dangers to "stability and national security." The New Order's "danger" referred to the menace of resurgent communism after its defeat and after the massacre in 1965–66 of hundreds of thousands of those accused of being communists. The danger arises from the maldistribution of opportunity and particularly of income in Indonesia that has come with the incursions of the international market. Nurcholish here expresses a distrust of destabilizing influences that he shares with his Islamic opponents, as we shall see. This opinion grows out of a warning spread by the government, the warning that both the government and the Indonesian public must be forever on guard against the attempted return of communists to power. Those who broadcast this warning point to the fact that in 1948, during the revolution, communists fought the forces of Sukarno. Despite their defeat, the Communist Party subsequently regained its position, reclaiming power to such an extent that in 1965 many expected them to win control of the government through elections. Just at this moment, the communists were massacred. Now, it is feared, communists will emerge again.

Nurcholish speaks of the danger of cults rather than the danger of communism as a way of introducing his criticism of religion. Cults, in his view, are a stunted form of religion. One must open religion up; he proposed making it as inclusive as possible. He suggested a way for Muslims to accept the religious life of others. The Qur'an recognizes two other people of the book, Jews and Christians, to whom prophets appeared bearing the word of God. Mohammed is the seal of prophecy, the bearer of the perfected message. But Muslim men are allowed to marry Jewish and Christian women, in acknowledgment of the line of prophecy common to their religions. In the interest of inclusion and of the spirit of religion, Nurcholish wants to show that the God of the Muslims is also the God of others. It is in the first place a question of the name of God: "Because 'Tuhan' [the Indonesian word for "God"] and 'Tuhan' can have different meanings. As an example, the 'Allah' of Arabs before Islam differed from the 'Allah' of Islam. Among other things, the 'Allah' of the Arabs had children and associates [in English] who were all 'served' with offerings and prostration by humans. While the 'Allah' of Islam has the sense of God who is the only God, who is pure; according to Max Weber it is 'pure monotheism'—strict monotheism [in English] as is cogently stated in the Qur'an, the well-known Surat Al Iklhash."⁵

The name of God confuses. Nurcholish claims that the name is not relevant. "Allah" once meant not the monotheistic god of Islam but a god of the polytheistic tribes before the foundation of Islam. What is important is that there is a single source of truth, regardless of the name given it: "Everything that is true comes from the same source, that is Allah, the Truest [*al-haqq*]. And all prophets and apostles [*rasul*] bring the same message. The difference is only in the form of the response, depending on the time and place of the apostle. Thus there are no differences of principle."⁶ It is a question of identifying "the same source." That is only in part a question of prophets and apostles. Thus the divine message was brought not only to Christians and Jews but also to Buddhists, Hindus, and others. For those who have *iman*—faith—there are no great differences. Nurcholish follows an Arabic interpretation that gives Muslims the right to marry not only Jews and Christians—people of the Book—but Chinese, Japanese, and others because "they too have holy books which contain the basis of the *Tauhid* [unicity] of God, who is uniquely One."⁷

The names of God can be confusing. The important thing is to understand that one cannot know God in his uniqueness, his lack of duplication. To try to do so is to fall into the error known in Indonesian as *berhala*, which means to picture God, to create an image of him, perhaps a material image. This for Nurcholish is the Muslim equivalent of alienation. Humans worship what they create; this means that they no longer control their own productions. He calls this *alienasi*, as he Indonesianizes the word *alienation*.

Nurcholish Madjid had some defenders. They formed one group of Muslim intellectuals on the Indonesian scene. I want to examine his opponents, however. They were numerous, but for the most part the arguments they put forward to challenge Nurcholish coincided. One assertion was that Nurcholish, in accepting that religion had undesirable effects and citing Westerners who made the same claim, no longer spoke from Islamic suppositions. According to Drs. Nabhan Husein: "It meant that he put in place a principle of use to measure a truth. This is the same as putting religion in the position of a tool [*instrumen*], subordinate to the criteria of the society concerned. When the society is flooded by change, a religion [Nurcholish thinks] has to be reexamined. And so on through the ages. A foundation of thinking of this sort might be compatible with certain religions but not with the Muslim religion."[8] Such thinking, according to Lukman Hakiem, is based on a faulty understanding of the unknowability of God. Allah cannot be known, but He can be experienced. Working through contradictions, as he says Nurcholish does, using a method he labels "Hegelian," leads those who are naive into doubt, philosophy, and secularism. He claimed that Nurcholish's misunderstanding is based on his inadequate translation from Arabic.

Another critic, H. M. Hasballah Thaib, M.A., warns, like many others, of the danger of raising doubts through the use of inappropriate methods for the study of Islam, particularly secular ones: "Many people are already made nervous about their faith when *la ilah ilallah* [the first phrase of the confession of faith] is analyzed to mean 'There is no god [*tuhan*] except God [*Tuhan*].' Not to mention saying that 'God never named himself Allah; only humans did that.'" Hasballah goes on to criticize Nurcholish for using Cartesian methods: "Imagine if someone who believed in Islam wanted to look for the truth. Would he have to leave Islam first? What would be the result? He would clearly be an apostate. In this way we see that *scientific research* [in English and italics] raises real danger when it is used in the area of faith."[9] He concludes by finding fault with Nurcholish's translations of the surat Al Imran and other parts of the Qur'an: "In his piece, NM frequently plays with Arabic words that have multiple meanings to the point where changing the meaning just a trifle can deceive the Muslim community, especially those who do not really understand the language of the Qur'an."[10]

If Nurcholish is at fault, so too are Westerners who study Islam, usually referred to in these writings as "orientalists." Hasballah Thaib enumerates their faults. Like Nurcholish:

a. They are not willing to accept the truth of Islam.
b. They have an insufficient grasp of Arabic.
c. They do not understand Islamic law.
d. They look at Islam through Jewish or Christian lenses.[11]

Another critic explains why orientalists are so influential: "After the West felt itself defeated in its attempt to control the Islamic community through political imperialism, the West struck out on another path. Among other things, they launched an attack from 'within.' For that they made an analysis of Islam in order to find its weaknesses (according to their assumptions). Then they disseminated this widely within their own areas and in the midst of the Muslim community itself in order to shake the faith of the Muslim community in its religion."[12] This writer points out that various Muslims who have studied in the West have exposed this strategy. The term "orientalists" lacks the specificity it has in Said's famous book and has little to do with Said's notion of scholars of the Middle Eastern tradition. In the works of these Indonesian writers, only occasionally are orientalists named, and even then the line of connection between a particular scholar and his influence on particular Muslims or, for that matter, the ideas of particular orientalists, goes unmentioned. Western scholars of Islam such as Jacques Berque, who are known to be defenders of Islam, do not appear. But vagueness of reference does not prevent the term *orientalist* from being consistently pejorative.

Several critics leveled the charge of orientalist influence against Nurcholish. A couple of them charged that he does not acknowledge his sources. Were he to do so, said Abu Ridho, it would mean acknowledging that many Muslim scholars who were students of Western orientalists are still under the control of their teachers. One must understand that the students of orientalists are their tools, scattered throughout every Muslim country and constantly under their control.[13]

Misquotation and mistranslation are often said to result from the influence of orientalists. Daud Rasyid, M.A., points out that, in their study of the Qur'an and Hadiths, Muslims have a certain method. They follow the etymology of Arabic words in order to be precise about their meanings, whereas Nurcholish does not. Rasyid claims further that: "Those who are not disgusted by the contents of the thought launched at them will be stunned by the feverish use of foreign terms and the philosophical delivery. . . . [They] 'will be stunned and accept the ideas.'"[14]

In this context, anti-Semitism arises. Daud Rasyid points out that Nurcholish is not the first to return from abroad with shocking ideas. There have been others. And there have been secularists of this sort in the Arab world as well. One of these is the Egyptian Thaha Husein, who claims, Daud Rasyid says, that Mohammed, rather than receiving the Qur'an from God, wrote it himself. Thaha Husein, he says, claims that there is important Jewish influence on the Qur'an. He made these assertions "following the suggestions of his teacher, Durkheim of the Sorbonne University in France, who was the director of his doctoral thesis."[15]

Daud Rasyid repeats the charge of orientalism. He quotes Prof. Dr. Ismail Raji al-Faruqi from Temple University in Philadelphia, whom he claims "fell directly into the clutches of Jewish [*Yahudi*] Zionists in the study of Islam, from the giving of scholarships and professorships, and who was murdered by Zionist agents and who advised Muslims not to study Islam in the West." The problem, Faruqi explains, is that America "was accustomed to taking in exiled intellectuals who went against the mainstream in Muslim countries and who were later given positions in the U.S. as university professors."[16] Rasyid concludes that Western orientalists do not use scientific methodology, which would insist on objectivity [*obyektif*] and an honest approach to Islam.

Returning to Nurcholish, he says that Nurcholish has mistranslated important words and has not followed the etymological methods that pertain in the study of the Qur'an and Hadiths. The results could be serious if, for instance, one translated in such a way that it was no longer necessary to fast. Rasyid notes the declaration of Allah that exposes the tricks (*trik-trik*) of the Jews and of those who study Islam with the Jews, who twist the lines of Allah with devious turns of the tongue and stunning philosophical statements so that people will accept them as the truth. Maybe this is Nurcholish's aim so that everyone will think that the duties contained in the *syariah* are unimportant and it is no longer necessary to carry them out.[17]

He goes on to criticize Nurcholish's claim that the designated "people of the Book" whose women Muslims can marry include not only Jews and Christians but also Buddhists, Hindus, and others. This conclusion, he says, is the result of another of Nurcholish's mistranslations. He ends by asserting: "Finally, how difficult it is to [have to] say that Nurcholish forces himself to be arrogant toward Islam but does not have the capacity [*modal*] for it. It is even harder to say that Nurcholish, who claims to be rendering a service to Islam in Indonesia, in fact damages Islamic thinking. The most difficult thing to say is that Nurcholish is a Zionist agent who ruins Islam from within."[18]

Daud Rasyid assimilates Nurcholish to others who have returned from study abroad. Lukman Hakiem blames Nurcholish at length for having studied at Chicago: "It was at Chicago that Nurcholish made the acquaintance of Prof. Leonard Binder, a fanatical Jew who proposed to this Indonesian Muslim intellectual the title Doctor provided he deny the role of the Muslim community in Indonesian life in the past and the future."[19]

Certain critics charged that Nurcholish spoke as a secularist. But secularism in their estimation merely delivered Nurcholish into the hands of Jews. If we assume that the secular, by contrast to the sacred, is open to argument, then a close examination of the criticisms leveled against Nurcholish shows that his critics do not really locate him in a "secular" tradition but in an alien, blasphemous "sacred" tradition, a system of falsified faith. It may be that he is open to argument within the limits of Cartesianism, but he is outside the possibility of argument with genuine Muslims, oriented as they are to the sacred word and understanding it according to prescribed principles. Nurcholish is not merely weak in his command of sacred Arabic, they say. His weakness is a sign that he translates the sacred books by other principles, those of orientalists. He is relocated or reoriented elsewhere, toward another sacred, in the sense of another foundation of translation and method of thinking, though of course only a secularist could speak of "another sacred." Nurcholish's deviation from *kiblat* opens onto the secular; the secular is another *kiblat*, another set of principles that makes it impossible for him to exchange views with those who think in genuinely Islamic terms. At the same time he continues to communicate with those who are unaware of what informs his thinking. He can only corrupt belief, according to this view.

Some writers in the monthly magazine *Media Dakwah*, where much of the criticism of Nurcholish was published, no longer consider Nurcholish to be a Muslim, but no one claims he is a Jew.[20] According to his critics, Nurcholish is the agent, more often than not unwitting, of orientalists. He is in their power, unreachable by argument. In that sense, too, Nurcholish's understanding of the Qur'an is a mistranslation from only one point of view. The Jews who have, in the understanding of Nurcholish's critics, mistranslated the Qur'an have done so willfully. Their nefarious intentions are fully transmitted in Nurcholish's discourse. The Qur'an may be mistranslated, but the words of Jewish orientalists are not. Generations after their studies were made, their work shows up intact without any slippage in translation from English or French or German into Arabic and from there into Indonesian. Unwitting Indonesian Muslims, duped by these studies, repeat the intentions of Jews who lived generations before on different continents.

There is no mistranslation at all. On the contrary, there is a path of translation that is always accurate, preserving the inimical intentions at its origin. These bad intentions differ from those one encounters in daily life. One can reply to or even correct threats in daily life. But there can be no exchange of views with those of another orientation. They are under the control of others far away in time and place. Nurcholish at best could repent rather than modify his opinions. For their part, his critics could be influenced by him only at the cost of accepting something that would remain incompatible with everything else they think; alternatively, they could change their entire manner of thinking. Words that originate from another *kiblat* cannot be assimilated within the true Islamic understandings of Nurcholish's critics. Taken in, they destroy one's capacity to understand correctly.

Many of those who responded to Nurcholish stress that Islam is tolerant and that Jews and Christians fare well under Muslim rule. The converse, they say, is not true. They do not fear the presence of non-Muslims within Islamic society; rather, they fear that someone or something shows up through the intervention of Nurcholish and others trained by orientalists. This someone, the originator of the dangerous messages, remains abroad. They do not object to the presence of Jews themselves. For all practical purposes, there are no Jews in Indonesia, and no one claims that there are.[21] Rather, they fear Zionist influence, and they conflate Zionists and Jews. Furthermore, Zionist influence has nothing much to do with Israel. The misconceptions of orientalists originate in Europe or America, not in Israel, and it is not clear what political benefit there would be to Israel if, for instance, Nurcholish Madjid gained influence in Indonesia.[22] Zionist influence means harm to Indonesian Muslims through the actions or speech of those taken to be Indonesian Muslims controlled by those at a distance.[23]

Media Dakwah is not an organ of "fundamentalists" insofar as that word means religious figures who insist on a scripturalist interpretation of the Qur'an.[24] Rather, it is an organ of "modernists." Its chief ancestral figure is Mohammed Natsir, who was an important Islamic reformer. An Islamic modernist in the Indonesian context meant someone who, in the 1930s, in the name of Islam and of the Indonesian nation, advocated the establishment of Western-style education rather than qur'anic schools, who worked for the emancipation of women, which meant favoring modern dress and education for them, and who, upon independence, preferred including all groups of the archipelago in the nation to establishing a state ruled by Islamic law.[25] *Media Dakwah* continued to welcome changes in Indonesian society. It looked on the new conglomerates to be found in Jakarta as promising vehicles for the spread of Islam. It introduced prayer sessions and religious instruction into conglomerates run by Muslims and into certain government banks. Yet *Media Dakwah* thought corporate enterprise largely favored Indonesian Chinese at the expense of small-scale Muslim traders. Its objections to "capitalism" seem to be linked to their concerns about the "Chinese" (this term refers to people merely of Chinese descent, often, indeed, of mixed ancestry, who are culturally and by citizenship Indonesians).[26]

Media Dakwah was founded by members of the Indonesian elite, people who had benefited from Western-style education and who had worked to enlarge opportunity for those considered less privileged. In the 1930s and 1950s such people were eager to benefit from Western learning. If their attitude has changed, that is in part because the notion of the foreign as it impinges on Indonesia has changed. "The foreign" is no longer a source of ideas whose assimilation by Indonesians led to independence and promised to generate economic and social development. It is now identified, in the first place, with the market. The writers of *Media Dakwah* are not against the market as such, but they recognize that neither the elimination of the communists nor the introduction of an internationalized economy has closed the gap between themselves and "the people," now the underclass, in whose name the revolution was fought; rather, the opposite has happened. The assumption that others, foreigners, knew how to construct a just society and that the adoption of methods, means, and ideas from abroad would lead to a united national community has been shaken.[27]

Nurcholish Madjid addressed such reformist, modernist Muslims, saying that it was time to go beyond them. In turn, *Media Dakwah* devoted much space to Nurcholish. The cover of one issue largely given over to him bears the title "Where Nurcholish's Thought Comes Out" and shows someone entering a maze. At the end of the maze is a Star of David. This refers to hidden twists of the tongue; issuing from Nurcholish's mouth, these take effect at a distance, misleading others, who then end up as Jewish Zionist agents.

Media Dakwah has no monopoly on Indonesian anti-Semitism, but it is noteworthy for its position near the balancing point of a debate about Western influences and Indonesia. The writers and audience of *Media Dakwah* constitute a group that is (or was once) open to Western ideas, that does not absolutely oppose the introduction of the global market and the changes it brings, and that favors technological change. It is also anti-Semitic. *Media Dakwah* points to another sort of anti-Semitism, one that does not issue from communal tension or from the suspicion of traders in a peasant society, but rather from conditions of communication that fall under the rubric "globalization."

Martin van Bruinessen, perhaps the leading Western authority on the current state of Indonesian Muslim thought and organization, suggests that Indonesian Muslim support for the Palestinian cause, particularly since the Six Days' War, is one reason for the great increase in anti-Semitic material during the Suharto period. He is surely correct, though, as he notes, the conflation of Jews and Zionists is inaccurate and unnecessary, making anti-Semitism aberrant.

With the defeat of the communists in 1965–66, Muslims, who were instrumental in the overthrow of Sukarno and who supported the efforts of his eventual successor, Suharto, hoped to find their influence increased in the state. For a long time, they were disappointed. Suharto promoted a number of Christians to important positions in the military and the government, a move that some Muslims resented. When he also granted concessions to Indonesian Chinese in order to attract their capital, these signs of favor led some to complain that, though Muslims formed the majority of the nation, they were politically marginalized. As the New Order came to an end, Suharto turned more and more to Muslim groups for support, but resentment about being kept out of power persists among certain of them, particularly those who write for *Media Dakwah*.[28] Other Muslim groups and leaders, including Nurcholish Madjid, found a place for themselves with Suharto.[29] One must take into account the changed place of religion in the Indonesian state. Before the New Order there was much less conflict between religions than certain Muslims, at least, felt to be the case in the 1990s. Since then, such conflict has developed into serious violence in certain regions.

In general, religious sentiment or at least activity has gained in strength in Indonesia as the left has been eliminated from the political scene. There have also been reports of many (one cannot say how many) former leftists who became Christians or, less often, Muslims to avoid the consequences of having been party members. Moreover, with the end of populism as practiced by Sukarno, some of that movement's ideological fervor passed into the mode of religion. At the same time, new divisions have separated Muslims from each other. In the Sukarno era the main distinctions were between Muslims closely tied to local traditions and the proponents of "modernization." Nurcholish Madjid directed his remarks, we have noted, at the latter, in the name not of regionalism but of a changed world in which the "modern" no longer could comprehend Indonesian realities. In my opinion he reflects the segment of the population whose point of reference is, first of all, the large city and for whom the contention between reformers of another period and their rural opponents is without much relevance.

This does not mean that the majority of Indonesians, neither those living in the regions nor the urban lower classes, have been forgotten. *Media Dakwah*, for instance, sometimes sees them within the context of a certain embourgeoisement; it reports that the conglomerates who support Islamic activities in their businesses appreciate the "increased discipline" that regular prayer and sermons produce in their employees.[30] For the most part, however, it regrets that the great underclass, assumed to be Muslim, is not represented in national or even local affairs. Nurcholish's remarks, in fact, address the failure of Islam in its present condition to appeal to these very people, people he wishes to raise in the social scale and whose actions he fears if the situation remains as it is. He speaks of toleration for Christians, Buddhists, Hindus, and so on, calling on the power of a certain Islamic belief to encompass others, including this neglected underclass. His toleration would make possible the inclusion of everyone currently a citizen by law in the nation. The danger he sees when he speaks of cults is not from Buddhists or Christians, but from the underprivileged, who might disrupt national security because of the "gap" between them and people in Nurcholish's own class. These potential disrupters of the social order are usually referred to as the *massa*, the masses or the mob, and they are thought to be Islamic. The power of the state and the nation to encompass its citizens is more severely challenged by their discontent than it was by the regionalism of the early period of the republic. The implicit assumption of the debate on tolerance is the lessened ability of the Indonesian nation to encompass its citizens through the assumptions at work in the founding of the nation. Islam, in some form or another, is needed to accomplish what people fear the state no longer can.

In the view of *Media Dakwah*, the Indonesian Chinese pose a problem because they incite the underclass. The writers of *Media Dakwah* also fear the "gap" between the middle class and the underclass. They, like many Indonesians, focus on division caused by inequities between wealthy Indonesian Chinese and poor Muslims. This formulation conceals the non-Chinese middle class, to which the writers themselves belong. It perceives Indonesian Chinese to be the cause of disruption and popular discontent. The writers of *Media Dakwah* both justified the anti-Chinese rioting of 1998 in terms of the need and long suffering of the people and, at the same time, feared it. In their opinion, once the underclass has proper Muslim leadership, which was blocked under the New Order, the problem will be solved.

For Nurcholish, toleration of Christians and Buddhists, meaning "Chinese," is one issue; the question of cults is not altogether another. The cults he fears would be Islamic, appealing to the underclass. Many middle-class Muslims fear Islamic "fanaticism" in a way that is not always different from the sentiment of some Americans. To include and tolerate Indonesian Chinese in the nation would ideally make them less alien, and thus neutralize them as an object of unwanted attraction for the underclass. Indonesian Chinese would no longer incite envy and desire, and therefore no longer incite fanatical, "fundamentalist" Islamic notions, which express that envy. To propose a more tolerant form of Islam is to oppose cults and to prevent Indonesian Chinese from (indirectly) playing a role in their formation.

Nurcholish wishes to renew Islam so that it can play its necessary political role. His opponents wish to return Muslims to power by overcoming those who have prevented their accession to it (particularly Indonesian Chinese and Christians) and who have thereby prevented the full inclusion of the Muslim underclass in the nation. They want a Muslim political party that would speak for this underclass in Islamic terms. They perpetuate the thinking of an earlier period in Indonesia, when the various cultural strains of the nation each had its own political party. Despite these differences, the underlying problem for both *Media Dakwah* and Nurcholish, as for the entire Indonesian political class, is the "gap" between the middle and lower classes. In the issue of religious toleration, questions of class and religion intersect.[31]

The state's insistence on religious tolerance is part of its policy of overcoming differences within the category "Indonesian." The first of the Five Principles, or Panca Sila, of the Indonesian state—"God is One"—requires Indonesians to be believers. They can choose between the five religions recognized by the state: Islam, Protestantism, Catholicism, Buddhism, and Hinduism, each with its own department within the Ministry of Religion. This first principle was adopted to appeal to Muslims, who wanted a stronger Islamic basis for the state but were unable or unwilling to have a provision obliging Muslims to follow Islamic law adopted at a time when to do so threatened national unity.[32]

Tolerance is guaranteed within the framework of the state. This is the outcome of Indonesian nationalism, in particular, the result of an attempt by Sukarno to include all the peoples of the archipelago in the nation. If the monotheism of the first principle, belief in one god, was understood to include nonmonotheistic religions, this happened because the Five Principles, taken as a whole, were thought of as making a place for all the peoples of Indonesia. Perhaps also it was because of the syncretism Sukarno practiced, which had its roots in Javanese tradition, whereby diverse and even incompatible ideas were routinely brought together as proof of the power of the kingdom.[33] Later Sukarno announced other principles, such as NASAKOM, an acronym of the words meaning "nationalism," "religion," and "communism." These incompatible elements were nonetheless joined in a unity that found its force in the nation. The proclamation of NASAKOM was also an attempt at inclusiveness, another word for which is *tolerance*, a word borrowed from English. The very capacity to hold together disparate elements proved the power of the state and the nation. It attested to the state's cultural and even religious force, beyond its political power.

Why Panca Sila survived and NASAKOM did not is a question to be answered by political history. In any event, syncretism was out of date in the New Order. Although syncretism derived from Javanese tradition, its force outside Java, in the nation as a whole, rested not on a fundamental belief in Javanese ideas but on belief in the state as the heir to and even continuation of the revolution. If the monotheism of the state's first principle could also comprise Hinduism, for example, that was not merely thanks to political compromise. It was because the nation itself, realized during the revolution, had a capacity to include its peoples. Under this dispensation, Muslims could be satisfied with the strict sense of "monotheism," while Hindus could be assured that somehow it applied to them as well.

From the beginning of the Indonesian state, then, there have been multiple *kiblats*. If in 1945 it was possible to ask Muslims to moderate their claims in the interest of national unity, that was because the prestige of the revolution made conflict between Indonesians insupportable. Now the Islamic faction represented in *Media Dakwah* asserts that its status as a majority within the state gives it the right to decide the terms of toleration, and that in religious terms. Nurcholish, for his part, is not content with a purely national source of ethnic inclusiveness; he too turns to Islam. One is left wondering what is considered to be fundamental. The wavering between principles reflects the inability of the state to continue to incarnate the revolution in the minds of Indonesians.

Nurcholish continues Sukarno's impulse to include. But to ask after the basis of tolerance is also to show its limits. Nurcholish does not mention communists, but his references to the "gap" between classes is a coded reference to the possibility of their return, no doubt in a different form. If he wants to include "everyone," that does not mean everyone under any definition. His notion of tolerance coincides with that of the state. It includes all Indonesians, but only as spelled out by the first principle. Nurcholish wants to include Christians and Buddhists within the limits of acceptability of Islam and of the Indonesian nation. If some of these are former communists, they are not acceptable as such. *Media Dakwah* fears the inclusion of the same groups, and it is more forthright in its insistence on exclusion.

At the time of the state's founding, the problem was to make national identity prevail over regional and religious definitions of personhood. Today, in the conflict over toleration, the problem is different. With the prosperity of the New Order, class differences have emerged. These are obscured by the place of the Indonesian Chinese, who were integrated into the Indonesian economy by Suharto in return for their investment but were kept out of the national universities, the government bureaucracy, and the armed forces. This left them vulnerable to being considered the wealthy *tout court*, obscuring, as I have said, the newly prosperous non-Chinese. There is also the fear of a return to power by communists, who are unrealistically blamed for social unrest. By identifying the Indonesian Chinese and resurrected communists as the chief causes of disunity, the people we have been discussing maintain their belief that unity of the nation is still a possibility. If only the rich and the ineradicable force of communism did not threaten us, the nation would be unified, and there would be no need to discuss toleration.

Questions about tolerance and about the foundation of the nation are raised together.[34] In this context, one's opponents do not voice ordinary disagreements. They seem, rather, to speak from somewhere else, from presuppositions out of reach of certain interlocutors. To this complication are added the complications raised by voices meant to be kept out of the discussion entirely, including the voices of communists somehow left over after the massacres and imprisonments of 1965–66, and, for some, the voices of Indonesian Chinese and of "the people [*rakyat*]," who, as the *massa*, the masses, threaten to speak in the form of uprising. It becomes a question of whom one hears and whom one is afraid of hearing.

In this situation, one does not fear statements themselves, but rather the origin of the communication. Van Bruinessen tells how a religious scholar from a remote eastern island of Indonesia complained about cassettes that recorded recitation of the Qur'an. The recordings were perfect; the Qur'an was chanted as it should be. People listened to them enthusiastically. That troubled the religious scholar. Instead of chanting the Qur'an themselves, the people of the island listened to the cassettes. Their faith weakened. It was, he said, the result of a Jewish plot. It was entirely a question of the origin of the recordings. Nothing in the recorded words themselves indicated their origin. Everything that could be recognized was as it should be. And yet there was something else, something unrecognizable about these perfect recordings. This scholar found there a distant origin. He saw it as a communicative force with the power to put words in the ears of believers and make them want to hear these words over and over again. This he labeled this the work of Jews.[35]

The subtle mistranslations of Nurcholish likewise arrive from some distant place, according to his opponents. He cannot be convinced to recognize their perverse source, and the source, rather than the content of the translation or mistranslation, is truly at issue here. Were Nurcholish himself to be the origin of mistranslation, his intentions could be read, and he could be corrected. He, however, says something that makes his opponents certain its origin is not with him at all; the real source of the message is far away. The consequences of hearing this message, like the consequences of listening to the cassettes of the Qur'an, are potentially catastrophic. The messages have a power that cannot be guessed at and that extends far beyond the effect of what they seem to say. In that sense, the true sources of the message remain as unrecognizable as the identities of those who fabricated the perfect Qur'anic chanting on the tapes. Nurcholish is said to be the bearer of singular effects that could mean anything other than what they should mean.

Seen from one side, Nurcholish is the bearer of obscure, distant, and catastrophic messages; from the other, he is a man who wants to save his country from the menace of violence and even disintegration by bringing something as yet unheard of. For people who trust him, his message is limited and precise. To his opponents, he represents the possibility of a messiah—unwanted, of course—because what he says contains the possibility of meaning anything at all; all possibilities, including those as yet unknown, are open.

This messianic possibility arises out of the disturbed horizons of the Indonesian nation. Yet the unknowability of Nurcholish to his opponents cannot wholly be reduced to that disturbance. Not only is Nurcholish oriented to falsehood, but the term *Jew* indicates a source of falsehood that is as potent in its consequences as it is difficult to locate. Though "Jew" and "Zionist" are conflated in this way of thinking, Israel is not considered to be the source of Nurcholish's errors. The places named—Chicago, Paris, Germany—are merely stopping points for Jews, whose place of residence is unimportant. It does not matter whether they are American, French, or German; what matters is that they are Jews.

One cannot derive the Jewish "elsewhere" from the complicated array of diverse *kiblat*—communist, Buddhist, and so on. It is beyond all of these, unlike them in that those with such an orientation—Jews—are not explicitly part of the Indonesian scene. One comes across them only by chance, it seems. One knows the *kiblats* of non-Jews, but the Jewish *kiblat* designates an "elsewhere" without an indicator. What might it have to do with other voices and other *kiblats* found today in Indonesia?

References Abroad

There were, of course, Dutch Jews in the Dutch East Indies, as well as descendants of Jews from the Middle East. A synagogue remains in the port of Surabaya today, but the Jewish community was never prominent in the Indies.[36] In any event, present-day references to Jews do not refer to actual populations. The Jew is neither an unwanted figure who already exists in Indonesia nor is he the excluded one, which would imply that he could at some point become an element of the local population. The Jew as object of anti-Semitism remains abroad, and it is assumed he always will, his references being Zionism, orientalists, and qur'anic pronouncements. Only his effects are feared.

Westerners often compare the Indonesian Chinese population to Jews because the Chinese are a minority that came from abroad and because many of them are traders. One might imagine that anti-Semitic thinking would cast them in the role of crypto-Jews. This is not the case. Chinese are seldom identified with Jews,[37] but on at least one occasion the Jew showed up in the pages of *Media Dakwah* when churches were burned as a result of conflict between Muslims and Indonesian Chinese.

There is a long history of contention between those termed "Chinese" and other Indonesians. Under Sukarno Chinese education and the use of Chinese characters for store names were banned. Indonesian Chinese have been encouraged to replace their Chinese names with other names, usually Javanese or Arabic, and many have done so. They are, in the eyes of mainland Chinese, indistinguishable from other Indonesians. But they are accused of having favored the Dutch during the revolution and of being less than reliable in their fidelity to the nation, as evidenced by the popular fear, widespread before the change of regime in 1998, that they would expatriate

their capital during the economic crisis. On the one hand, they are acknowledged as Indonesian citizens, Indonesian by culture and language; on the
other hand, they are distinguished as separate by small identifying marks,
such as the initials WNI (Warga Negara Indonesia), which stand for "Indonesian citizen," and by other terms indicating the distinction imposed on
them by their fellow Indonesians.

All of this might favor an identification of "Chinese" with Jews. This
happens only vaguely, but it does so at a specific, significant point in the
discourse. In March 1997, *Media Dakwah* devoted an issue to anti-Chinese
riots in which churches were burned in certain Javanese cities and their
surroundings. In Rengasdengklok, the Pentecostal Church was burned. In
the area as a whole, four churches were set on fire. So was a bank, and many
shops were looted. Outside the city, a *vihara* was also burned. This last
event attracted international attention, because an Australian photographer
from Associated Press Television was present when a statue of the Buddha
was hung by the neck from an arch at the entrance to the burning temple.
His recording of the event was shown on CNN.[38] Nonetheless, the attention of *Media Dakwah* focused on the churches, not on the *vihara*. It also
reported similar events in nearby cities. The magazine was upset because
Muslims were blamed for the fires and the riots. It did not deny that Muslims set these churches and shops afire, but opined that these Muslims were
justified in doing so. The problem began during the fasting month, when
an Indonesian Chinese called Cik Gue (*Media Dakwah* writes it "Cigue";
for convenience I will follow that practice) complained because she was
awakened by the beating of the drums in the mosque, calling believers for
the optional prayer often made during the nights of the fasting month. Here
is an account of the incident by a local Muslim teacher:

> At 2:55 A.M. people here usually strike the drum, announcing the time to
> prepare breakfast (early because it must be before dawn). This lasts for five
> minutes, until 3:00 A.M. This has gone on for years. Cigue had a toothache and
> for some reason swore at the kids in the mosque, using dirty words: "dog," "pig,"
> "stupid." Then she called the police, and the police straightway took down the
> names of the boys in the mosque. After the police came she [Cigue] overacted
> [in English], feeling she had protection. So she cursed some more. Finally, the
> masses were angry, she was beaten up, and the police could no longer break up
> the masses. As time went on more and more people came.[39]

If Cigue, rather than the rioters, is to blame for the riot, it is not merely because she lost her temper and her husband threatened to call the police. It is also because she acted with the confidence of one who was "protected" when she made her complaint; she was able to act with impunity toward Muslims because she felt that the governmental authorities were on her side, favoring Chinese. Muslims are a majority, but they are blamed for the faults of others. Another local religious teacher says of the same riots: "We are very disturbed that the Islamic community is blamed for the incident; always blamed, forced into a corner. Why not blame the people who triggered it [*menjadi pemicu*]? The ones who triggered the flare-up were not Muslims. Why should it only be Muslims who are pursued? . . . Because if indeed the Islamic community is to blame for the flare-up, it's only for the smoke. The fire is them (non-Islam—editor). I said the same to the police chief."[40] These speakers do not claim that the churches were connected with Cigue. It is unlikely that Cigue belonged to more than one of them, if to any at all. Rather, Cigue's bad temper is taken to be characteristic of "Chinese." Typically, these speakers claim, Chinese do not respect the customs of their neighbors. The subtitle of one article states: "Those of Chinese descent act without regard. This triggers unrest and deep hatred." Some Javanese often accuse their Chinese neighbors of keeping to themselves and not respecting Javanese ways.

"They," "Chinese," cause the trouble while we, Muslims, take the blame. By making this claim, a writer registers his complaint about the actions of the police who subdued the Muslim rioters, and perhaps also about the national papers and their coverage of the riots.[41] Chinese are also accused of cheating in the marketplace, substituting eighteen- for twenty-four-karat gold, not giving full measure when they sell vegetables, and so on. All such complaints stem from a general conviction that the Muslim majority in Indonesia, while so often showing tolerance toward others, is not only taken advantage of by those they tolerate but is ignored and abused by its own government.

The result is an accumulation of grievances that Muslims say they have every reason to think should be corrected by the government. They do not invoke equal protection under law but the feeling that the government is by rights theirs since they are the vast majority. They complain that their protests to the government are never rightly heard; instead, such protests only attract suspicion. They perceive themselves to be the victims. But the burned-out churches indicate to others that they are intolerant and at fault. If they act against the Indonesian Chinese and not against the government, it is because they identify with the nation; though the government is not in their control, they think of it as symbolically their own. It is Chinese who prevent it from being more than symbolically theirs.

Another religious teacher complained that when the regent in his community issued a permit to build a new church, the Christians, meaning Chinese, built one almost twice the size, even adding a second story.[42] He presented himself as a defender of the regulations, of the national government, implying that Indonesian Chinese enjoy better relations with officials because Chinese bribe the officials. The teacher is not against the law; he is for it. But when local officials do not enforce the law, they, Muslims, must enforce it themselves, even if they do so, paradoxically, with illegitimate violence. Chinese are contemptuous of the country and are not fully Indonesian. It is not a question of legal citizenship but of moral status. "They," "Chinese," should become Indonesian in the full sense by participating in the community while respecting the rights of the majority. "We," Muslims, are ready to defend the law even to the point of taking on the opprobrium of the government, of public opinion, and of the police, the agents of the law.[43] We act out of desperation. It is not simply that only violence is left; in the absence of law enforcement, to act outside the law is to institute it. When Chinese understand that they cannot bribe officials and cannot act outside the community, the law will work again.

The events at Rengasdengklok and the other places nearby are, in the view of *Media Dakwah*, not merely the result of accumulated past grievances: they are an indication of trouble to come. They reveal the presence of a "time bomb [*bom waktu*]." A riot is the call of people who have become convinced that they are powerless and unheard. This religious teacher, who instructed some of the rioters, says that the trouble in Rengasdengklok began in 1978 and has been continuous. "But these are sharp pebbles, a time bomb they have planted." He explains the machinery of the time bomb by saying it concerns questions of the economy, business politics of the Chinese, social questions, and many questions that concern religion. All this adds up to the point where

> there is jealousy and there are many questions that concern religion. Indeed, they have not put up any new churches. But houses that have been turned into

churches . . . [ellipsis in original], these are numerous. Yeah, these are new churches, new churches. I told the regent straight out and the chief of police. It was the first time I was "arrested"; I wasn't really arrested, just questioned [*dinterogasi*] and asked for explanations. After, there were indications of people in their twenties [i.e., possibly his students].

And then?

Ya . . . [ellipsis in original]. I said there are no new churches. But there are many houses that have turned into churches. The time bomb issue; the people [*masyarakat*] urged the council of religious scholars to protest the church built by Oklih. Oklih is the Director of Pantura Bank.

What is at issue?

The regent's permit is for a church of 400 square meters, but they built 730 square meters, and they made it two stories. The regent and his assistant do not allow churches to be built larger than the church in the regency capital [Karawang]. But this is actually the biggest church in West Java. Everyone knows that they have contempt for the regulations. We even met with the Council. Write this down: we are not antichurch, anti-Christian.

You mean an attitude of tolerance?

Really we live next to them in peace. But procedures have to be gone through. There should not be [a permit] for one limit and then a church built for more than that. There, that's the time bomb if the officials don't deal with it. We asked that the government tear down what's over the limit. But it's never been done. The regent himself doesn't understand. He just knows that Oklih built a church within the procedures. So that's the symptom that something is hidden in the background.

You mean things have accumulated?

He then goes on to speak of the beating of the drum in the middle of the night. People should understand that it is the fasting month, he says, and restrain their feelings.

Religious conflicts are the culmination of other problems. These budding conflicts are represented by a sign: the multiplication of churches. Like the act of building churches larger than those permitted by law, these churches have no legal standing. As a result, one cannot tell for sure whether they exist or not. The religious scholar says the Christians have built no new churches; then he says that homes have been turned into churches. Asked how many churches there are in Rengasdengklok, he an-swers: "A lot. Officially there are only four. But this does not include resi-dences that have been made into churches. I don't know exactly the number because they do not have official permits. They aren't registered."[44] These churches symbolize a series of grievances. Their appearance has an inevita-ble and autonomous course of its own. What is a house one day is a church the next. Churches simply appear, and no force can stop them. People do not know how many there are. The "time bomb" has exploded. At this point we have moved from discussing an individual "Chinese" who "trig-gered" the burnings with her complaints to the workings of a force whose agents are nameless and whose places of appearance are uncertain.

Media Dakwah reproduces photographs of burned-out churches with captions that indicate their significance: "A Church the Victim of Unrest: They are built on a magnificent scale often without legal permits."[45] Indo-nesian, which lacks both tenses and a plural form, permits one to say "it was built" and "they are being built" in the same words. The effect is to make a unique case, the church in the picture, typical. Not merely is the church like others in its display of extravagant expenditure, but seeing it in a photo-graph (already, of course, a form of duplication) and reading the caption links it to multiple examples. One departs from the historical event and even the narrative, which is to say, the connection between Cigue's reaction to the drumming in the mosque and the accumulated grievances that mag-nified the significance of the incident. The account slips and expands, so that more churches threaten automatically to replicate, with, in conse-quence, more arson to come. This is the "time bomb" not only as it was but as it will be.

Churches as symbols of past grievances are one thing. Churches that continuously appear out of homes have a tinge of the uncanny. Burning them down does not solve the problem. It merely indicates a moment of provocation. The implication is that the churches will continue to appear and that they will be found unbearable again sometime in the future.

"Write this down, we aren't anti-church, anti-Christian," the religious teacher tells the reporter. He thus asserts that burning the churches was an action directed against Chinese, not against Christians. The congregations of these churches were likely to be mixed, yet the churches are thought of as the work only of Chinese. Chinese are thought to have bribed government officials, and Chinese are thought to have paid for the churches. Churches that were not "magnificent," that did not display the amount of money invested in them, might be merely Christian. Money forms the "gap" between "Chinese" and "us" that causes the "time bomb": "they" have it and "we" do not. But it is also formed by the refusal of Chinese to mix with their Javanese neighbors. "Chinese" in this sense signifies wealth and exclusiveness.

Indeed wealth, at least "Chinese" wealth, is thought to lead to exclusiveness. Here is a report from the team of Indonesians who investigated the events at Rengasdengklok. The writers of *Media Dakwah* are unlikely to find it objectionable:

> Kim Tjoan [the husband of Cigue], Cigue, and their children are thought by the people of [the neighborhood] to be a family that does not mix much with their neighbors. Small incidents related by their neighbors show the objections and difficulties of the family in mixing socially. Mrs. Weskorni, the wife of a teacher, one of the figures of the neighborhood, knows Cigue to be a difficult person. "Earlier, when the Chinese were poor, they did mix [*bergaul*], but now that they have their own store and house they are remote. In fact, they live right in our midst," she said. When Cigue talks with the neighbors, she only goes up to the fence of her house.
>
> Once there was an incident: a sweet sop fruit ripening in Cigue's yard was picked by a neighbor's child who was also of Chinese descent. This event raised problems between the two families. Cigue could not contain her feelings, said Oen Ceng Bouw, whose house is right in front of Cigue's. Cigue charged Oen Ceng Bouw's child with being a thief.[46]

The gap between Chinese and other Indonesians might be thought to provoke jealousy. But the logic is not exact. If other Indonesians want what Chinese have, they do not want to have it in the same way. In anti-Chinese riots in Java, stores are often looted and the goods then burned. Not to keep the goods for oneself is a way of showing that what Chinese value is not what one values oneself.[47] One remains uninfluenced by wealth. Cigue and her family are charged with allowing wealth to inflect their relations with their neighbors. When they were able to own their own shop and their own house, they set themselves apart. For a child to take a piece of fruit from a neighbor's tree is considered part of the way that neighbors share belongings. Cigue came to think differently. She no longer "mixes," which means not only "talks with" but also mixing property. She and her family live apart. They no longer talk to their neighbors, and they no longer understand them.

Wealth leads to separation. But "in fact, they live right in our midst." It is a strange prejudice that wants those who are disliked to take a larger part in the community. Of course, the anticipated result is that, once such people mix, they will no longer be upset when they are awakened by a drum before dawn. The complaint is that, without such mixing, Chinese become strangers. These Chinese are not different by custom or descent. Nor do they begin by being different: Cigue was once "like us"; when she became wealthy, she became not merely different but unreachable. Separation is intolerable, not merely because it causes difficulties between those still living side by side but because, even before there are problems, those who have become strangers take on a ghostly tinge.

The complaint is that such people are still present, yet are removed. Where does Cigue keep herself when she is not mixing with Muslims? She is rumored to be insane.[48] This report of insanity is actually a hyperbolic form of the statement that because Chinese do not mix, they do not understand "us," save that here the statement is comprehended through a reversal: "We do not understand them." There is a connection between the spectral churches that keep appearing out of houses, which is to say, out of nowhere, and the spectral neighbors who, because of their idea of property, keep to themselves and thus choose to live "nowhere": wealth marks Chinese as not merely different but as having an incomprehensible provenance.

Chinese are often thought to be wealthy when they are not. They are the repositories of imaginary wealth not merely in the sense that they may not own anything more than their neighbors but in the sense that their wealth is incomprehensible, coming as it does from other sources than those thought to be available to Javanese. A Javanese who finds something unusual, perhaps a number printed upside down by accident on a train ticket, might well use that number to bet on the lottery. If he were to win and to become wealthy, it would be a mark of the way in which the supernatural favors him. It would give him a new and honorable position within Javanese society. His wealth, unlike Chinese wealth, would come from an uncanny force whose provenance, though not known, is at least usable and integrated into everyday life. Chinese wealth removes Chinese from the society of their neighbors and comes from a source not open to these neighbors.

The "elsewhere" of Cigue, alone with her possessions, is not the same "elsewhere" as the source of a winning lottery number. It is not available to her Javanese neighbors. She is, in that sense, more than merely "odd [*aneh*]," the term used for the misprinted train ticket that indicates a possible uncanny source for the numbers. Though still so termed, she is beyond that category as it functions between Javanese, and thus she is unlocatable. Nonetheless, her neighbors remain acutely aware of her. From this perspective, the problem with the gap between presumably wealthy Chinese and their Muslim neighbors is not that it is unbridgeable but that it is not wide enough. What they, Chinese, have is apparent to us. We are bothered by it. Across this gap there seems to be continuous communication, but not of the usual sort. "We" are bothered by them, by the strange appearances of their churches and by their strange relation to property.

That Chinese wealth is thought to estrange may be merely an effect of the intrusion of the market. The market is not at all foreign to Muslim traders, however. There is also the charge that " 'Chinese' are a minority in the nation while we are the majority, and yet they are wealthy and we are not." The authors of a study of the riot in Rengasdengklok note that several Chinese there were favored by the government. They point out the open secret that, to do business, one needs to have various government permits and that Chinese, and not Muslims, got these, usually in return for officials' receiving shares in the companies owned by the Chinese applicants.[49] Furthermore, economic development during the New Order "favored Chinese more than others."[50] To point to real economic differences, however, is not to explain how the rivalries between Chinese and Muslim traders become generalized or how they function in a national setting. Most important to us, it does not explain how economic rivalry yields a view of Chinese as somehow uncanny.

The conflict between neighbors is also a conflict between co-nationals at a certain point in time. The gap referred to is nationwide; it is the division between rich and poor Indonesians. Economically, sociologically, such a division marked the very inception of the nation. It was always intended to be closed, however. Inherent in the idea of "the people [*rakyat*]" was the belief that the educated class would lead them out of poverty and ignorance. The populist policies of Indonesia's first president, Sukarno, fostered this idea. With the New Order of Suharto, however, populism was set aside in favor of Development (*Pembangunan*). The expansion of the market in fact benefited most people; the amount of poverty, for instance, was drastically reduced. It also marked the strong development of a well-to-do middle class, including both Chinese and non-Chinese. The gap is the wound dealt to the unity of the national body by this augmented class division. It is blamed on Chinese, the richest of whom were, in fact, favored by Suharto in order to encourage them to invest in Indonesia. As I have said, to blame Chinese for being wealthy while "we" are not is to conceal the well-to-do non-Chinese middle class.

In Rengasdengklok, the separation of the rioters from their government is in fact a separation dividing two groups of Muslim Indonesians. Yet those who support the rioters say the division is caused by Chinese. They do not hope to cure the nation of ethnic Chinese by initiating a campaign of "ethnic cleansing"; they hope to cure the nation of its own estranged, ghostly members by reintegrating them, making them obey the rules. This action would reunite the underclass with the national government. Until the time when that reunification takes place, Chinese will be attacked for having caused a rift.

Recognizing "Chinese" means identifying a certain "strangeness," as we have noted. The youth, Hendra Kurnia, who beat the drum and was cursed by Cigue said this about the couple: "It's not because they are Chinese that I don't like them. Nor is it because their religion is different from ours. It's because they act and they think strangely [*yang aneh*]. They never act like good neighbors. In front of Kim Tjoan's house there is another Chinese, Ceng Bouw. He is totally different, wants to be a good neighbor and likes to shoot the breeze [*ngobrol*] in the neighborhood-watch guardhouse in front of the meeting place for prayer."[51] This youth uses the word *aneh*, meaning "strange," a word that also means "supernaturally strange," as I have noted. For him, Chinese who do not spend time in talk with their neighbors are uncanny. He recognizes them as neighbors, but he sees in them something else as well. This "something else" is not exactly difference, if that means positive difference. Rather, he senses that the man or the woman in front of him, who does not speak, is concerned with something he cannot grasp. He complains of their *watak*, their nature. Asked if he had been taught by someone to dislike Kim Tjoan, he replies: "No need to be taught. The others here have the same feelings about Kim Tjoan because his *watak*, his nature, is like that. So that's why he gets it like that. In fact, if we could, we'd tear his house down to the ground so he would never come back." The strangeness of Kim Tjoan is apparent. His qualities are visible to everyone. Because of this he invites violence. He is recognizable as "strange," "odd," different from what one would expect, not entirely recognizable. Hendra Kurnia denies that he dislikes Kim Tjoan because he is Chinese. If he were not "Chinese," however, one might ask if his *watak* would be so apparent. The riots spread because the strangeness of Kim Tjoan is assumed to be shared by other Chinese. The uncanny finds its locus in the man's ethnic identity. Hendra Kurnia sees in Kim Tjoan something he cannot recognize, and he knows how to call it: "Chinese"; more precisely, " 'Chinese' who do not mingle with their neighbors."

Although "Chinese" such as Kim Tjoan are spoken of as if they were uncanny, it is not clear that their eeriness is of the first order. In the charge "they do not mix," one sees the "gap" between classes made concrete. The Chinese, perceived as being uncommunicative, refuses to acknowledge his Muslim (and non-Muslim) neighbors. If Kim Tjoan were a good Chinese, like his neighbor Ceng Bouw, he would chat or "shoot the breeze," meaning he would say nothing memorable. This, indeed, is the habit of Javanese between themselves and their neighbors.[52]

In most Javanese cities, the well-to-do live on the main streets. Behind these streets narrow lanes run through crowded quarters where people of various classes live. In the late afternoon the people of these quarters, rising from their siestas, stand outside and chat in a desultory way. It is an example of the "mixing" referred to. In 1981, when I lived in Surakarta in Central Java, I took a bicycle ride late one afternoon along some of these narrow paths. At a certain point, I got down from the bicycle to turn it around. As I did so, I heard a woman, only a few feet from me, say, "Ah, he's turning around." She might have been surprised that a middle-aged white man would be riding a bicycle at all, even more surprised that I appeared in this remote lane in front of her house. In place of an expression of surprise— indeed, I believe, to prevent such—she said instead exactly what I was doing, as though naming my activity accounted for it and for me. Other times on my bicycle I had been pelted with stones; on foot, I was frequently verbally assaulted. When, however, I addressed my assailants in Javanese, merely saying the Javanese equivalent of "hello" or reprimanding them gently in the proper speech forms, they were instantly polite and, although they did not apologize for their behavior, seemed to put it out of mind. These are examples of how a stranger (I am tempted to say, "the" stranger) is incorporated into language, in such a way that he loses any potential to incite surprise. By speaking, I located myself alongside the good Chinese: the alterity I initially displayed was obfuscated.[53] The effect of mixing is to give Javanese a feeling of peacefulness (*tenterem*) and the sense that nothing disturbing will occur. Not to engage in this practice is to make oneself into an object of suspicion, whether one is Chinese or not. Mixing, then, is a way of obscuring differences. Not mixing makes differences not apparent but suspected.

The reassurance provided by such nearly contentless speech is not permanently effective. Whoever is in the position of the stranger in a Javanese setting can again become *aneh*, odd, the stranger, as the testimony concerning Kim Tjoan shows. When this happens to Chinese, they are left at the focal point of a certain fascination. Chinese wealth is imaginary, as I have said, in the sense that, whether or not Chinese have money, their relation to it is mysterious. They keep wealth to themselves; it is the material form of their *watak*, perhaps. The "magnificence" of their churches is visible, yet it raises the question of the secret sources of their wealth. When revealed, this source is corrupt, but even discovery of the source leaves unexplained the Chinese ability to take advantage of "our" government when "we" ourselves cannot do so. Wealth places Chinese in a different world. It keeps "us" from seeing ourselves in "them." "We" cannot simply ignore it. Indeed, it rivets attention. The gap, as I have said, is too easily crossed in the mode of the uncanny as the riches that make Chinese turn their backs on us come into imagined view.

The result is the terrifying impulse of Hendra Kurnia thinking of Kim Tjoan: "so that's why he gets it like that. In fact, if we could, we'd tear his house down to the ground so he would never come back." The uncanny is unbearable. In fact, Kim Tjoan's family was driven out of the neighborhood. He was sentenced to three and half years for incitement of racial sentiments; his wife and daughter were forced to move to Jakarta, where at last report they lived in poverty.[54] Their house, instead of being razed, was bought by a nearby Islamic school.[55] This approaches ethnic cleansing but does not equal it, for other Chinese were left untouched. Several residents mentioned Ceng Bouw, a Chinese who was protected by a Muslim family during the riots, in order to illustrate the good relations between Muslims and Chinese in their neighborhood.[56]

If there is no ethnic cleansing in the mode of the former Yugoslavia, it is because Chinese are seen ambivalently. They too are Indonesians. Many Muslims rioted against them, and many Muslims protected some of them. The desire to have Chinese be "normal" is as great as the desire to eliminate them. The Indonesian idea of the nation is, indeed, based on its ability to assimilate its peoples, to reconstitute those, including Chinese, into Indonesians, no matter what their birth or their mother tongue. Marriage alliances across ethnic groups, for instance, indicate the strength of the nation. Before the birth of the nation, the ancestors of today's Indonesians could not intermarry in this way. Precisely this rupture with the family of origin begot Indonesians out of the many people born into one of the hundreds of groups that inhabited that nation of islands. Chinese, however, often are treated as though they are not entirely Indonesians, though intermarriages do frequently take place between them and other Indonesians.

The political entity created by the liberation of Indonesians from their own origins was the *rakyat*, the people. No one is born a member of the people, nor is it a sociological category. A farmer, for instance, is not a member of the people because of his profession, his place of birth, or the language he speaks. He becomes a member of the people by a performative act. In the Sukarno era he was one of those the president addressed either in the great stadium of the capital or over the radio. When Sukarno, who styled himself "the extension of the tongue of the people," spoke in their name, those listening, even when hearing certain ideas for the first time, found that these ideas did indeed express what they thought. At that point they were members of "the people."

The empty talk of the late afternoon does not produce "the people." Indeed, its purpose is to blur social differentiation of any sort. The fact that the stranger could appear, however, making such empty talk necessary, indicates that new sorts of social definition can occur when Indonesians are faced with something odd. The *rakyat* is formed out of such a possibility. It needs the oddity of someone who speaks and, as with Sukarno, after the fact it needs a number of people to recognize in his words, and in himself, what they had always intended and always been. During the revolution, not necessarily Sukarno but local leaders of small bands formed the focal point of the *rakyat*, each acting in the name of "Indonesia." Their followers became members of "the people," members of a new nation whose form of expression was inchoate but anticipated new political and social forms. The revolution, from the viewpoint of this example, can reoccur. The *rakyat* can reemerge. The insistence on "mixing," which suppresses such a possibility, indicates the pressure for such a formation to reemerge.

The populism of the Sukarno period ended with Suharto's New Order. The people were without a form of expression. At the same time, by the 1980s differences in wealth led to pronounced differences between classes. At this point, we have arrived at the "gap" so widely discussed in Indonesian society in the later years of the New Order. It expresses the fear of the middle class that "the people" will reemerge. These fears shaped the development of events and prevented the *massa* from becoming the *rakyat*. At the same time, the continuous suppression of the underclass and the idea of the gap left the underclass confronting "Chinese." The "odd" figure who did not mix, whose difference was feared and who fronted for the middle class as a whole, was at once a failed and a rejected leader who could announce another *rakyat* or "the" *rakyat*.[57]

In the evolution of events from the drumming of Hendra Kurnia to the burning of churches by large numbers of youths, we see the failure of "the people" to form themselves. Bereft of true leaders, guided only by speakers who mention the "time bomb" after there has been an explosion, "the people" advance to destroy the property of those who are thought to impede the restoration of what they once had: a reflection of themselves in others who were the means of their identification with the nation.

Jews are never mentioned in *Media Dakwah*'s several interviews or in reports from the scenes of church burning. In the issue of *Media Dakwah* that tells of the anti-Chinese riots in Rengasdengklok and nearby Tasikmalaya, however, there is a report about a countryside religious school in the same area said to teach heterodox beliefs. Students from orthodox religious schools attacked this heterodox school and chased out the teacher. On the ceiling of the mosque there was a star, reproduced in a photograph and said to be a Star of David. Nothing at all indicates that this school had something to do with Jews. Literature found in the remains of the school simply indicated that its leader had expanded the confession of faith and had pronounced himself the Imam Mandi, a heterodox version of the messiah.

The reporter concludes his piece: "The case of Buki [the name of the religious teacher] indicates that the *provokasi* of Islam and its community never ceases, both from Jews and Christians (QS 3: 120). For years Buki was a thorn in the side of the Tasik Muslim community. From the moment the officials did not act quickly enough, at a certain time the masses lost control and it all exploded."58

This is the logic of the time bomb all over again. But this time the provocation includes the heterodox pronouncement of the coming of the messiah. There is no reason to think that there is Jewish influence here. If anything, judging from the presence of a mosque, from the name of the foundation that supported the school [Yayasan Marganingrat], and from its doctrine as *Media Dakwah* reports it, it resembles the Javanese version of the Imam Mandi. It is not said to be Jewish itself but to be a "link in the Network of the Jewish International [*mata rantai Jaringan Yahudi Internasional*]" and part of an "organ of conspiracy [*organ konspiratif*]" to crush Islam. The title refers not to Jews but to their traces ("Jewish Traces in Tasikmalaya"). Once again, the reference to Jews is made by the reporters and is not said to be part of local interpretations.

The introductory piece to the articles of this issue speaks of "Christianization and various networks such as Jewishization and Chinese conspiracy [*konspirasi*]—with motives of trade that ceaselessly try to crush Islam in this country; it's really obvious, right in front of your nose."59 The Jew, in this piece, appears not as a figure that arouses the resentment of the lower class but as part of an interpretation of society by middle-class modernist writers. He appears not in life, or even in local accounts, but in the medium of *Media Dakwah*. He is only vaguely adduced in these reports. He does not appear as a Chinese, a Christian, or even a heterodox Muslim. Chinese, Christians, and heterodox preachers are not substitutes for Jews, nor are they Jews in disguise. One cannot trace a direct connection between Jews and those who are part of the Indonesian landscape, no doubt because Jews remain unrecognizable. In the way that the face of the despised Jew disappears into that of the valued Arab, the Jew, when his influence reaches Indonesia, retreats from making a direct appearance. Even to call these Chinese and Javanese Jewish "agents" is too strong; they merely bear "traces" of Jews.

The Jewish effect, in these incidents, is a feeling of intolerable menace that cannot be accounted for by the accumulation of past grievances. Buki himself never makes an appearance, and, of course, whatever Jew was thought responsible for the Star of David, however indirectly, does not. No one expects this Jew to appear. The Jew, we have said repeatedly, remains absent from the scene. In that sense, the Jew figures even more strongly than reclusive Chinese as the nonreflecting mirror of the Indonesian Muslim underclass. The very distance of America, Europe, and wherever else Jews are thought to live helps to bring them onto the Indonesian scene. They come to mind at the point where one cannot account for the force of appearance—when one's opponent seems to say amazing things or when painted stars appear in mosques. The absence of the Jew means that he can never be directly addressed. His effects mean that he is nonetheless present and in communication with certain Indonesians. They are affected by Jews, but they cannot make themselves felt by those Jews through their own initiative. It is the situation that pertains between Kim Tjoan and his neighbors, but in an exaggerated form.

When Nurcholish Madjid was accused of having been influenced by orientalists, this meant that what he said, whether he knew it or not, originated in the distortions of Jews from another place and time. His errors were not a matter of his intentions; thus his pronouncements could not be corrected. What he said was not a matter of interpretation; one needed to search for the distant factors that compelled his speech. Resting outside interpretation, Nurcholish's message could not be understood. One can say that it was singular even if it was recognizable as the type of something that others, such as the Egyptian Thaha Husein, had said before. It was, in that sense, mere repetition of the same. Its singularity, pointing to an impossible source of (un)truth, was the possibility of any message whatsoever. Mistranslations might even foretell the messiah in the form of Buki.

The Jewish uncanny in Indonesia comes with the erosion of the national idea and the consequent feeling that "Indonesians" now have different sources of truth. The Jew appears (though that is not the correct verb; "reaches" would be more apt) not only from outside Indonesia but from outside the history of Indonesia, helping to make him unapparent. He acts out of nowhere. He is not a *revenant*, the French term that indicates a ghost as something that returns. To be such, he would, of course, have to be identifiable and actually to appear. As it is, each time a Jewish effect is felt, it is mere repetition of something that comes from no knowable origin and bears no form. The uncanny effect of Jews is thus different from that of Chinese. Chinese are a recurrent, indeed constant feature of Indonesian society. Chinese give the uncanny a body. Jews inhabit nothing in Indonesia. The word *Jew* in Indonesian indicates a menace. No form has been found for it. Jews are not specters but the threat of specters to come. Chinese give the Jewish threat of the coming of ghosts a body and thus a place in Indonesia.[60]

Buki is as close as I can find to a Jewish specter in Indonesia, though he is not that. If we are permitted to imagine the effects of a confrontation between him and his Muslim neighbors, what can we suppose they would find? In the thinking of *Media Dakwah*, Buki, were he present to do so, would embody the singular messages of orientalists. Were he capable of being present, one would see, without knowing exactly what one was facing, the effects of qur'anic teachings twisted out of recognition long ago somewhere else. Facing him, even in his absence, certain Indonesian Muslims find themselves no longer at home in their own land, and this feeling of alienation is even more thorough than when they confront Chinese.

Buki had his own teachings, uninfluenced by Jews. One can imagine that they were unique and that they contained a political program. Does his banishment then indicate the failure of the idea of the *rakyat*? That is, did a failure of the possibility of becoming other occur when the nation was newborn, when a peasant listened to Sukarno speak and found himself to be one of the people, his origin inconsequential? If, after Buki spoke, some of the people of Tasikmalaya found in his message what they seemed to think, as others did when they heard Sukarno, one could say that this possibility of becoming other—of becoming Indonesian in fellowship with all other Indonesians—is still alive. Buki, the individual, is gone. Chinese remain. Alas, they remain to embody the failure of that possibility. As such, they, among other figures, are established as Indonesian national ghosts, supplementing the numerous local spirits that inhabit the regions of Java.

It is not altogether surprising to find anti-Semitism without Jews; after all, it is not caused by Jews.[61] It is not surprising that Indonesian Muslims identify with their coreligionists in the Middle East. It is striking, however, that so many Indonesians conflate Zionists and Jews and that this conflation inflects their self-image or, rather, lack of one and comes to mark the limit of national identity.

FOUR

The Curse of the Photograph: Atjeh 1901

When I was in Aceh,[1] the province of Indonesia on the northern tip of Sumatra, in 2000, I was not surprised to find nearly every Acehnese I met strongly against the government. Most people supported the Free Aceh Movement, which meant they wanted to secede from Indonesia. They claimed an Acehnese identity in the face of the depredations of the Indonesian army, which for decades had killed, raped, and robbed throughout the province. I was all the more surprised, then, when I heard so few references to the Acehnese War, as the Dutch spoke of it. From the time of the Dutch invasion of the Sultanate of Atjeh, Acehnese conducted a fierce resistance lasting about forty years. It is not easy to establish a new identity, even when it claims to be grounded in an old one. Why, then, more references were not made to the war, and why, in particular, nothing like the jihad that was waged against the Dutch is being waged now—this despite examples from other places in the Muslim world—interested me. One cannot treat an absence directly. Looking again at photographs of the war waged by the

Dutch, I asked myself about the place of photography throughout the conflict, hoping that this necessarily oblique approach might suggest an answer to my questions.

Photography came early to the Indies, in particular to Java. As elsewhere in the world, it arrived in the wake of a tradition of pictorial representation that, according to Liane van der Linden, reduced the strangeness of the island and its population.[2] There were two aims of this form of representation: to show the place as it was and to be aesthetically pleasing. When photography began, it furthered this double aim. The first major use of photography by the state was in archeology. Under the influence of the Napoleonic inventory of Egypt and for the sake of the prestige of the Netherlands, the government wanted to show the great temples of Java, particularly the Borobodur. The drawings that had been commissioned for this purpose were thought to fail. They "were not considered suitable for scientific study, nor did they do justice to the artistic value of the Borobodoer."[3] The governor-general gave the task of photographing the monument to a photographer, Isidore van Kinsbergen, who had maintained a studio in Batavia since about 1860. There was little general interest in these pictures.[4] Yet at least from an artistic point of view, they were a success, inspiring Gauguin, for instance.[5] The double interest in scientific recording and in aesthetic rendering continued as the photographic inventory became one element in the general recording and, some say, invention of Javanese culture by the Dutch.[6]

Van Kinsbergen taught his photographic skills to a man named Kassian Céphas, who became the first Javanese photographer. Another story has it that it was not van Kinsbergen but another Dutchman, Simon Willem Camerik, who taught Céphas. Whatever the case, Céphas apparently learned photography from one European or another between 1861 and 1871.[7] He was subsequently hired by the archeological service to photograph many important monuments, including the Borobodur. There, he succeeded in the first aim, "to show the place as it was," but there was controversy about his degree of success in the second. Some notable Dutch authorities at the time felt that his photographs lacked the modeling that would show the beauty of the temples. They felt that his pictures were too stiff. Not everyone agreed with this assessment; the Jogjanese court retained him to photograph its members and to record its ceremonies. The controversy continues into the present. The French historian Claude Guillot said of Céphas's pictures: "With rare exceptions, all life seems to have disappeared. Nothing indicates a trait of character: there is no overall plan; all the portraits are taken standing, face forward, stiffly posed, under equal light. Images of dignity and not images of individuals."[8] He was answered by a Javanese, Yudhi Soeryoatmodjo, who argued that the images were not supposed to represent character and that faulting them for its absence would be a judgment foreign to the time and place. They were meant to show dignity. It is not a question of technical ability. The pictures show what the sitters intended, which was not "the individual characters" but what surrounded them: their regalia, the batik they wore, the positions of their hands, "all of which represented the tradition and identity of the Yogyakarta court."

These critics agree about the character of the photographs, but they disagree about their value. I say this in order to show that there was little problem in adopting photography in Java. The very mechanical quality of the camera may have enabled it to show what Javanese wanted it to show.

In any case, the most important achievement of the camera—memorialization—was precisely what all parties wanted. As the Dutchman J. Groneman said in his preface to a volume of Céphas's pictures of court ceremonies: "One day this shall belong to the history of the past. May then this book preserve the memory and manifold remarkable imagery of it."[9] That is exactly what happened. And that is because there was an accord of ideas about the aims of photography between the Dutch who taught Céphas, thus indirectly establishing a line of Javanese photographers after him, and the Javanese consumers of his pictures. The disagreement between some Europeans (not including Gauguin, for instance, who used his pictures) and the Javanese only shows how photography suited Javanese aims and even tastes.

All this sounds unexceptionable, but the compatibility of photography with the cultures of the archipelago should not be taken for granted, because photography was not adopted elsewhere in the Indies. I will now turn to one area where it found no place in local culture. My point, in fact, is to say why, when the camera, as an instrument of memorialization, ought to have been quickly adopted (providing always that there are no myths about its technology, as there apparently weren't in the case I will discuss), it was not. I hope thereby to say something further about the place of the camera generally.

To do so I will turn to the story of another photographer, this time Dutch, from a few decades later, but from quite a different place. In 1873 the Dutch invaded the Sultanate of Atjeh. Dutch ships anchored off the coast near the seat of the sultanate and landed their troops. The Dutch forces had only poor maps and guides. They got lost repeatedly during their first foray. They found themselves surrounded and attacked by Atjehnese snipers, whom they could not see. They managed to get to the palace grounds nonetheless. General Kohler, in charge of the expedition, standing under a nearby tree, was killed by a sniper. The Dutch forces retreated and did not return until the next year. When they came back, they brought photographers with them, members of the Topographical Service, whose job it was to help in gaining knowledge of the terrain but who also photographed the troops and the areas where they were found, as well as Dutch fortifications and, eventually, the results of Dutch victories.[10] Unlike in Java, then, photography in Atjeh was not a tool for the preservation of a culture but a technological device devoted to its defeat and to the recording of the remnants of that defeat.

The Topographical Service pictures reproduced in the book of Louis Zweers are not those used for the preparation of maps, however. They show the inside of Dutch forts, the position of the cannon, the cannoneers with them, the mortars and their accompanying soldiers, poised to shoot. They also show a team in charge of provisions positioned next to their supplies and warehouses and sailors in ranks on board their ships. These photos associate people and things: soldiers with their tools. They show installations new to the sultanate. They show the occupation of Atjeh, insofar as it had progressed, but more than that, they show the Dutch in the process of inhabiting the sultanate. These men belong in the landscape, in the first place because they have wrenched the land away from its inhabitants. There are pictures of soldiers at ease, in half dress, comfortable in their surroundings. They are in Atjeh, but the gap between Atjehnese and Dutch was surely greatly widened by the prevailing hostility between them. The Dutch did not drive the population out of the capital, which they named Kota Radja, City of the King, but they had little to do with Atjehnese. Given the hostility of the Atjehnese toward the invaders, the pictures of Dutch soldiers in Atjeh reflected back to them their presence in the sultanate in the absence of the usual reflection one gets from the glances one exchanges with local inhabitants, whether we are at home or in a foreign place. The lack of reassurance furnished by mutual looks was compensated for through the mediation of photography.

The Atjehnese War lasted perhaps forty years or more. No one is certain when war turned into a resistance movement sustained by small bands of guerrillas and individuals. Several times this conflict was declared over, only not to be. After Dutch forces took the palace in 1874, they thought they had won, but it was still more than twenty years before the large valley around the capital was cleared of resistance forces. At that point, in 1898, Dutch forces moved to Pidie, an area of the sultanate on the east coast. Their success there again led to announcements of the end of the war, but again this was not the case, and no one dates the end of that conflict before 1914. In 1901, General van Heutsz, the civil and military governor of Atjeh and later governor-general of the Indies, who, along with Christian Snouck Hurgronje, is given credit for the policy that eventually led to ending the war, moved to the next important site of resistance, Samalanga, in Pidie. By this time, the influence of Atjehnese *ulama*, or those learned in Islam, had risen considerably, and the doctrine of the holy war was widely influential.

"Atjehnese will never be defeated except by force, and then only someone who shows himself to possess power [*macht*] to make his will respected shall be the master whose orders they will obey." This sentence of General van Heutsz, widely quoted, is repeated in the introduction, pseudonymously signed, to a book written by a commercial photographer, C. Nieuwenhuis. Van Heutsz invited Nieuwenhuis to join his troops on their expedition to Samalanga, to record it. The writer of the introduction notes that in the Netherlands popular interest in the war waxed and waned, depending on major events. Much took place during what he thought was the final stage of pacification, a stage that he believed the Dutch public should be aware of yet was apparently ignoring. He hoped that the photographs would arouse interest and thus support for the war. In point of fact, the brutality of van Heutsz, of a sort repeated later on a larger scale by General van Daalen and carried out prior to his campaign in the clearing of the Atjeh Valley, aroused indignation in Holland. The book reports the burning of villages, for instance, and there is a photo showing victorious KNIL (the acronym for Royal Netherlands Indies Army) troops staring down into an Atjehnese fortification they had just defeated.[11] Atjehnese corpses are scattered over the earth. This photograph became the model for others taken later, as photographers fulfilled van Heutsz's goal of recording Dutch victories. Other photographs, showing Atjehnese women among the corpses, with only babies left as survivors, are even more difficult to look at.[12]

Nieuwenhuis was not self-conscious about his work. He says of himself that, thanks to the good offices of a certain Lt. Col. van der Wedden, van Heutsz, the civil and military governor of Atjeh and dependences, allowed him to be "a witness to the foremost events of the Samalanga campaign."[13] He wrote a short account of the expedition rather than an account of how he took his pictures, though he sometimes includes such information incidentally. He lists the participants in the march through the forest to the series of Atjehnese fortifications and describes the difficult conditions they encounter. His photographs are illustrations; he could well have written the book without including them, since one can comprehend his perceptions of the course of the expedition without them. He reports that he was the first photographer to be invited on such a military expedition in the history of the KNIL. His account shows him to be a nonsoldier who was much impressed by Lt. General van Heutsz and by the prowess of his soldiers. It was probably that admiration that gave Nieuwenhuis the courage to make the horrifying photographs he did of the Atjehnese victims of this aggression.

He records events that took place before the scene of the final battle without much feeling. At one point, for instance, the artillery destroyed an Atjehnese fortification. When Dutch troops reached a nearby village, they discovered that the inhabitants had fled when the fortification was destroyed. "The warships off the coast thus got the chance to successfully harass the refugees with their salvos."[14] The initial plates in the volume have captions such as "Panorama of Meuredoe," a place on the coast; "Naval artillery, 10.5 cm, on Glé Nang Roe," Glé Nang Roe being the mountain where fighting began; "Bivak Nang Roe," showing about two dozen soldiers posed in a group before an Atjehnese house where they apparently put up. And so on. But Nieuwenhuis also continued to use the camera to show things never before registered on film and to create a record to be used later, as photographers in Atjeh did before him. He describes, for instance, how in certain places there is practically no trail at all. "At 10:30 a.m. the head column reached Oeloë Oe; the artillery left the path and tried to find a better way to Gampong Ankieeng. But this path too was scarcely passable."[15] The way was rough, and it took a full day to march ten kilometers. At this point, the author inserts a photograph of the troops wading across a river for lack of a bridge. When a bridge does appear in the photographs, it is an Atjehnese bridge, a series of bamboo poles set in a line over a swamp, with another such series raised above it to be used as a railing. The soldiers balance their way across, but several seem to have fallen in the water.[16]

When the Dutch forces finally reached the enemy positions they sought, Nieuwenhuis took pictures of the approach to the battle. The line advanced, and he followed. But when the fiercest fighting ensued, he was unable to photograph it: "A fearfully obstinate fight now began of which I, alas, took no picture. My servants and the coolies who carried the apparatus were nowhere to be found; frightened by the rattling gun fire, they had run to safety in a sheltered place, and only with great difficulty, after the first storming, could I get my camera 'in position.'"[17] He does, however, picture the troops storming through a thorny bamboo barrier, up a hill to an Atjehnese fortification.[18]

Having missed most of the close fighting, Nieuwenhuis nonetheless was able to capture a picture of the immediate aftermath. This picture, "Photo showing the still-burning fortification of Batëe Ilië," shows Dutch troops looking down over the palisades onto Atjehnese corpses strewn over most of the ground.[19] There is still smoke rising from the firing of weapons, and this obscures a great deal. Nieuwenhuis has added numbers and plus signs, which identify: "1. Lance 2. Blunderbus 3. Grenade launcher 4. Oven 5. Rice Sack. + + + + Bodies of Atjehnese."

The taking of the fortress entailed fierce hand-to-hand fighting. The defenders would not surrender. The Dutch troops (which is to say Dutch officers, whose soldiers were largely Ambonese and some Africans) pressed on over the top of the fortress and fought inside. Nieuwenhuis describes the battle: "There now began a terrible fight, man against man. The enemy defended himself heroically, that has to be recognized, and they chose to the last man to die with *klewangs* [Atjehnese short swords] in their fists rather than surrender. The dreadful drama became more terrifying at each moment through the bursting of powder mines which, no matter how badly laid, the enemy now and then succeeded in exploding."[20]

Nieuwenhuis saw this event "close up." Still, he offers us a synoptic picture, obviously made afterwards ("they chose to the last man . . ."), from the point of view of an observer who saw it all, unobstructed by smoke or other obstacles to vision. He pictures the conflict as a conflict, that is, not as the sense impressions of someone who, "up close," cannot impose a structure on the confusing impressions that reach him. Furthermore, he does not fail to recognize the courage of "the enemy":

> Also the Atjehnese had a brave van Speyk in their midst who, still even then, before he could be bayoneted, found a way to stick a fuse in a big powder vat.

> I have seen this brave man, old and wrinkled, and, regardless of the wounds to our side caused by the explosion, I felt respect for the gray hero, who, rather than surrender, blew himself up with friend and foe.[21]

Nieuwenhuis thus remained clear about who was who, what qualities counted, and what happened. If he missed photographing all this, it was only because his bearers had run off. He apologizes. But there is nothing he describes that, it is implied, in theory the camera could not capture.

After describing the battle, he sums up his impressions:

> Whoever as a civilian and a peaceful citizen has seen the dreadfulness of such a battle close up shall never forget it. When our troops were positioned for the storming of Batéë Ilië, the fire power of the Atjehnese from Batéë Ilië as well as from Asam Koembang was deafening. The fort was covered and surrounded with heavy powder smoke. Then, the assault; the wild hurrah of the attackers, once or at most twice, followed by the prolonged and penetrating battle cry of the Atjehnese, Allah it Allah [no doubt they chanted *Allah la'ilah*], swept away by fanaticism into uncontrollable madness. In addition to this appalling turmoil of fighting and hellish noise, the sound of some shots, the clank of *klewangs*, steel on steel, then again a raw shriek; we can only guess whether it is the death cry of a friend or an enemy. From time to time there is a red flash, which for an instant interrupts the powerful rays of the sun, immediately followed by somber, dull thuds of explosions of powder, which again and again make clouds of powder smoke rise up; finally the noise quiets down for a moment, and then come the yells of the victors, Batéë Ilië has fallen.[22]

Here, battle as conflict is replaced by battle as confusion; often one cannot tell who is on which side. The explosions of light—brighter than sunlight—and sound overwhelm the senses. The picture of events changes, I believe, when, in the midst of his synoptic account, Nieuwenhuis remarks that he has seen the wrinkled old man just moments before he blows himself up "with friend and foe." He remarks on a detail of the man's features—his wrinkles—introducing a singular perception into an otherwise formulated account. This detail is associated with death, as though what he has seen and what happened are conjoined, but in an incomprehensible way.

This, indeed, is how we often think of the sublime. It occurs at moments when we have had a narrow escape from danger. Afterwards, we feel once again in charge of our cognitive powers. Before this recovery, "we flee from the sight of an object that scares us," Kant says.[23] Overwhelmed by a danger we cannot cognize, our cognitive facilities are exhausted, and we are faced nonetheless with something we cannot take in. At those moments, Kant adds, we experience "a momentary checking of our vital powers." Without vital powers, we are of course dead, though how we could represent that to ourselves Kant does not say.

Nieuwenhuis recollects how he admired, and thus in a certain way identified with, the brave Atjehnese man he saw just before that man's death. At this point Nieuwenhuis feels that he too could well have been killed. After we have made our way out of danger, according to Kant, there is a sense of well-being because we have escaped and because we know that our cognitive powers in fact do function, even if the overwhelming danger itself was and remains beyond our comprehension. We know that we are safe and that our mind functions. When we recover in this way, there is a moment of exhilaration, as we regain the ability to unify our thoughts. First comes a moment of disunity of perception experienced as death, if one so reads the "checking of our vital powers." Then, as Neil Hertz shows, in the descriptions of the experience of the sublime there is not only a consolidation of our cognition but a reconfirmed sense of personal integration. We have the feeling of having escaped death. We were "almost" dead, and finding ourselves not so, we feel more ourselves than ever.[24]

In the case of Nieuwenhuis, the moment just after the battle appears in his picture of Atjehnese corpses. Viewing it, one has no doubt who is who. The Dutch stand above looking down; the Atjehnese lie on the ground looking nowhere. This distinction, however, does not mean that the boundaries between the dead and the living, the Atjehnese and the Dutch, were always firmly in place. What follows Nieuwenhuis's moment of cognitive disorder—also, of course, a moment of killing—is a picture of corpses. It is a picture, that is to say, of the fate that Nieuwenhuis, so close to the battle, seems to have felt he narrowly avoided himself. All the more so since, although the corpses in the picture are all Atjehnese (there were seventy-nine of them), five Dutch soldiers were also killed, one of them a European.[25]

At the moment death occurred, it could not be shown. Just after, the corpses attest to its arrival. The photograph, then, shows the moment of consolidation in which what one avoided is illustrated, to the degree possible. It thus fulfills the role given to it when it was an instrument used to mediate what had never before been seen. Such confusion, when the Dutch first landed, brought the risk, sometimes realized, of death upon them. Here, in this picture, the camera shows it has not mastered but gone beyond those moments of confusion and captured what it cannot and could not understand.

This photograph was not viewed differently from the way we are accustomed today to viewing photographs, particularly those of bloody events. We see pictures of the victims of earthquakes, massacres, and starvation from around the world almost daily. It is commonly said that, shocked as we might be, we still, in effect, say to ourselves, "He is not me." In the end, we are satisfied and able to put these terrible images out of mind, though we of course do not want to admit our satisfaction to ourselves. Nonetheless, we enjoy seeing what we fear—the loss of ourselves—in order to be reassured that annihilation is not the case for us. This is the logic implicit in the sublime. It is important today because it allows us to manage an economy of identification—"we are who we see"/"we are not"—by which the mass of photographs from no matter where becomes available to us and for which we develop a taste. Every day we seem to need to see them.

To my knowledge, there were no Atjehnese photographers in the nineteenth century and probably none well into the twentieth. There was no one like the Javanese Céphas, who was taught photographic technique by a European and found a way to adapt it to his own condition. Naturally, the war itself was an obstacle to such a development, but it would not have been impossible. The Islamicist Snouck Hurgronje, for instance, could not have written his important ethnography, *The Achehnese*, without the help of his Atjehnese assistant. If, nonetheless, there was no Atjehnese photography, it was because the war was perceived by the Atjehnese side as a holy war (*prang sabil*). The doctrine of the holy war varies from century to century and even place to place. In Atjeh it meant that, under the prevailing circumstances, Muslims there had the duty to fight the unbeliever. One who died in the war against the unbelievers would not have to await the day of judgment to enter paradise. He would be instantly transported to that place, where he would enjoy all its pleasures. Under ordinary circumstances, the corpse in

Islam is buried, never cremated, because it will rise again on the day of judgment. At that time its hands, its mouth, and the other parts of its body will testify to the worthiness of the person, and on that basis he will or will not be allowed to enter paradise. The corpse of someone who died in the holy war was sometimes displayed for a few days in honor of the deceased and to stimulate others to go on the jihad. The corpse was no longer the lifeless remains of someone lost to the living. It was a sign that the person was now alive in paradise.

The corpses and the graves of those who died in the holy war thus lost their function as memorials. The graves of some killed were thought to contain a certain power that worshippers at these places might appropriate. However, the objections of modernist Muslim leaders from the 1920s on largely eliminated this practice. Today there are not only no memorials in Atjeh to anyone killed in the holy war against the Dutch (this could be for religious reasons), there are also no statues or plaques of the sort raised by Indonesian nationalists to commemorate the anticolonial revolution. The preservation of the memory of the martyr is of no importance in the unusual condition in which the notion of the holy war prevails.

However the involuntary recurrence of the memory of the deceased might be dealt with, it was not exteriorized in the form of memorials or stabilized by being embodied in stories of martyrs. There are such stories in the epic devoted to the holy war, but they are few, and often they do not concern Atjehnese at all, but others who died in other places. The war, sometimes claimed as the moment in which Atjehnese nationalism was born, has in fact been largely ignored in recent times and into the present, as Atjehnese are demanding their independence from Indonesia. This indicates the success of the notion of the holy war, in which gaining paradise meant for many Muslims putting the world behind one. Martyrs were apparently seen from their own posthumous point of view. Thus the photograph of the person, a memorial too, of course, had no place. Atjehnese had no interest in photography at that moment in their history.

When "risk" means "I might not be killed," rather than "I might have been killed" (the second response is typical, even instinctive, in cultures where the sublime is known), corpses take on a different sense. To the Atjehnese viewer at the time of the Dutch incursions, the view of corpses would not mean that the viewer had narrowly escaped, with the result that he is now even more himself. The image would mark at best the viewer's failure to achieve paradise and the neglect of his religious duty. The narrow escape that reinforces identity would be instead a moral reproach and a reminder of a worldly identity that the person was trying to shed.

The Dutch photographer who, in the midst of dead bodies, takes photographs and sends them home might share the glory or the opprobrium of the Dutch soldier. But the Atjehnese photographer who did the same would be sending nothing of importance. His association with death would not stimulate the imagination of risk, as the corpse would not allude to the destruction of the person, his loss, or the death that threatens us all and that we can imagine now through the photograph. The equivalent position for him, if there is one, would be paradise. Only there, in the place that eradicates death, loss, and suffering, could he send back pictures from an "elsewhere" that would stimulate Atjehnese to put themselves in the picture. Alas for us here today with our secular imaginations. We would find only one more tourist's snapshot. Lacking, then, a notion of the sublime with Western roots, developed with religious overtones, and having no room for such an idea, Atjeh did without indigenous photographers.

The Atjehnese, Nieuwenhuis said, instead of surrendering, died "*klewang*s in hand," swords in hand. Had they surrendered, they might have lived. It was not the pursuit of honor that led to their death, but the hope of gaining paradise. The *klewang* opened the gates. So doing, it had one of the functions of the camera: it revealed what no one had yet seen, in the way the camera helped to map uncharted land. The descriptions of paradise that assume its use are the major substance of the epic of the holy war. This epic testifies to the fact that, in the end, there was revelation and memorialization; after the end, there was still the world in which the epics were chanted. But there is a certain paradox in understanding the position of these texts. They pass on to others, later, whatever they might say. But they enjoin men to leave their families to find in paradise an existence that makes that break permanent. Paradise is not life on earth made perfect; it is life elsewhere, with all connection with earth broken. It is difficult for most people to imagine our own deaths without imagining those we leave behind; this is just what the texts that announce the holy war accomplish. They ask that they themselves, these texts, be forgotten. What the fate of the Qur'an itself would be I cannot say.

If the camera extended the power of the gun, the *klewang*'s relation to power was altogether ambiguous. One can rightly say that it extended the power of the Qur'an, turning its words into actions. But its power was also turned away from the world, and this was the chief message of the epic of the holy war: not the defeat of the unbeliever, but his death. And the unbeliever's death figured as the means to one's own. Furthermore, standing in relation to the Qur'an, the holy war was available to all Muslims without need for intermediaries. The *klewang*, then, was not governed by worldly centralized political authority. Even after Atjeh was finally considered pacified, up through the 1930s, almost to the time of the Dutch defeat by the Japanese, individual Atjehnese, coordinated by no general plan of resistance, would suddenly stab Europeans in the hope of being killed themselves and gaining paradise. The Dutch considered them mad, and from a secular standpoint there is a case to be made for that view. Madness puts the person who suffers it outside communication. We lack sufficient words for its various forms, and necessarily so, since we cannot see from the point of view of the mad; some of the mad suffer, others seem happy. But the mad by definition live in worlds that are unavailable to the rest of us. With these Atjehnese, long after Atjeh had been restored to order, its economy functioning, a nascent modern form of nationalism on the rise, family life again established, the older way continued. Killings continued. And always, it seems, by stabbing, if not with the *klewang*, then with the other important Atjehnese weapon, the *reuntjong*, or Atjehnese dagger.[26] A fetishistic power, again figuring in relation to death, phallic in form, but outside phallocentric organization, the dagger came to be used less frequently, but its use did not cease. This took place in an Atjehnese world that progressively refused to take the claim of the jihad to heart and that, therefore, isolated the perpetrators and led to the cultural forgetting of the holy war against the Dutch.

The camera assumes the presence of a viewer to see the picture and in some way to have it reflect himself back to himself. The *klewang* was a weapon whose goal, from a secular point of view, was to eliminate self-consciousness. In my opinion, the eradication of memories of the war as important elements in the politics and the identity of Acehnese shows that, by and large, it—the elimination of consciousness of self—succeeded. There is nothing in the logic of the holy war that can bring it to an end except the defeat of the unbeliever. However, without this defeat, and with the restoration of a functioning economy and the rise of ideas of nationalism, the promise of the jihad in Atjeh gradually lost its force for most. Eventually, few in this world saw what the *klewang* and *reuntjong* revealed when their mission was taken seriously. If one thinks that the *klewang* was used to eliminate self-consciousness, this, perhaps, is the sign that it succeeded—not, of course, by instituting the holy war in the heart of Acehnese society, leaving a place where Atjehnese could always find not themselves but the negation of themselves. Rather, success was accomplished by having a highly important segment of their history, which depended on the practice of the holy war for its energy and focus, remain suspended in Acehnese memory, remain, that is, without being incorporated into the dialectical development of Acehnese identity. The recitation of the epic of the holy war gradually stopped. And photographs, taken mainly by Chinese commercial photographers, appeared, showing Atjehnese who could afford to have their portraits made, attesting to a world where memory of a conventional kind was restored.

Before the conventional functioning of Atjehnese society was fully reestablished, the very lack of a wish to leave behind memory in the world made it possible for individuals to perceive death in the holy war as a goal that could be achieved through individual action, without the need for the candidate to imagine how he would be viewed by the community. They could thus continue their suicidal killing even when the community had lost interest in martyrdom. It is exactly this that made the Dutch feel that the acts of such people were not political but the effects of madness.

It would be better to accept the holy war according to the terms set by the Atjehnese and to follow their logic. The lines from the Qur'an that founded the jihad are these: "God has bought from the believers their selves and their possessions against the gift of paradise; they fight in the way of God; they kill and are killed; that is a promise binding upon God" (9:111). Dying in the holy war, one achieves paradise without waiting for the Day of Judgment. These lines were propagated not directly from the recitation of the Qur'an, however, but principally through the Atjehnese literary form called the *hikayat*, and in particular through the *Hikayat Prang Sabil*, the *Hikayat of the Holy War*, various versions of which were written in Aceh during the war.[27] It is by interpreting them in the tradition of the *hikayat* that we can return to consideration of the camera.

According to the great Islamicist, colonial advisor, and ethnographer Christian Snouck Hurgronje, to whom we have been referring off and on in this essay, the *hikayat* tradition was likely to have been of considerable length. He based his judgment on two *hikayat*s from the eighteenth century, which, he believed, were of such outstanding quality that many more must have preceded them. The earlier body of work had disappeared, however.

That disappearance was probably not an accident. The chanting of *hikayat* was done in such a way that the contents of the epic dissolved as listeners attended to its sounds. The *hikayat*'s prosodic structure made this possible. All *hikayat*s have the same strict structure, consisting of a line divided into two phrases, with a single rhyme at the end of the line and another bisecting the phrases of the line. *Hikayat*s were chanted to a single melody with two tempi, fast and slow. As it was explained to me, one follows the rhyme scheme, which, along with other things, such as the tempi and the melody, breaks up the meanings of the line. An example:

> *Hantbm / di gob / na di geutanjòë / sabòh / nanggròë/*
> Never   by others exists by us one land
> Dua / RAJA /
> Two KINGS

Here the rhymes occur in the syllables underlined as well as at the end of each line. The linking of "us" (*geutanjòë*) with "land" (*nanggròë*), rather than with "others" (*gòb*), with which it is contrasted, is a first example of how the sense of the sentence is broken up in favor of conveying the sounds of the words. Rhyme divorced from meaning in this way makes it seem as if certain words respond to patterns set before the construction of meaning and without reference to what is said. All the more so, of course, because of the repetitive nature of the prosodic structure. The final rhyme, for instance, is likely to go unchanged for over two thousand lines. Similarly, the melody is likely to begin in the middle of the line and to end there as well. It too is repetitious; one melody was repeated 662 times in a *hikayat* of 2,117 lines. Furthermore the tempi are likely to be used so that they contrast with what is portrayed. Thus a battle scene might be recited in slow tempo. Atjehnese describe listening to chants delivered in this way with the word *mangat*, "delicious." They devour the contents, as it were, taking them in, as they drift in and out of the performance, listening when they are hungry to do so, as it were, and resting when they are satiated.

The decomposition of the contents might seem merely an aesthetic pleasure, that is, one sealed off from the rest of life in the interest of enjoyment. But it is not exactly that. The epics were the major archives of Atjehnese history. In effect, Atjehnese were devouring their own past. One can see this in one of the *hikayat*s that Snouck praised. That *hikayat* describes the most revered Atjehnese king as a coward. A European account shows the same man dispatching elephants to trample to death anyone the king thought a threat to himself. In this context, it is easy to understand the *hikayat* as an instrument of defense, set against whatever menaced Atjehnese, whether it be the king or the past more generally.

The long-term effect of *hikayat* recitation was to eliminate history. But no society can continue without its archive: its genealogy, at the very least, its tracing of kinship, is necessary to its very structure. Were the *hikayat*s ever to have been decisive, permanently effective, Atjehnese society would have disappeared. I argue that, in effect, this is what happened. But not before the war with the Dutch.

The structure of the *hikayat*, its modes of recitation and hearing, stood in contrast to everyday speech. In the first there was the alternation of the two reciters' voices, echoes of each other, at best, rather than replies, tending toward music. Heard or overheard by listeners, they produced a pleasure leading out of the world as meaningful sound decomposed. In everyday life there were alternating responses as each speaker in turn listened and replied, engaging speakers with each other and thus locating them in the present world. It was a question of one set of rules or another, marking off two linguistic realms. These were not merely coexisting registers, to which one could turn as one chose. They were antithetical. One could "speak" in the language of the *hikayat*, but what one said was then not presented as speech—as, for instance, speech is in opera, especially after Wagner. Rather, to say something "in *hikayat*," as it were, would be to decompose what was said. The prosodic structure of the *hikayat* was the opposite of what has been posited for the Yugoslav epic, for instance. It was not an aid to memory but a means of setting aside what was said, to the point where the success of doing so can be judged by the disappearance of the *hikayat*, a tribute not to its failure but to its success.

Prosodic form seems to have remained constant. Whatever was set into it was eventually lost. What remained was the form itself, at hand to take on all sorts of things, whether historical events, stories arriving from outside Atjeh, or fantasies. The only important modification came with the Atjehnese War. With it came the definitive end of the *hikayat* tradition. After that point, no more were written, or at least none that ever became popular. And this is because a final pleasure was made possible, one that no longer depended on the reduction of sense to sounds, but rather as based on the sealing off of the picture of paradise in another form and another language, a sacred language, indicating something attainable in its full form only after death.

The *Hikayat of the Holy War* in its most popular version is the story of a young man who overhears his elders, who are speaking of the holy war, quote the lines of the Qur'an I have cited. These lines are, of course, given in Arabic and then paraphrased, rather than translated, in Acehnese. "Hearing the line from the Qur'an, Moeda Bahlia felt a yearning. . . . It was as if he were already dead." He decides to go to the holy war. He has a dream of entering paradise. When he awakens, he tells his elders the pleasures he saw there and how he met the nymph who will be his wife. He then goes to battle. There "he chopped away like lightning running through clouds. The unbelievers collapsed front, back, left, and right. . . . [Until finally] Moeda Bahlia then became drowsy, his body weak and without energy. He had no one left with him, and so he joined his fallen comrades."

The lines from the Qur'an are exempt from the prosodic structure of the *hikayat*. They are chanted in Arabic according to the rules that govern Qur'anic recitation. With this, the decomposition of sense becomes a rhetorical device, a way of intensifying what is said about paradise. It shows that no representation is adequate to the description of heavenly bliss. As an attempt to indicate something that cannot be comprehended, these recitations might constitute a step in the logic of the sublime, except that another tradition altogether intervenes. The pleasures of paradise await, sealed off by their setting in holy Arabic, immune to the sort of listening that the prosodic structure of Atjehnese offered before the war, while the Atjehnese language itself becomes merely a way of inadequately paraphrasing inalterable holy truth.

Within the *hikayat* there are a series of images of the nymphs, the rivers of paradise ("Along the river bank all was green and white," 242), jewelry, and even the market ("The market was not a place where things were sold but a place of pleasure for every day. [There were] fine clothes and diamonds for hands and toes," 243), and so on. These are related by the boy to his elders and by the reciters of the *hikayat* to their listeners. These pictures thus have viewers. But their point is that they mark not the end of the world but rather a stimulation to the suicidal end of their viewers, who are told about them to incite them to join the holy war, to destroy themselves there. They are photographs in a way, but photographs that contravene the idea of photography as we commonly understand it.

The purpose of these images is to stimulate listeners to find the originals by going to the holy war themselves. I do not want to say that they are photographs avant le lettre, however. Photographs, at least of the sort we have seen, depend on the logic of the sublime. One sees death and one escapes it in the very act of doing so. One is reconstituted as oneself, even more coherently so than before. These pictures have the effect of dissolving the viewer/listener. He is not to regain himself. Thus the *hikayat* no longer functions as a *hikayat* did before the war, as an antirepresentational machine, but as a literary form promoting representation. Before the holy war, the *hikayat* was assumed to be always available as a defense against the world, turning its events into senseless pleasure. After the holy war, sense and pleasure were conjoined. There was now only one topic, and it was meant to be pictured and preserved. But the preservation of images was meant to be only temporary. It was to last until the original was found. One does not recover from the description of paradise or the fighting of the Atjehnese War feeling more oneself. The aim, on the contrary, was not to recover at all. Instead, inspired by the *hikayat*, one would be compelled to go and actually destroy oneself. The separation between oneself and whatever it is that produces a feeling of sublimity is neither attained nor sought. The *hikayat* is now at odds with social life. It attempts to separate the listener from the world and to prevent his exit from the pleasure of listening.

The subject who could completely enjoy the pleasures the *hikayat* now promised, of course, is the dead person in the photographs we have seen. With the invention of this new subject, the *hikayat* form became a funeral ritual, but a peculiar one. It lacked the aim of such rituals—to turn the memory of a deceased person from involuntary to voluntary memory, re-trievable at will, a transformation that insures it will not appear as an invasion. Instead, the aim was to exhaust the viewers/listeners of the *hikayat*, to effect their disappearance from the earth without regard for their memorialization. They would survive only in paradise, the last memory of them being the moment of transition as their earthly identities were shed. With the success of the *Hikayat of the Holy War*, there would then be no body of people left whom one could imagine as guarding the memory of the deceased. Of course, I do not claim that the idea of the holy war was totally successful in Atjeh. Many Atjehnese survived. But there is evidence that the concept of the holy war was pervasive at the time. Had it not been so, had there been instead an idea of martyrdom as it is understood now in the Palestine of what we call "suicide bombers," whose aim is as political as it is religious, the memory of martyrs would have survived. But that is not the case. There are no memorials to the holy war in Aceh today. Nor is the war much referred to during a historical moment when the inhabitants of the Province of Aceh, opposing Indonesia, claim to be no longer Indonesian, but Acehnese.

Without memorialization—which means there is no intent or expectation that a viewer will see the photo later, perhaps after the death of both the photographer and the photographed—there can be no interest in photography. It took decades after the war ended for Acehnese to become photographers themselves. This does not mean that there were no photographs of Atjehnese, however, as we have seen. But these photographs were neither for nor made by Atjehnese. They were made by Dutch photographers for Dutch consumption. They were made on various occasions, one of which is of special interest. When Atjehnese surrendered, Dutch often photographed them, no doubt to create pictures that, when viewed in the Netherlands, would build support for the war there. It was not only Atjehnese who were photographed. There is a photograph of a man called Demang Léman, an important figure from the Bandjarmasin War, photographed in shackles ten minutes before his execution. Rob Nieuwenhuys, who reproduced this picture in one of his volumes of photographs, says of Demang Léman that "he looks at the photographer [one might rather say, "camera"] uncomplainingly, almost indifferently, but in any case, without fear."[28] Surrender, when not followed by execution, was not always final. Teuku Umar, the most famous warrior chief of the Atjehnese War, surrendered and was made an ally of the Dutch; then, after he had been heavily armed by the Dutch and had defeated many of his fellow Atjehnese, he changed sides again. Dutch troops then hunted him down. Hundreds were killed on both sides before he was slain. His wife, Tjut Nja' Din, who was nearly blind, replaced him as head of his followers and fought the Dutch fiercely. Then one of her bodyguards, who had also been the bodyguard of her late husband, led them to her. The Dutch photographed her also. It is said that "she behaved savagely, screaming, cursing, spitting."[29] In the picture she is scarcely indifferent. But what is interesting is that she is not facing the camera. Her hands are bent in the gesture of Islamic prayer. She is beseeching God, still full of fury. Here, God has replaced the camera as the one who, in her estimation, sees her.

I think this is true even of others who surrendered and who faced the camera. One need not be anguished facing God. One might be indifferent to one's captors, as Nieuwenhuys said of Demang Léman, and as can be seen, for instance, in a photograph Nieuwenhuys reproduces of a group of chiefs who have surrendered. The man second from the left in this picture has three *klewang* slashes on his face. When he smoked, the smoke issued from five places in his head. This extreme disfigurement does not prevent him from having the same expression as the others. They have none of the shame of the defeated. They look straight at the camera, but it is evident that they are not defying their captors, nor do they appear defeated. Demang Léman leans on the chair, relaxed despite being bound. The chiefs stand erect and look straight forward. The energy of their bodies, apparent in their posture, is transferred to their eyes. They are not subjugated in attitude, but neither are they conventionally defiant. If they are defiant, it is not toward their executioners but toward anyone who dares return their gaze, understanding that moments later they will die and that this knowledge informs their look.

Defiance is not the exact word for them. They are, I believe, indifferent. Which is to say that they do not anticipate the return gaze of the photographer or of those who will see the photographs. Their images will be preserved, but they will never see them. They are, in that sense, about to disappear, and they do not regret it. Their disappearance is a curse of a sort. These people still have the holy war in mind. They face viewers who do not understand them, and who, as *kafirs*, promise only savagery in all its senses. But the indifference of those photographed does not stem simply from the impossibility of mutual understanding occurring across such a gap. It derives also from their comprehension that their own disappearance forecasts that of their viewers. Their indifference says, in effect, that whoever sees their images meets an empty gaze. It is "empty" not because it lacks life but rather because it does not anticipate a response. The presence of the potential viewer is of no value to these subjects because they do not value memorialization. Whoever sees these pictures and understands what they mean will lack a reflection of himself in the gaze of the photographed subject. The viewer thus disappears along with those invested in the jihad. Such is the curse.

These photographs, of course, belong to the archive of Atjehnese history. Their curse seals that archive, protecting it against anyone who interrogates it. They mark the line between a culture where the sublime is established and one where it is not. Nieuwenhuis, seeing the old Atjehnese man just before he blew himself up, knows that the man now is in a realm to which he, Nieuwenhuis, has no access. He knows he cannot comprehend anything about the state of the man after that moment. But he has a name for the elsewhere, "death," where the man is, he knows, now to be found. He, Nieuwenhuis, is on one side, "death" is on the other.

Dead, however, is not the word Atjehnese of that era accepted for the man's condition, and consequently they did not accept the difference between themselves and the overwhelming power that Kant claimed was produced with sublimity. Their elsewhere was not that of the Dutch. It is not a simple matter of contrasting beliefs, however. Atjehnese produced an elsewhere out of language. In the context of discourses within Atjeh, between the *hikayat* and everyday speech, the *hikayat* for a while was ascendant. The *hikayat* achieved that place, however, only by incorporating an element foreign to its structure. The jihad of that time was the culmination of a process of the elimination of history already contained in Atjehnese literature, but which could succeed as far as it did only by modifying the prosodic structure on which it depended. Doing so, it introduced a reference analogous to, but in competition with, the power said to produce sublimity. Eventually, with the introduction of modernity through nationalism, Atjehnese came to share the cultivation of the sublime which Kant said was necessary to it.

The line between the two systems is not absolute. Photographs of captured Atjehnese show that one infiltrated the other. The persons in the photographs, now, of course, long deceased, still tell us that they ignore us, that they are dead in a way beyond our capacity to understand or even to put aside by saying that we do not understand as we turn to Atjehnese history. It is this persistence that, I believe, prevents a jihad in Aceh today of the sort that Atjehnese practiced earlier.

FIVE

The Hypnotist

The tsunami that struck parts of Asia in December 2004 struck hardest in Aceh, the province of Indonesia on the north coast of Sumatra. Three years afterwards I took a trip through the coastal cities with two friends, Arief Djati, who works with an NGO in East Java, and the anthropologist Joshua Barker from the University of Toronto.[1] One of the hardest hit was Meulaboh, on the west coast. Meulaboh had sixty thousand inhabitants and lost about a quarter of them. Statistics are imprecise because to this day (2010) people there are not sure who is missing and who is not. Even three years after the disaster, a junior high school girl came to the house of a friend looking for her, though the girl had disappeared in the tsunami. A place where no one is absolutely certain who is alive and who is dead one would think would call for attempts to separate the two. And this, we might assume, through mourning, putting the dead in the past, and through the reestablishment of "normality," meaning the domination of the present and the functioning of institutions. Acehnese society does function now: $8.1

billion dollars of aid for Aceh was pledged; houses, roads, and schools were reconstructed; and government was resurrected. That is one story. But in Meulaboh the restoration of institutions brought with it a normality other than had existed before, one that, rather than separating living and dead, largely integrated them (which is not at all to say "assimilated") and led to a revision of the idea of death.

There were, in fact, two disasters that struck Aceh. The tsunami is one, the other is the *konflik*. *Konflik* is the word *conflict* Indonesianized and made part of the Acehnese language by phoneticizing the spelling. It is the name given to the struggle set off by the depredations of the Indonesian army, which for nearly thirty years assured the Indonesian government and President Suharto's family and associates of Aceh's resources, and along the way raped, looted, and killed. It was opposed by an Acehnese force called the Free Aceh Movement (GAM). One cannot understand the aftermath of the tsunami without understanding that it is also the time after the settlement of the conflict. We will come back to that. For the moment, let us turn to some aspects of Meulaboh today.

Normality implies familiarity. One has expectations as one goes through the day, and these are met. But it is possible to expect the unfamiliar and to have a place for it. This, indeed, is not surprising to anthropologists, particularly to those who work where supernatural appearances are common. It is more or less the case in Meulaboh today. It was not so before the tsunami. There are entities in Meulaboh that had no existence before; at the same time, there are fewer uncanny manifestations.

If one looks at the way mourning takes place and the conditions of today, one sees why. There is a difference in Aceh between how men and women respond to the death of people close to them. This is long standing. Acehnese indigenous culture was formed in the rice-growing areas. From there Acehnese migrated to the coastal areas and elsewhere, where a different sort of society was formed, particularly in coastal cities such as Meulaboh. But the migrants carried with them Acehnese practices, including those surrounding death. What I saw in Meulaboh in 2007 and 2009 matched what I saw in a rural village of Aceh's east coast in 1962 to 1964: for instance, in Meulaboh we met a woman who had lost her two teenage daughters. Three years later it was evident that she had in no way come to terms with this loss. She searched for them for two years, and she visited the mass graves daily. Even after three years they were seldom out of mind, she said. She does not differ from the women I knew in the interior rice lands of Aceh some fifty years earlier.[2] They still grieved for their children years later. But they did not believe that their children might still be alive, as the woman from Meulaboh sometimes does.

Men, by contrast, are proud to be able to master their feelings. It shows the strength of their belief in Islam. To mourn would be to protest against what God has given. This leaves them unable to give much comfort to their wives. Women's grief is taken to be a sign of their weakness. Men pity them for this and do what they can to help them. But the comfort that their sort of Islam provides—that death is God's will—does not avail. Nothing men say can help their wives. No doubt it is like this with death anywhere. But in Aceh, given the scale of deaths, it is even more difficult. The sympathy and sociality that a grieving person ordinarily depends upon become doubtful when, for a while, people think that *kiamat*, the final day, has arrived and society itself has ended.

I do not think that these women recover from the death of their children. No substitutes are acceptable. They hold onto the singularity of their loss. They could not do so for as long as they do, perhaps, if they could not at the same time make use of it. Women do not dispute what men say about religion. They certainly think of themselves as Muslims and have no doubts at all about it. But the singularity of their loss gives them something else. For men, the deaths of their children are examples of the way God works. As such, their dead children are comparable to others who have died; they fall under a type. But Acehnese women, in my experience, allow themselves to suffer, while their husbands do not allow themselves that possibility. Women somehow know that the significance of each lost child is unlike that of any other. It is, in that sense, inexpressible. Knowing something their husbands do not know, or at least do not formulate, gives women a source of authority within the household—a source that is all the more powerful for never being articulated and therefore never a subject of dispute. They cannot and do not justify their feelings. But their loss gives them a moral justification nonetheless, which sustains them in disputes with their husbands.

It is only a seeming paradox to speak of "them" when what is at issue is the singularity of each death, the singularity of each mother. What "they" feel is not necessarily incommunicable (though it might be), but it is has no place in the discourse of their husbands. The husbands recognize this, but they are powerless against it. Men defend themselves by trying to suppress their wives' feelings, but their religious discourse has no prise on their feelings. In the rural areas, reinforced by traditional economic relations—women owned home and rice land; men had to leave the village to trade, usually, in order to supply their families with money—women traditionally had an undefeatable source of power and even authority, authority because men too shared the loss of their children and recognized it, even if they thought that women were wrong in their reactions to it. But they could only protest that their wives should not react "emotionally," as they said. They had no other argument and not much in the way of tactics. There was a continuous battle between men and women, which women won, but never decisively. The irresolution of this war depended on a certain sensitivity of men to women, a respect for them ambivalently sanctioned by religion as practiced in Aceh, which makes the situation differ from some other strongly Islamic societies. And it depends on women's respect for the Islam preached by the men. They defer to men, but they do not obey them.[2]

Economic arrangements were, of course, different in the coastal towns, which served mainly as entrepôts and where women did not own rice lands or the family house. But it is evident that men and women in Meulaboh continued to face death differently. The tsunami did not change this, but, as is usual after a disaster, the assurance of authority of all types was shaken.

In normal times, in villages, at least, the effect of women's determination not to give up what they had lost was a certain supernaturalism, particularly the appearance of spirits in curing rites, which men disapproved of but women found compelling. The refusal to mourn, as one might expect, led eventually to the formation of ghosts, the return of the dead in another guise—a form rendered more exactly in French as *revenant*, literally "returned," "returning." These "returned" were usually disguised as the spirits of women, vaguely from another time and another place, but within Aceh. Men, bolstered by the rationalizing of modernist Islam, protested against these rites, but they could not eliminate them. But the return of the dead in this form was, at least, a solution to something that, in my estimation, has no solution. Revenants appeared in curing rites, where they saved ill people from death. Their use as a denial of death is clear.[3]

This, however, was not the case after the tsunami. In the first place, loss was no longer taken in silence and privacy. Too many people were in the same situation. Loss became multiple though not comparable, or typical rather than singular. At the same time, the sublimation of lost people into spectral figures who save from death was less probable after the tsunami. For the woman of whom I spoke, the loss of her children still in 2007 remained unaccepted, bare, crude, simply the event, unrepressed and thus not transformed into cultural productions. It is as though, without the fabrication of revenants, cultural production itself no longer continued. There is then no place to put the dead apart. Either they are not buried, most of the missing either never having been found, or, if found, they were buried in mass graves and not identified. As a result, the city continues to contain the missing.

Meulaboh is full of people thought to be alive, remembered as such, though many surely were swept off by the tsunami. People are aware that they themselves, like everyone in the city, do not know who is alive and who is dead. As one young man told me, "Everyone knows that no one knows who is dead and who is alive." Knowledge of this fact is normal, at least in the statistical sense of that word, and not a pathological failure of memory or cognition. There are thus "living-dead," people whose status as alive or dead is unclear. One does not know and cannot reestablish facts of life and death.

One might expect that the benefit of the doubt would go to the assumption of death. Those one has not seen oneself would be assumed dead until shown to be otherwise. But the assumption is made in the other direction. We see this in new figures that, if not exactly seen, are possibly experienced. One of them is the hypnotist, whom we will soon discuss. Just now it is enough to know that hypnotists walk the streets and are said to have been experienced by people who, however, have never seen them or who cannot recollect having seen them but know they have been affected by them.. In such a case, what value is cognition? It is a question not of the presence of something dead but of a figure whose presence is not subject to cognition of any sort. And this is the situation not merely with the hypnotist but with the missing. They are not seen, but they might be present somewhere, and one might eventually meet them. One holds interior conversations with them, and one speaks about them, saying, as one woman told me, perhaps they merely lost their way. One does not rely on the workings of one's senses to know they exist, but they might exist nonetheless. They exist through a rational deduction: "Everyone knows that no one knows."

It is hard, but not impossible, to distinguish these living dead from ghosts. Specters are treated differently from living beings, at least in Aceh. One can communicate with them only by extraordinary means—in trance, in particular—and they have extraordinary effects; in particular, they cause illness and cure it. One communicates with the living dead of Meulaboh, however, as one communicates with the indisputably living. One speaks with them, for instance, but only in one's mind, without an actual confrontation. But the lack of confrontation does not lead to identifying the effect of memory as just that. The widespread idea that the city is populated with people thought to be alive but no doubt actually dead, the lack of clear division between living and dead, simply adds those remembered to the current population of Meulaboh. There is no other place to put them. The argument is circular—the lack of established difference between living and dead allows memory of the probable dead to seem to confirm their living existence.

One's memory of the missing is like the memory of others in Meulaboh of those they have lost. Before the tsunami, death meant that the survivor had to suffer alone something she could not adequately communicate to anyone. In 2007 memory of the missing had led to the conclusion "I do not know, and no one else does either." Beyond the lack of recognition of the dead and the living as such, there is an awareness that one's own knowledge is doubtful, all the more so since this is said to be true of everyone else. Where memory of the dead would before have confirmed their absence, the shared, thus confirmed and accepted fact is that absence means merely uncertainty. People remembered do not necessarily belong to the past; they might be alive. The word *might* is introduced into a process that once would have established a difference between living and dead. Now, so long as memory is strong, to remember means to pull the missing into the society of the living. Possibly.

In some parts of Indonesia, ghosts are commonly experienced, but by definition they are set apart from everyday life. The ghosts I know of in Indonesia often haunt specific locals, the site of their stories. The living-dead of Meulaboh have no fixed locus. When one finds a ghost, one finds a presence that should no longer be there. When one becomes aware of a living-dead, as one might when one looks for a friend only to learn that she has disappeared, one comes across an absence where one had assumed the opposite. But even then one cannot be sure the missing person is dead. Her mother suspects her missing daughters are merely lost. The absence of these figures is not definitive. These, the living-dead, are the inverse of ghosts. The ghost upsets the idea of being by existing after the extinction of the person. The living-dead of Meulaboh have a similar effect, but by opposite means. They produce an ambiguous absence by not decisively dying. Because of their indecisiveness, they have to take a hyphenated form, one that links the two terms only in order to establish an oscillation between them.

There is a difference between the uncontrollable memory of a lost loved one resurging at unexpected moments and the condition of Meulaboh, continuously populated by numerous persons whose absence one learns about by accident and who are not only people one was close to. The living-dead are announced, not by themselves, as are ghosts, but by others who report them missing. Their locus is social, then, rather than personal or private. One expects to find someone, and one is told that no one can. One thinks of a schoolgirl looking for her comrade years after the tsunami, coming to the girl's house and only then finding out from her mother, who herself is not sure whether her daughter is alive, that the girl cannot be found. The abrupt failure of expectations does not settle the matter. The mother thinks her daughter might still be living. The testimony of those who ought to know is insufficient to establish the fact of life or death. The place of confirmation of essential knowledge becomes the source of its uncertainty. But out of that another certainty arises: *everyone knows* that no one knows.

The living-dead are not lost to the social. Indeed, that is a part of their definition. Meulaboh in 2007 held the dead alive. It not only refused to put the missing in the category of "the dead," it incorporated them in a way not different from the way it makes those up until then considered foreign part of itself. "Alive" applies to whoever is thought to inhabit the city. The dead, the living-dead, remain a part of it; "the real is the rational."

Women probably are at the origin of the belief in the living-dead, but men share it with them, believing also that no one knows who is alive and who not. Men continue to say, in a conventional but sincere way, that their religious belief carries them through the deaths of those close to them. They refuse to grieve, refuse to allow the memory even of lost children to affect them. As I have said, this traditionally reinforced their authority and left them free of a need for ghosts. After the tsunami, with the dislocations of social life, a different sort of figure, not supernatural and not necessarily uncanny, depending on how one wants to understand that adjective, appeared.

There is, in particular, the hypnotist, who walks the streets, touches someone's elbow—women are the victims in the accounts I heard—and takes her jewels. I heard of such a hypnotist in Jakarta; the figure does not originate in Aceh. It is a story clearly set in the context of Indonesian urban street crime. Judging from the word, scarcely Indonesian, it may have its source in the international world. It was adopted in Meulaboh for reasons peculiar to Aceh after the tsunami. In any case, the woman does not know she has been robbed until later and has no memory of the moment of the theft.

This story is borrowed, but it has local references. The army closed Meulaboh for three days after the tsunami, under the pretext that rebels would steal weapons. During that time it was looted, soldiers and others taking, among other things, jewels and even clothes from the corpses of women. The story of the hypnotist is clearly connected to this event, but the intermediate connections remain murky. The hypnotist is not presented as a conventional specter, known from curing rituals and easily identifiable as supernatural. The hypnotist lacks the tinge of the uncanny for those in Meulaboh who told me about him or her. He is accepted as a constant part of everyday reality, rather than intruding on it as ghosts do. Whatever sense of déjà vu he might bring with him is not remarked.

Spectral presences served a purpose for both sexes before the tsunami. For mothers who lost their children, their ghostly return could be an ambiguous source of satisfaction. Disguised as specters, they brought illness but they were nonetheless present. After the tsunami, lost children sometimes reappeared in dreams, but there seems to have been no particular resurgence of the supernatural. Rather the contrary.[4]

Even for men who disapproved of the stories of ghosts, the stories confirmed the difference between life and death. Thus in a square where, it is said, a thousand people had gathered after the earthquake, only to be carried off by the tsunami waves, people say there are no ghosts. Just a couple of hundred meters from this square is a disused Dutch cemetery. Before the tsunami, a boy dreamed of a tall Dutch soldier who demanded a fried egg. He got it. A trishaw driver, riding past the graveyard one night, again before the tsunami, was terrified to see figures standing in the cemetery. Yet in the square where so many perished, it is claimed that there are no ghosts. Perhaps there might have been in the first few days after the event. At that time, some people heard children calling for their mothers. But this, they say, might have been the voices of those still alive. No one is prepared to say that they heard the sounds of apparitions.[5]

Ghosts in Aceh are said to ask for something that they lacked in life. It is something trivial—a glass of water, for instance. Curing rituals are carried out to find out what the possessing spirit wants and to fulfill the wish, making the spirit vanish. Ghosts are desires without bodies; they lodge in the bodies of others for lack of one of their own. What would a spirit do with a glass of water if she had no body to drink it with?[6] The treatment of illness is the path not merely to hearing their demands but to discovering their existence. Spirits, desires without body, thus without voice, find a voice through the curer. The curer, in trance, allows them to use her voice. The spirit, then, lodged in the body of the sick woman, exits by finding a means of expression in the body of the curer. The ghost then disappears, and in theory the woman is cured.

As I have said, the desires stated are trivial. One does not have a sense of a life unfulfilled—there is nothing tragic about wanting a glass of water. Nor does the spirit announce the loss of a particular individual. The spirit has a name gained in life, but no one knows its biography. The force of the demand, its seriousness as judged by illness, is disproportionate to what is asked for. The object demanded is close to worthless. However, a communication is made, which is not reducible to what is said but which is important for the path it traces from the spirit to the patient to the curer to the world. What cannot ordinarily speak, speaks in trance. And when it does so, someone dead speaks to the living world, only to vanish afterwards. The worlds of the dead and the living interpenetrate only to become separated. The line between them is thus emphasized.[7]

Acehnese ghosts belong to ordinary life. One dies thirsty because in ordinary life one is sometimes thirsty. The life that produces ghosts is so ordinary that one does not ask what prompted thirst or what caused the person's death or why the close sequence of the two events. One assumes one knows how the person's life was lived. The tsunami dead, however, are products of an extraordinary time. They are not exactly spirits without bodies or even bodies without spirits. Their transformation into the dead is incomplete by the standard of previous conventions.. On the one hand, because of their great numbers and because they were unidentified, their bodies lacked the traces of life that create respect. They were frequently discovered under strata of debris from destroyed buildings, trucks, shafts of wood, and more, making them only another now useless article. They were collected, thrown into trucks, then dumped into enormous pits, which were covered with debris. It was simple to confound these bodies with the debris that is said to have killed the living being and that was used to cover them. The *arwah*, or life force, ordinarily dispatched in the funeral, with the dead then awaiting the day of judgment, had merely vanished. The two poles, body and life force, usually related after death by their separation, as in the case of ghosts, no longer referred to each other.

Revenants appear among the living but do not belong there. They thus mark the separation of living and dead. When this separation was not in place, a possibility arose that before the tsunami was never considered. "Everyone knows that no one knows who is alive and who is dead." This formulation, heard three years after the tsunami, is important not only because it states the lack of boundary between life and death but also because it does so, in the first phrase, by stating a condition of knowledge, "everyone knows that no one knows," that, we will see, was subject to evolution. This phrase pictures a mental condition, an uncertainty about knowledge in general as a social fact. As the memory of particular lost persons gradually— very gradually—faded, this condition remained.

We return to the consequences of accepting death as a brute fact, occurring on a major scale in a single moment. With that, there was no fear of the corpse and no respect for it. The army took charge of collecting the bodies and, as I have said, was accused of having stolen women's jewelry (woman traditionally wore their riches in the form of gold ornaments) and even their clothes. It is one thing to blame the army, which was generally feared and even hated throughout Aceh. It was another, however, to tell how volunteers—who, it is said, came principally from the metropolis of Medan, a day or two days' drive away, and from surrounding villages to help clear the devastation—were also said to have stolen jewelry. Indeed, they were accused of cutting off the hands of bloated corpses when swelling prevented the easy removal of bracelets. These stories are lurid, but they were not told as a scandal. Nor did I meet anyone who knew of someone accused of these thefts or of the pursuit of anyone who might have done so.

The bodies had no trace of sacrality. The residue of life that would have produced it was not recognized once the bodies were merged with debris. The people of Meulaboh themselves were said not to have participated in the theft because they were too busy looking for relatives. They recognized those they had known and knew that they did not recognize others. The body as it was in life was at the center of their perceptions. Others, coming from outside the city, saw only cadavers. It was, finally, this view that prevailed for everyone, it seems. To produce a revenant, a body must first be identified as the site of a deceased personality. Without that, it lacks the capacity for desire, the trait around which the Acehnese ghost takes shape. The grotesque distribution of the bodies, dangling from trees or electric wires, or with only limbs or heads protruding from piles of debris, for instance, surely contributed to depriving these cadavers of their personalities. There is no doubt that people searched for those they knew. But it seems that the overwhelming fact of countless nameless dead—one remembers that about a quarter of the city was lost—meant that the aggregate view was established in people's minds. The people killed, said one man amongst others, one who had himself lost all his grandchildren, were killed by debris. They suffered the effects of garbage (the same word as for debris), and they were deposited in heaps with garbage and, as I have described, were treated just like garbage. They were literally worthless—worthless in social life, worthless as material, deprived of moral value. They were without intrinsic value, thus without the ability to claim the valuables that clung to them. Those who robbed, then, were not considered as having a predilection for theft, as "thieves," therefore, or even as being in need. They simply recognized the scene they had come across.

Yet new forms appeared in the city. One man told me in 2007 that things are not the same as before. He no longer knows everyone, as he did before. There are people he does not know. This is a way of saying that he recognizes that he does not recognize certain figures. If the uncanny is the mere appearance of something one knows one does not recognize, then this is uncanny. In these societies, the uncanny usually appears in the form of spirits, thus as set apart, though even here, the setting apart of ghosts means that they are recognized for what they are rather than being the cause of uncertainty of recognition. Thus whether Acehnese ghosts are uncanny is an open question. The possibly uncanny, in any case unrecognized figures

on the street stimulate nothing more than the remark that things are different now. They do not need either ritual banishment or political action.
Another such example is traffic. Traffic is said to be disorderly. Once again,
as after World War I in Europe, traffic, easily visible public order, is
thought to be disorderly. As such, it causes uneasiness. This is, in the first
place, a doubt about the strength of authority to create order. It is also a
fear of being overwhelmed by an irresistible force, again one of the elements
said to produce the uncanny. But, as in Europe, this uncanny manifestation,
if it is that, leads to nothing more than caution when crossing the street.
One might surmise that one sees the living-dead, but these are not beings
returned from the dead with the characteristics of death. They are merely
alive but unrecognized. To my mind, these examples illustrate the uncertainty given by the general proposition "Everyone knows that no one
knows." They exemplify the normality of the presence of the living-dead
and the acceptance of one's own uncertainty. As such, they lack the attribute
"uncanny."

After the tsunami, one sees a movement from the uncanny in the form
of ghosts to anonymous persons on the street. Whether the nameless are
also uncanny is uncertain. One has to chose—without any possibility of
doing so definitively—between two possibilities. One might see the new
manifestations found in public spaces as a transformation of a constant, perhaps innate, sense of the uncanny, where any instance of recognizing that
one does not recognize is uncanny. Or one might think that there has been
a reduction of the uncanny after the tsunami, one whereby the introduction
of the possibly dead into daily life goes practically unmarked and what before would have been uncanny manifestations are now merely anonymous
persons. Along the way, one notes that the acceptance of anonymity in this
society is a major transformation. Catastrophe, in this instance, rather than
isolating its victims, has brought them into the contemporary urban world.

The possibility of accepting the living-dead, of making the dead part of
living society, is in part made possible by the structure of Meulaboh. Meulaboh was settled by people from various parts of Sumatra—Batak, Mingaka-
bau, and others as well as Acehnese. The mixture of peoples resulted in a
new creole, built largely out of Minangkabau but known by its label in
Acehnese as "Guest Language" (*Basa Djaméei*).[8] That is, these peoples are
guests in Aceh, but that would include the Acehnese themselves, who for
the most part came from the inland rice lands. The creole they use, "Guest

Language," takes the place of both Malay, the lingua franca, and Indonesian, the national language that developed out of Malay. Across ethnic lines, each speaks a language that is neither his own nor the national language. In one city, though on the other side of the Acehnese border, in 2007 we spoke with a Chinese married to a Sumatran woman, a Batak. The Chinese spoke to his daughter in Batak, though his children speak Teocheow, and to us, for lack of a "native" language, in Indonesian. Indonesian, the national language, here was used as a lingua franca. And that is the point; these people live in ways similar to the way life was led under colonialism, in the famous plural society of John Furnivall, where each group had little in common with the other, and they met only in the market. Indeed, the coastal societies of most of what is now Indonesia were plural societies even before colonialism.[9] However, the antiquity of the arrangement can give a distorted picture. Immigration into the west coast of Aceh is recent. There are no long-standing traditions in which the first settlers have a privileged place, while everyone who comes afterwards is a "guest." Rather, everyone is a "guest," including ethnic Acehnese, in whose language the "guest language" is named. Everything seems translatable here, since it passes without the resistance of an established language that belongs to the place. Everyone speaks the language of the other, the "guest." Everyone is welcome without regard to nationality. In Singkil, another of these coastal towns, we met a man born in Burma whose mother was a Saudi and who arrived in Aceh unintentionally—he was a boat captain and had been arrested by the Indonesian navy, imprisoned for over a year, and then released on condition that he act for them as a translator. He married a poor woman born in Singkil. He was widely praised because he never displayed jealousy. He knew everyone but he kept out of their affairs, and that was what he was praised for. The Chinese man I mentioned had a similar view of life. He told us he got on well with his neighbors regardless of their origins, but the condition was never to speak to them more than once a week. Otherwise there could be trouble. It is a strange place where the perfect "citizen," if one can use the word, is one who stays out of the lives of others and who, as a foreigner and belonging to no local community, is valued because he does not threaten to impose his ways. The perfect "citizen," then, does not participate in politics. The people of these cities, it seems, live their lives to the greatest extent possible outside the public realm. In such a place, one does not speak of the "assimilation" of peoples to the place or the political order but rather of their "integration." Where provenance does not count, where nationality does not count, not only whoever but also, it seems, whatever enters is capable of being integrated. This was the situation of Meulaboh in 2007, where the living-dead were the latest immigrants.

I am not describing paradise when I speak of the integration of everyone and everything. These societies have known violence, such as church burnings, on occasion, and in particular the massacre of Communists in 1966. And it has long been said that one has to beware on the west coast. Many die from poisoned coffee, or so they say. Since the coffee shops are public places, much frequented, and serve excellent coffee, this is another example of how the mixture of peoples is at once possible, accepted, and even pleasurable but also thought to be dangerous. Everyone lives together, but to peer across lines of division is ambiguously to invite disaster.

In Meulaboh there is always the possibility of crossing the lines of difference, as we will see again. Moreover, when people spoke of not knowing who is alive and who is dead, there was an undercurrent of excitement or perhaps celebration. It keeps everyone part of Meulaboh, even if it is a transformed city as a result. If the need to mark the transition from life to death is avoided, that is not only because factual knowledge is absent. Nor is it only because people do not want to give up the dead. Women traditionally did not want to give up their children, but they did not deny their deaths. Partly it is because a principle of these societies has been activated. Under the conditions created by the tsunami, the unknown dead have been conflated with immigrants and made part of Meulaboh rather than being set apart.

With this in mind, we turn to the figure of the hypnotist. In the story of the hypnotist, as in that of the tsunami, women are robbed. These women are not dead but alive, at least they are at the beginning and at the end of their encounter with the hypnotist. What they are in between those moments is unclear. The hypnotist is an especially powerful street criminal. Indeed, as I have mentioned, the idea of the hypnotist probably came from metropolitan Indonesia, where street crime is an important topic and where hypnotists are said to be found, operating as they do in Meulaboh. The idea was borrowed after the tsunami, which makes it seem likely that the looting after the inundation stimulated its borrowing. As in the accounts of the tsunami, a person is overcome by an unprecedented or at least an unknow-able force. But the critical moment of death is obscured and indirectly indi-cated through loss.

The tsunami was so massively destructive that the world disappeared. The references or associations assumed when one sees one element of the city—a street, for instance—were gone. The victim of the hypnotist has no memory of the event. It is set apart from her life in the way that the tsunami both was unexpected, even unknown, and created a nearly unrecognizable world. Neither event has any connection with anything previously existing in the lives of the victims, as is the case with traumatizing events, which, when retold, seem to be relived rather than being put in the past from the point of view of the speaker. Indeed, in one place Freud explains the repeti-tion of events in speech and in dreams as an attempt to master them. Mastery means that the event can be recalled at will. When memory is involuntary, the force of experience causes involuntary repetition. When destruction is repeated or represented, albeit in a disguised form, as in the case of the hypnotist, one thinks the repetition is an effect of trauma. Not being able to be conceptualized, thus given a place in mental life, it reappears.

A traumatic representation is disturbing and disrupts normality. The hypnotist, however, had an assured place on the street—as assured as that of any street criminal, which, indeed, is what he was assumed to be. He is as normal as any criminal. The criminal, one might say, makes disruption "normal" in the sense of explicable and without mystery. The hypnotist, as a hyper-criminal, as it were, seems to be half way to the normalization of the tsunami.

Remade as a story of criminality, the tsunami in the form of a hypnotist gives the tsunami a place geographically (the public sphere) and conceptu-ally (the criminal). It belongs on the street. It reestablishes references that disappeared in the massive waves of overpowering water. As such, it is not a repetition of the event or a retelling of the experience. At the same time, insofar as it changes destruction and in particular death into material loss, it preserves that moment through displacement and no doubt consolidation, in the manner of a dream. It keeps hold of death and gives it a place in a disguised form, as the dream conceals the dream thought in order not to disturb the sleeper.

As in a dream, elements from different moments are combined in the story of the hypnotist. The hypnotist repeats the robbing of the corpses. So far as can be established by repeated inquiries, robbers of corpses have never been identified, and there has been no attempt to do so, any more than there has been an attempt to apprehend the hypnotist. The agents never come to light. One might say that of the "tsunami" itself, which remains a word with at best an indefinite content, as we will see.

The hypnotist kills no one; every victim escapes. It could be a version of what Neil Hertz has called "the sublime turn." There catastrophe is evoked and a figure is fabricated that allows the power of the disaster to be recuperated for those who tell the story. It becomes a story of how one "almost" lost everything. But, of course, the accounts of the hypnotist, if they are a retelling of the catastrophe, are disguised, just as is the hypnotist himself or herself or itself. In the sublime turn, there is always one who, having just evaded death, now takes the excitement of that moment into his voice to tell the story. In Meulaboh the story is not told by its victims but by those who have heard of others who, at third remove, have heard from its victims. Moreover, what one has escaped from is considerably less than the massive death imposed by the tsunami. It is thus not the power of the tsunami that powers the telling of the story. Rather, the tsunami is vastly reduced in its effects, and this enables the easy telling of the story that is necessary to myth rather than the compelled retelling of trauma or the use of hyperbole in narratives where the sublime turn occurs. It is, of course, not surprising that a notion of the sublime should not be at work outside the cultures where the notion developed. One might say the same of the notion of trauma.[10]

The hypnotist has never been seen. Can he then consolidate disaster? We say something is "a figure of." But the hypnotist is not a figure; he is the absence of something; the word stands in a place where its referent never shows up. But "something" is assumed to have been there. This in itself makes him like the tsunami in that the tsunami has not yet been satisfactorily conceptualized. What the word means remains unclear. It is as though the very word *tsunami* is too powerful to utter safely. Therefore one invents another term. And with that other term, which also keeps the referent at bay, the effects are reduced. The "real" loss sustained by an encounter with the hypnotist is considerably less than the damage of the tsunami. But this loss nonetheless suggests the lethal force of the latter. In one way or another, for one purpose or another, this lethal force is installed in Meulaboh.

If the hypnotist followed the logic of trauma, he would disappear once he had been accepted as part of normality. It seems, indeed, that the hypnotist had disappeared by 2009. At least one heard no more about him. But his disappearance did not mean the end of the problematic he embodied. It did not mean that death was no longer embedded in Meulaboh but that its expression took another, even more generalized form.

One might think of the hypnotist as a supernatural being, yet he is not like the figures that appear, for instance, in curing rites. The ghosts of Aceh are found in the family and the village. The hypnotist, by contrast, is encountered in a public place. He is not treated as another sort of being but as an ordinary human, albeit with the ability to blot out memory. The specters of curing rites are responded to by curers, who go into trance in order to communicate with them. There is nothing like that here. Nor is there any attempt to banish or to exorcise the hypnotist, as one would a specter. One responds to him unconsciously. No one remembers handing over her jewels. But the transaction is otherwise normal. The question of whether the hypnotist takes his booty or it is handed over does not arise. Either way the transaction is like those that occur in normal life except, of course, that one cannot recall the event. Aside from that, the hypnotist is a figure like the thieves who inhabit Indonesian city streets.

The hypnotist is known, then, only by his effects and never through experience as it is remembered. He leaves in one's mind only the feeling that something happened, though one cannot reconstruct the details. One would not know that there had been an event at all if it were not for the material loss. Loss is doubled: loss of memory, thus of experience, and material loss. One knows only that some event, something, happened, but what, who? Something is held in mind, but one can't give it content.

Once again, ghosts are different. They are experienced: one hears them speak, and they leave traces. They are anachronistic. Their endurance beyond death is the source of the fright they cause. The hypnotist, by contrast, is like the living-dead. He has never been put into the past; he appears rather than reappears, as it were. But, of course, he does not ever "appear." He only indicates that, in the place where, surely, he did appear but nevertheless was not seen, something is missing. Where, surely, there was something, now there is nothing, a "nothing" marking what one lost and a 'nothing' meaning the hypnotist himself or herself or itself also is not. The hypnotist in that sense almost figures the living-dead. They are possibly alive, possibly dead. They are something, they are "here," but they cannot be found. Their very negativity indicates their existence. The impossibility of this, finally, gives rise to the oscillation between the terms *living-dead*. Death and life, something and nothing, change places. If there is such a thing as Acehnese metaphysics, its question after the tsunami is not "Why is there something rather than nothing?" but "Can nothing exist?" The hypnotist answers that "nothing" is "something."

There is nothing particularly unusual about a city populated with the dead. They exist elsewhere, particularly in societies with extended longevity. I am seventy-three as I write this. Perhaps 89 percent of the people I have been closest to in my life are dead. I continue to speak to them and they to me, and this is not unusual. An old people's community might resemble Meulaboh in this respect. What is unusual is to have a figure such as the hypnotist. My transactions with the dead are identifiable as such. I remember certain people: what they said, what I said to them, what I "heard" in a book and what I said to it. Transactions with the past are normal for people of the type I assume are reading this piece. But transactions with the hypnotist are extraordinary. The hypnotist makes room for existence where there is no sign of it and has never been. Where, for instance, do the goods stolen from the corpses disappear to? No one thinks to ask. No one thinks they can be recovered. One could not hope to find them, because they are "elsewhere," *ailleurs*, as one says more definitively in French. They have disappeared "there," never to be found again. There is a realm of loss. Contacted by a figure from that realm, one loses—loses ones possessions and loses oneself. It is only logical that, if the dead are mixed with the living, one will have transactions with them. To do so on their terms, one becomes one of them, but only for the moment.

The line between life and death still stands, but one can cross it. Just there is the importance of the hypnotist. It is the figure that allows everyone in Meulaboh who knows the story to know that, since he or she might be the hypnotist's next victim, he or she is part of a scene that includes the absent, that is, the dead, and does so without the need to put them definitively apart. One has transactions with them, one crosses the line and crosses back again. That is not an imaginary journey to the land of the dead or an anxious feeling that the dead have returned as menacing ghosts. It is not even the workings of involuntary memory or the innocuous workings of memory under conscious control. Rather, the hypnotist shows that death continues to mean loss and, though the living-dead are ambiguously distinguished from the living, they are still part of living society. The nothingness implied in the Western sense of the word *death* has to be modified.

The hypnotist forms an other, even an absolute other, who incipiently and even right now affects us. When he does so, one cannot consolidate this loss by saying "I am dead" or "I was dead," not because the sentence is impossible but because at that point one lacks voice. One "experiences" the hypnotist; in a certain sense one dies and lives again in perhaps the only possible way that distinguishes life and death and yet does not absolutely separate them: by knowing that one has effaced all memory of oneself in the alternate state. The "experience" of the hypnotist's victim belongs to someone unfindable, thus unrecognizable. Someone who at once is "me," the hypnotist's object, the person who lost riches, and an unknowable "I," someone who is unknown to the social, conscious "me," who, if this "I" has a voice at all, is always inaudible, at least to everyone except, possibly, the hypnotist.

The hypnotist, installing death on the street, causes the evolution of the effects of the tsunami. It is not a question of the historical, singular loss of a person. Not like the woman who lost her daughters and whose memory of the tsunami focuses on that loss. It is, rather, a generalization of destruction, of loss, and of death. The loss of a person perhaps always seems unjust, unwarranted, or unfair, since it is "my" loss, thus exceptional. But the loss expressed by the hypnotist is a loss that potentially affects everybody. It is a normality or a condition of life in Meulaboh. It normalizes death as a property of the living.

In place of a consolidation of loss followed by an attempt to regain it in memory or to forget it, there is the evolution of a community, one that contains the dead, as we have many times repeated. Their inclusion should raise problems of contamination. If "we," the living, associate with the dead, if they are not sacred, that is, if their memory is not set apart, put into the past, then there should be cognitive disorder or anxiety. And, indeed, from a conventional point of view this has ensued. But in Meulaboh we reach a point where to say that is to insist on our own ontology and so to miss the chance to see another normality.

SIX

"Tout autre est tout autre"

> If all essents went up in smoke, it is the noses that would differentiate and
> appreciate them.
>
> —HERACLITUS, Fragment 7

The "Other" Revised

The "other" taken into account by ethnography has been the peoples of
different cultures. That type of otherness is suspect today, suspect to such a
degree that the practice of ethnography, particularly in the United States,
has been revised. One is not surprised to read that an American anthropologist has lived in a part of the world remote from her country, has become
fluent in the language, has spent years there, and has discovered no important differences, at least once the anthropologist attends to the persons she
knows. When ethnography takes this form, it can be accused of undermin-
ing its own first assumptions. In France the conclusions drawn from this
state of affairs have been brought to the fore with such force that many
ethnographers feel that their discipline is threatened. The opening of the
Musée du Quai Branly was also the closing of the ethnographic section of
the famous Musée de l'Homme. The rich collections of the latter were

transferred to the new museum. "Really, one could think one is dreaming. Everything one reads on the subject is unbelievable," wrote the eminent anthropologist Louis Dumont when the project was announced.[1] It is "unbelievable" that the ethnographic museum might disappear. It, according to Dumont, makes the work of ethnographers available to the public. It forms a part of their instruction. It tells them, he implies, of the peoples of the world. Without it, they would be ignorant. One is in a world of dreams if one thinks one could live without ethnography.[2] The anthropologist Jean Jamin published an article at the time, "Is It Necessary to Burn the Museums of Ethnography?"[3] the answer would be "yes" if the ethnographic other is not merely out of date but morally and politically suspect as many think.

The question was the nature of the value of the museum objects. The new museum was seen by anthropologists as an art museum. But this was disputed. The purpose of the museum, said President Chirac in his address at its inauguration, was to honor peoples formerly despised. The new museum would "render justice to the infinite diversity of cultures" and in doing so would "manifest a different regard for the spirit of the peoples and civilizations of Africa, Asia, and Oceania." One might think that the ethnographic museum from which the bulk of the collections came, the Musée de l'Homme, had done just this. It is the calling of ethnography, indeed, to "render justice" to the diversity of peoples. But listening to President Chirac, one has the impression that the ethnographic museum had to be dismantled for there to be "a new view" of diversity, both of "peoples" and of "civilizations." And of course the diversity displayed at the Musée de l'Homme reflected the understanding of peoples under colonial rule. An entirely different approach was called for, one that would dissipate the aura of colonialism the old museum emanated and so put the relation of France to its former colonies on another basis.[4] That the new institution does not have a more descriptive title reflects the inability to find a suitable term for ethnographic artifacts that have become aesthetic objects.

Throughout his speech Chirac spoke in pairs—sometimes it was "peoples and civilizations," sometimes "arts and civilizations." There was no dispute about the word *civilization*, as there might have been fifty years earlier. But between "art" and "people" there was a choice to be made. Ostensibly there was to be room for both, but most ethnographers are not clear

that room was left for their study. There had been a passionate debate between ethnographers, on the one hand, and art historians, curators, and
dealers, on the other. It concerned first of all the designation of what was
to be in the new museum. The objects were mainly (but not entirely) from
the Musée de l'Homme.[5] Were they, then, still to be used to illustrate the
lives of peoples, or were they now to be shown for their aesthetic value?
One question was how best to understand "others" (not to mention who
exactly these others are or were); another was how to "honor" them. It was
necessary to "multiply points of view" in order to give a certain "depth" to
the "arts and civilizations of all the continents." In order to do that, old
views had to be "dissipated." Not only the outdated views of ethnographers
but those of the general public were in question. The prejudice against ex-
colonial peoples had to be erased, and this would come about by showing
the cultural achievements of these peoples. The word *other* persisted here,
but it passed between the "other view" ("ours," the viewers) and the change
in the status of the others ("them"), those to be viewed otherwise.

Between the things to be seen and the viewpoints, there is an unsettled
relation in the president's speech. To see the exhibition would be to change
the way one sees, but the directions this would take could not be stated
in advance. The established way of placing "the other," the ethnological
viewpoint, was clearly to be discarded. And this in the interest of views
"more open and more respectful, dissipating the fog of ignorance, of condescension, and of arrogance that in the past has so often been present and
has nourished suspicion, contempt, and rejection."

"Condescension," "arrogance," "suspicion, contempt, and rejection"
would be replaced by admiration. And with this the credit for the objects
would fall to the nations where the objects had been made. Ethnic designations were kept, but they now had the status of, for instance, "medieval"
in "medieval art." One admired these objects while bracketing the beliefs
surrounding them as belonging to the past. Credit no doubt would be given
to France for making this gesture—no doubt particularly so because the
high aesthetic value of the objects reflected the refined taste for which
France is well known. France could be proud that the objects, though nearly
all collected under colonialism and often of disputed ownership, formed a
part of its "patrimony."

Objects were at the center of the museum, as they are in most museums.
But for some time social anthropologists had lost sight of objects.[6] Instead

of classifying peoples through their things, or seeing the inner motivations of peoples through objects, anthropologists had turned to the direct study of society. For some time, anthropology in France too had developed in this direction, especially, but not entirely, outside the museum. This, however, by itself did not seem to excuse anthropologists from furthering a view of others said to be morally, culturally, and politically out of date. The museum stood for ethnography. It was not that ethnography was to be eliminated, but that it would have to take other forms. There was to be a place for this in the museum, as attested to in particular by the participation of Lévi-Strauss, after whom an auditorium in the museum was named. But the director of the museum had clearly indicated that objects without aesthetic value were not to be included.[7]

For many anthropologists, the closing of the ethnographic museum seemed to mark an end of an era; where it left ethnology was unclear. Tracing the treatment of objects in ethnographic museums placed the dilemma in perspective. It is just this that Benoît de l'Éstoile has done in a study of French ideas of the other as seen through the evolution of the museum.[8] I will follow his schema in the following paragraphs.

De l'Éstoile begins with the *cabinet des curiosités*, the collections of odd, unclassified objects. He cites the study of Krystoff Pomian on the collectors of the Renaissance. Pomian shows that some of these objects from far off places were "collected not for their use value but because of their significance as representatives of the invisible, of exotic countries, of different societies, of strange climates."[9] These objects eventually were separated from those considered art objects. The cabinet of curiosities contained things without a principle of selection. According to de l'Éstoile, they amounted to an encyclopedia of the world. Some objects, collected in far-off parts of the world, came to indicate distance and things unknown. This resulted in a generalized other, more or less the equivalent of something, anything, unknown, and from anywhere.

With the rise of science, the objects became classified and separated from art objects. The attempt at classification is at the beginning of the ethnographic collections. From the start, ethnography almost literally domesticated, gave a home to, the strange. It reduced its strangeness by showing its rationality or its place in scientific thinking. It is just this endeavor that is thought no longer to be necessary and, worse, to classify in anachronistic

ways. Those of us who believe we show contemporary ways of life and escape this anachronism are not thereby freed from the charge associated with
it: that we do not let others speak for themselves. The new display of old
collections might, in its way, be a more direct form of communication between cultures if only it could free itself from the aura of the primitive, as
Jacques Chirac wished, and if it could be bound to national "heritage."[10]

The germ of the conflict between ethnography and art was already present at the separation of the cabinet of curiosities from the art gallery in the
seventeenth century: objects to be considered scientifically, on the one
hand; those to be appreciated aesthetically, on the other. Often objects were
contested. Were they to be considered evidence of historical and cultural
development, or were they to be seen as art? Objects from the Americas
collected for the Louvre in the middle of the nineteenth century because
they attested to the origins of art were transferred to the new Trocadéro
Museum at the end of that century, when it was decided that they did not
in fact do so. They did not show "a great page in the history of humanity
but another art altogether."[11]

The Musée d'ethnographie du Trocadéro, founded in conjunction with
the Universal Exhibition of 1878, developed the natural science project in
evolutionary terms. The thinking of the time consolidated a hierarchy with
"savages" at the bottom. But the museum's collections and classifications
had other consequences, as well. Jean Jamin points out that "each piece
collected, classed and presented in the museum not only counted as a witness [of the history of humanity] but also counted as proof." Rivet, the
director of the museum, according to Jamin, used the word *proof*, a word
taken from the law, as a way of "giving ethnology the task of rehabilitation
of oppressed and marginalized cultures"[12]—"proof," then, of the value of
otherwise unappreciated cultures. This appreciation, however, did not
change the centrality of the focus on origins; the origins of civilization and
the origins of art were at the heart of the idea of collection. Aesthetic value
was even considered a danger by Rivet, since focusing on it could mean
bypassing the collection of everyday objects useful for the classification of
ways of life.[13]

Meanwhile, ethnology evolved under colonialism, and the idea of the
"other" became progressively differentiated. The Colonial Exhibition of
1931 represented the ways in which colonialism "gave value to natural
wealth left unexploited by natives." This included the peoples themselves,

who were said to be in the process of development under colonial aegis. Thus the static view of "races" that were once and for all whatever they were originally gave way. Ethnography had the task of completing this encyclopedia. "Art négre" was included because it was thought to be sufficiently ancient to show the origin of this evolution.[14] This showed the way to the study of aesthetics particular to specific cultures. And in so doing it removed the ethnographic exegesis of art from the continued popular belief in a generalized and savage other. Thus, for instance, Michel Leiris, an important collector of objects for the ethnographic museums and a friend of Picasso, remarked of one of his friend's masks from the Ivory Coast that it has "a combination of quasi-geometric elements, each of which can be perceived in a relatively autonomous way and at the same time takes the value of a sign in the whole of a face imaginatively reconstituted by the viewer."[15] Once one knows that a face is not an imitation of nature but a construction made out of quasi-geometric units, one can arrange these units mentally and find a face.[16] Plastic elements become read as signs. Reading them one reaches a face, but without the code one cannot read and is left with the generalized, hence possibly with the savage. There is a particular aesthetics, not "ours." Through it one understands the object as a mask with a particular designation. Without this, the mask appears to represent an inchoate intention, a nightmare of the uncivilized, perhaps. Yet if one appreciates it, it seems to speak of something we cannot grasp but intuit nonetheless. It is beautiful, we say. But once we know the code, we know what the mask "says." Kantian ideas of beauty and pleasure then do not apply. Nor do ideas of savagery; both are banished in favor of understanding. One needs ethnography to generate such understanding.

But popular understanding did not evolve along the same lines as ethnography. The latter showed the specificities of different cultures. The former remained invested in the spectral and global otherness out of which ethnology had emerged. Thus the importance of "art négre," meaning certain objects of Africa and Oceania "discovered" to be art, a discovery confirmed by the interest of artists such as Picasso, Matisse, Vlamink, and others, but to which both the English translations—"black arts" and "Negro arts"—seemed still to apply. The word *art* indicated something worthy of appreciation. What went with the other term was an understanding of this art as "savage" and even magical. The "Rapport general" of the exposition of 1931 notes that "It does not take much imagination to evoke bloody ceremonies of suppressed cults, monstrous celebrations in the glades, strange marriages of love and death behind these masques and sculptures."[17] Beauty and savagery then contended or perhaps reinforced each other in popular appreciation of the objects.

The history of the treatment of the objects under consideration is full of ambiguities. On the one hand, ethnology stood accused of racial stereotyping even when it worked against the generalized view of "savages." On the other, aesthetic interests displaced ethnology, ignoring the place of objects in social life, and thereby were accused of ethnocentricism for bypassing local ideas of aesthetics and for neglecting the peoples who made the objects, thus leaving them open to prejudicial judgments. There is also the question raised by the seemingly inexorable aesthetic attraction of objects said to be "fetishes," which were in the main religious and magical objects in their places of origin. Though the savage other apparently vanished, the objects that sustained interest in it remained attractive under another name without raising the question of whether there is a connection between the magical and the beautiful. The idea of beauty and the idea of the wild are also mixed in Kant, for instance, the beautiful being originally wild or, in French, *sauvage*. It is not surprising, then, that the beautiful and the "savage" should appear together. In the Quai Branly, magic is entirely subsumed under a generalized aesthetics. Something is worth looking at even if one knows nothing about it.

French ethnology had sidestepped the problem not by avoiding the topics of magic or aesthetic appeal but by focusing on a broader issue. Paul Rivet, describing the project of the ethnological museum and its research, wrote, "The most humble tool, the most imperfect, the crudest pottery is as much, or even more worthy of study . . . than the most finely decorated vase."[18] Not long before, Apollinaire had complained about the results of such thinking. Speaking of the Musée de Trocadéro, the predecessor of the Musée de l'Homme, he said that it hid the aesthetically valuable and for that reason was practically not visited. The museum, he noted, had "a great number of masterpieces by African and Oceanean artists." But, in a phrase that anticipated the criticism of the Musée de l'Homme, he said, "The collections are mixed in a way to satisfy ethnic curiosity [*curiosité ethnique*] and not aesthetic sentiment."[19] This was precisely the charge repeated later, particularly by Jacques Kerchache, an art dealer and friend of Jacques Chirac to whom credit for the idea of the new museum has been given.[20]

The opening of the new museum, then, brought a conflict of values: aesthetic versus ethnographic. The latter extended far beyond the limits of the discipline, if one listened to the argument of anthropologists. Their cry at the closing of the ethnographic section of the Musée de l'Homme was heartfelt. Thus Louis Dumont, whom we quoted above, continued in a column in *Le Monde*:

> Until the eighteenth century, "art" was understood as mechanical arts, crafts-manship, and the "beaux-arts." Since then, the last has been elevated to coincide with absolute Art, but many artists continue to think of themselves as artisans. One can say that in speaking of *arts premiers* one actually imposes a modern notion of "beaux-arts" on cultures that do not recognize the term. Would you separate the parietal art of Lascaux from craftsmanship? To obtain an abstract equality with that which comes out of our own culture, one proposes to look at the beaux arts from other places with the presuppositions of bourgeois parvenus.

Either one sees objects in the terms given by their fabricators and thus "understands" them, or one sees them falsely. The falsity consists in impos-ing an aesthetic and an idea of place that belong to a certain culture, one among many, that of the culture within which the museum was established. Differences between cultures are obscured, the result being a false view. The charge against ethnographers, in return, is that even their differenti-ated view of peoples is now out of date. The differences they insist on are irrelevant in the world today, and, once again, they leave open a route toward prejudice.

The argument is complicated and even ironic. On the one hand, the case against the ethnography museum is that it consolidates a distorted view of the other—distorted either because despite itself it fosters ideas of savagery or else because it furthers views of cultural identity frozen during colonial times and now out of date and demeaning. The argument against the art museum is similar: it imposes an aesthetic in place of an interpretation on objects and thus on peoples, and it is ethnocentric.

Before the closing of the ethnology section, popular interest in the mu-seum had declined considerably: in part because the museum was underfi-nanced; but in part also because what drew crowds to it before seems to have evaporated. Interest in the ethnographic other had dissipated, surely

in large part because of the work of anthropologists, who meticulously de-
lineated the reasonableness of the societies they studied, but also because
the peoples who had made the objects were known under their ethnic
names, which now, instead of making them seem exotic, left them entirely
without connection to museum visitors. The peoples to be honored by the
new museum were peoples whose ethnic designations were subsumed under
national designations. The slippage from ethnic to national identities
matched a change in European popular mentality, one aided by the presence of former colonial peoples in the metropole, where they were known
not as speakers of Wolof, for instance, but as Senegalese or simply as Africans. It is the designations on their passports that determine who they are,
not their ancestry. And if they have no French visa, they are deported to
their "homeland," which is a state. The state, not even the nation and certainly not ethnicity, determines identity both politically and, though to a
lesser degree, in the museum. It is true that ethnic designations are still
attached to museum objects, but the honor falls to citizens of states.

The new museum designed to honor certain peoples is clear about who
is honored. It is the heirs of the people who made the objects, thus linking
ethnicity and the state. But who exactly are these heirs? Speaking of Nok
sculptures made two thousand years ago but claimed by the Nigeria of
today, Anthony Appiah comments:

> When Nigerians claim a Nok sculpture as part of their patrimony, they are
> claiming for a nation whose boundaries are less than a century old, the works of
> a civilization more than two millennia ago, created by a people that no longer
> exists, and whose descendants we know nothing about. We don't know whether
> Nok sculptures were commissioned by kings or commoners; we don't know
> whether the people who made them and the people who paid for them thought
> of them as belonging to the kingdom, to a man, to a lineage, to the gods. One
> thing we know for sure, however, is that they didn't make them for Nigeria."[21]

The famous Benin sculptures are known as such, but does the honor fall to
Nigeria, where the capital of the Benin kingdom was located, or to the
neighboring state, Benin? How can national identity claim the fabrications
of the peoples who lived in the area before the nation and before colonialism? Is there necessarily an "heir" at all? If there is, how is it that such
objects are inherited? By their influence on subsequent artists? By genealog-
ical connections between peoples? By the pride of the peoples of a nation
in those who lived there before them? By seeing and liking them?

The new museum claims a universality for these objects; anyone from anywhere is capable of appreciating them on the basis of a general idea of beauty common to people as humans. The national designation, once accepted, leaves ethnographic analysis in the place, at best, of art history. It might explain social conditions of another time, but such knowledge is optional in considering the value of the objects. Once the important designation of the object is national, thus part of the political world of today and so part of the world as a whole, value comes to be measured by a universally valid aesthetic. Enjoyment of these objects opens to all: Parisians, not to mention those from any place in the world who might visit the museum, as well as peoples of say, Nigeria, among those designated as the "heirs" to these objects. Whatever ritual purpose the objects might have had is a matter of the past and is only incidental to their contemporary status. They are beautiful now—they were so then and there, now and forever and even before, the future included, for all times and all places.

Universalism of aesthetic appreciation comes into being along with the diminishing of cultural differences of all sorts. A former curator and then director of the Musée national d'art moderne, Germain Viatte, who guided the Quai Branly to its completion, thought that the foreign was unavoidable in Paris. One is "constantly confronted" with it, and right here. "One cannot cross through our cities without being constantly confronted with cultural alterity." But familiarity dissolves exoticism; mere alterity is left. The exotic evaporated; the foreign was no longer strange. But there are still "exotic cultures," and one therefore needed a new sort of museum to respond to this "change of comportment of our European countries with respect to exotic cultures."[22]

The exotic, limited to the museum, differentiated from the people at its origin by the renaming of these people, still has a place. Anthropology has been accused of exoticism. But now exoticism will have a safe place within art. The museum will preserve the exotic, whereas anthropology, contrary to the charge against it, reduced it to the familiar. The work of anthropologists, in this view, is complete. Being already familiar with alterity, one no longer needs anyone to explain it. "They" are now understood.

But there is still a "they," those one sees in Paris from the ex-colonies, in particular. And behind "them," as it were, in their past or at least somewhere else, the exotic persists. It is now, however, sealed off in the museum.

In the museum as it has now been constructed, the exotic does not infect present-day immigrants. The universalizing of aesthetic appreciation valorized now by the museum has drained the exotic from them. They no longer raise specters.

The Quai Branly, of course, is designed to further good relations with the ex-colonial countries. The charge against it has been ethnocentricism, imposing as it does a particular notion of beauty. The further question is whether the political aim itself is achieved. A view rather different from that of President Chirac was given by the former Minister of Culture and Tourism of Mali, Aminata Traoré. She had this to say in an open letter sent to the French president on the occasion of the museum's opening:

> So our works of art have the right to the city just where we, in the aggregate, are forbidden to stay. . . .
>
> The art works that today take the place of honor at the Musée du Quai Branly belong first of all to the disinherited peoples of Mali, Benin, Guinea, Niger, Burkina-Faso, Cameroon, and Congo. They form a substantial part of the cultural and artistic patrimony of the "without visas," some of whom have been shot dead at Ceuta and Melilla, and the "without papers," who are daily tracked down in the heart of Europe and, when arrested, sent back in handcuffs to their countries of origin.
>
> In my "Letter to the President of France" concerning the Ivory Coast and Africa in general, I cite the Musée du Quai Branly as a perfect expression of the contradictions, incoherence, and paradoxes of France in its relation to Africa. At the moment when the doors are opened to the public, I continue to ask how far the powers of this world will go in their arrogance and the theft of our imaginary.[23]

Indeed, anyone who lives in certain areas of Paris, rounding a corner, is all too likely to find a group of police surrounding a *sans papiers*, usually African, but often enough Indian, Pakistani, or Chinese as well. (The list is incomplete.)

"Honoring" the peoples who made the objects displayed in the Quai Branly thus in no way ameliorates the economic and political views that lead to the deportation of migrant workers from France. One wonders if the Kantian notion of beauty does not reveal its "savage" foundation too clearly when applied to the art of the museum. If so, it all the more effectively conceals prejudice under the name of the beautiful while preserving it. From this point of view, prejudice would no longer be the direct rejection of the objectionable foreigner. Rather, the idea of savagery would be held in concealment in certain cultural forms, honorable ones, and then applied, no doubt unconsciously, to those who are its "heirs" and so remain contaminated—"under the skin," so to speak.

This, at least, is one possibility. But I do not think it is the likely effect of museum display. One can turn to someone interested in museums in general and the ethnographic in particular for another view. According to Georges Bataille, in 1930 museums produced the desire to be what was on display: "Today museums are a great and unexpected success," not only for their riches but also because they offer "the greatest spectacle of a humanity liberated from material cares and devoted to contemplation." On Sunday he observes the crowd exit from the Louvre: "One has to keep in mind that the halls and the objects of art are only a container of which the contained is formed by the visitors: it is the contained that distinguishes the museum from private collections."[24] What visitors see, or rather, comprehend, is not what is given to them to see. They see something else, and this something else is given by their identification with the figures they have "contemplated": "The canvases are only dead surfaces, and it is the crowd that produces the play, the bursts, the glints of light described technically by the authorized critics. At five on Sundays at the exit of the Louvre, it is interesting to admire the flow of visitors visibly animated by the desire to be the like of the celestial apparitions which their eyes still hold in fascination."[25] Bataille speaks of the visitors to the Louvre, but his remarks refer to the peoples whose artifacts appear in ethnographic museums as well:

> When a natural of the Ivory Coast puts polished axes from the Neolithic in a container full of water, bathing them in it, offering poultry to those he believes to be "thunder stones" (fallen from the heavens in a clap of thunder), he only prefigures the attitude of enthusiasm and the deep communion with objects which characterizes the visitor to the modern museum. The museum is the colossal mirror in which man contemplates himself finally in all his faces, finding himself literally admirable and abandoning himself to the ecstasy expressed in all the art journals.[26]

The impulse behind the museum is universal, in Bataille's view. But the museum itself is not. He notes that the first museum was founded by the Convention in July 1793, thus during the Terror. "The origin of the modern museum was thus tied to the development of the guillotine."[27] He implies that here is an effect of the crowd (a notion as recent as the possibility of anonymity) in the museum. Viewing "in private," one is known to others and thus more surely to oneself. In a crowd, it is said, one loses one's identity and thus loses oneself to the objects. If this happens in the ethnographic museum, identification with the objects is strengthened by ideas of evolution, which say that those on display were earlier versions of oneself.

It is not by accident that Bataille speaks of the stone axe and the guillotine. There is a violent, even revolutionary element. The possibility of identification with the other upsets established hierarchies, particularly when that other is foreign. This passes through objects. It might be indirect, but it is not less radical for that. The items displayed might be beautiful and presumably free of contemporary political significance, but the hierarchy of taste, one of the foundations of social hierarchy, will be upset. As Nélia Dias, the author of a history of the Trocadéro Museum, remarks, "Everything happens as if the valorization of certain types of extra-European art inevitably brought with it the questioning of the occidental idea of art and, consequently, of that of the art object."[28] The museum offers a potential source of value outside the normal. And the acceptance of this value makes the viewer like those who made the objects or who are pictured in them, no matter how "savage" they might be.

Jacques Kerchache, who first had the idea of the Quai Branly, originally wanted "tribal arts" put in the Louvre. Apollinaire before him had the same idea.[29] To do so would change the hierarchy of tastes. Finally, Kerchache was successful in having a place made for them in the Louvre, thus putting these pieces on a par with "masterpieces." It is not clear that the objects currently in the Louvre will remain there. Meanwhile, the Quai Branly establishes their special worth. But the hoped-for radical change suggested by Bataille does not occur. The assimilation of such works remains equivocal, since the change in taste does not bring new sorts of people into the top of the hierarchy, with the exception of a few brought there for window dressing.[30] Nor is it clear that today it reformulates tastes. Instead, it establishes the French "patrimony." France no longer owns the colonies, but much of their most valuable cultural productions are subsumed by France, they belong to it, not simply by legal or illegal possession, but through excellent French taste, which appreciates beauty.[31]

Seeing oneself in the other, as Bataille described, of course is not geographically or culturally limited. But when and how it takes place depends on prevailing conditions. When Sartre wrote about such a moment in 1948, it was the beginning of the era of decolonization. In an introduction to an anthology of poetry in French from the Caribbean and Africa edited by Leopold Senghor, Sartre wrote:

> Here [in their poems] erect black men look at you. I wish you to feel as I do the shock of being seen. Whites have enjoyed three thousand years of the privilege of seeing without being seen. . . . Today these black men look at us and our look returns in our eyes; black torches in their turn illuminate the world.[32]

No one had ever thought there could be a return of looks between whites and blacks. Then, through poetry written in French, it occurred. In retrospect it seemed it could always have occurred and no doubt did. But it went unnoticed. The result for whites of being seen in the eyes of the black other (n.b.: singular) is to discover that "our whiteness seems to be a strange, pale varnish which keeps our skins from breathing, a white jersey [*maillot*] worn at the elbows and knees, under which, if we could remove it, we would find the true human flesh, flesh the color of black wine." At the time when Africans were accused of practicing magic, for whites to allow themselves to exchange looks with Africans would mean seeing that they were them, just as the visitors to the museum saw themselves as what they saw there. The result was said to be political revision, even revolution. To see the return gaze of Africans is to no longer count on the unself-conscious rightness of white everyday lives. Something else is lodged in them, to which they are blind. For Viatte in Paris, this moment, now wrapped in familiarity, is much less possible. He easily meets the gaze of the "Senegalese," so defined by his passport. But for Sartre in 1948, without this encounter, whites were blind to themselves. Their sight will be returned when they see Africans *en face*. And when it is, everything will be different. Thus the possibility of the ethnological other, in the museum or not, in another time.

This moment is linked to the ideas that governed the foundation of the Musée de l'Homme, particularly the idea of the "document." The document was at the heart of the museum, according to Bataille and to others who published in the review *Documents* in 1929 and 1930. These included Paul Rivet, the director of the museum, and Georges Rivière, who described the aim of the ethnographic museum in that journal. Rivet, according to Jean Jamin, saw the museum objects as "documents." They were the "proof" needed to put peoples in evidence. Jamin uses the term interchangeably with "material witnesses." The anthropological use of "document" came to mean its use value, to use Marx's term, adopted by Dennis

Hollier in speaking of *Documents*.[33] "Use value," in this context, has a double significance. For ethnographers, it meant the equal value of objects, seeing them without judgment. Their aesthetic worth, for instance, did not matter; what counted was their provenance. As such, a document was irreplaceable. It is there that it joins the idea of use value in Marx. Use value is always singular. In Marx, it occurs before the exchange with other objects, in the course of which an idea of value necessary in exchange is produced, thus mixing objects comparable rather than unique. In the ethnographic conception of the time, only the place of the object in its original location matters. The idea leads easily to the notion of context. An ethnographic object might be inexchangable, but it could be explicated by describing its place. The idea of place was slippery—after all, contexts are variable.[34]

The document is not a representation. Rather, it forms part of whatever it documents; it belongs to the time of its origin. But as a document, it is removed from its provenance. It thus "refers," one says, to its origin, being at a distance from it. But it does not necessarily bring with it its original context when it makes this reference. It only attests to the existence of its provenance, to the object belonging to that moment and that place. Whatever reflections it might stimulate do not belong to it as document. The document says what it says; as a document, it is incontrovertible in saying, "This belongs to that time or place or event." The question it raises is not its sense but its validity, the degree to which it can be accepted as authentic. Whatever associations it might provoke are irrelevant to it as a document. As a document, it refuses all speculation.

For Bataille, the ethnographic museum offered radical possibilities linked precisely to the change of context that occurs when an object becomes a document without becoming an object of exchange. The document, in refusing all substitutability, nonetheless stimulates associations that have their provenance outside of it. Take, for instance, a piece entitled "Les Pieds Nickelés."[35] It is about mischievous comic-book figures favored by French children at the beginning of the twentieth century and about the Aztec god Quetzalcoatl. Bataille's two pages on them begin, "A Mexican god, thus Quetzalcoatl, amuses himself by gliding down the mountains seated on a small plank. More than anything else expressible in the usual repertoire of words, he always seems to me to be one of the *Pied Nickelés*." The God (Quetzalcoatl) amuses, and "moral liberty" depends on amusement. There has to be something to render us this necessity, Bataille says. And he finds it in the *Pieds Nickelés* and regrets that it is mainly children who read it. But the *Pieds Nickelés* have had a constant appearance among children of all social classes since their first appearance in 1908. "I can't help being crudely taken with the thought that men, not at all savage, not having paradise at their door, have generously erected playthings [*fantouches*] into gods and have reduced themselves to the role of playthings, to the point of regarding curiously, but with a big knife, what is inside the stomach of the screaming plaything." And, he concludes, "an individual is not a plaything, he is a player, or he is both at once. . . . Amusement is the most crying need, and of course, the most terrifying, of human nature."

If amusement is the "most terrifying" need of human nature, it is because to cry with laughter is to put the serious, hence the authoritative, aside. One might kill without justification and without condemnation. This is the world of everyone before they have the identities that come with adulthood, the world of children. What in France is relegated to children, Mexicans have given to a god. Something ridiculous, a *fantouche*, only serious to children, is taken seriously by "Mexican" adults, even given an ultimate seriousness, one that offers no justification and so is indistinguishable from amusement. And in doing so, children show a possibility that adults decline. The latter, in France, refuse to elevate the amusing, the ridiculous, into gods. It is to their detriment. Mexicans satisfied their need, but we do not. Or rather, adults recognize the need for amusement, since they give the *Pieds Nickelés* to children. But then they take it away. " Life is not a burst of laughter, educators and mothers of families in effect say to children, not without the most comical gravity, Then, with a light hand they give them the *Pieds Nickelés* to browse, but with the other, they brutally take them away." Amusement is restored but brutally kept in check. Seriousness reigns.

Quetzalcoatl was a serious possibility for French people so far as Bataille was concerned, because seeing his image awakens something out of their own past. Here this past is not contained in the history of all humanity but is limited to those who read *Pieds Nickelés*, and not necessarily all of them. If one sees Quetzalcoatl in the usual ethnological way, he stays where he was—in "Mexico," as Bataille used the term. But conjoined to a figure known in childhood, the result is not nostalgia for that time but the presence of the Aztec god. Quetzalcoatl, for that instant at least, lives and works in France.

The lack of seriousness of Quetzalcoatl in Mexico becomes important in France. It does so via the memory of another moment when amusement was taken seriously. All that is needed for amusement to become serious again is the making of a correspondence. But the *Pieds Nickelés* are only one possible point of conjuncture with that god. And it is not sure that Bataille meant that the same conjunctions work for everyone. In the museum people fill in what they see. It is, as we have said, no doubt an effect of the loss of identity said to occur in crowds. (We recall that, for Bataille, the museum is coterminous with the revolution, thus with its crowds.) The loss of identity allows a correspondence that would not be made if one were contemplating Quetzalcoatl in private. But there is no assurance that everyone fills in what he or she sees in the same way, no assurance either that each finds his resemblance in the same figures in the Louvre. One cannot know if the trigger setting off conjuncture is the same for everyone. The singularity or "use value" that Bataille insists on makes it impossible to establish. All that one can say is that there is a moment of conflation of what one sees and what one knows in one way or another, a conflation not necessarily brought about by resemblance or any other attribute.

If we follow the way in which Quetzalcoatl on his sled is seen through the *Pieds Nickelés*, we see that, almost paradoxically, the very singularity of the object taken from elsewhere is the source of its effectiveness in communicating to those who see it in the museum. Quetzalcoatl "makes sense" only if we use that phrase loosely, as it is used in common speech. Its "sense" is its capacity to be confounded with the *Pieds Nickelés*. Quetzalcoatl seems then somehow to light up, to stimulate further thinking. This figure from elsewhere, now in a museum, then refers to France, or rather to a France as it might be and even mentally is. Precisely as a document from elsewhere, it inflects life in France. No archeologist of Mexico, I am sure, would recognize this figure as Bataille presents it. And that is also a source of its force. It escapes Mexico to remake "the French." It speaks to them, telling them that "they" are "us." Or, more precisely, that "we" are "them." We are them already; we did not know it. To be so it was not and still is not important to believe in Quetzalcoatl in the way that one believes in God. It is not even necessary to lay bare the source of correspondence between this figure of Aztec origin and something hidden in "us." It is only necessary that the connection be somehow, in one way or another, felt and thus set into operation.

Precisely because the document has no sense as such other than this peculiar and limited form of reference, it offers itself as a challenge to recognition. As a result, the form used to recognize it outside its provenance is far-fetched, in a literal sense; idiosyncratic in its logic, unverifiable, and quite probably different for each viewer. As such, there is no assurance that one can necessarily find a biographical reference to explain the connection. One can only say that Bataille thinks it is the case in this instance. It seems necessary that there be a trajectory of the object through the viewer, but what if any associations are made cannot be established with assurance.

At the same time, it is important that Quetzalcoatl was seen in the museum of ethnology. The museum gives the terms by which one domesticates this moment. By "domesticate" I mean here "give a home to" the perceptions the museum has stimulated. The "elsewhere" or foreignness of the object to oneself is relocated geographically and culturally. Taking the term for one's own, one has a relation with this place. It is in this manner that the ethnographic museum could upset European cultural hierarchies. There is something foreign inside these remade hierarchies, and there is something inside ourselves, though forgotten and thus foreign to us, that allows us to find ourselves within the new structure. The museum catalyzes their juncture. Inadvertently, of course.

This is the other found in the ethnographic museum. But it does not take the form that ethnographers would give it. When Rivet used the word *document*, he meant something quite different, closer to a notion of authenticity, which then would be reduced to the schema that would be imposed on objects, granting them generality.[36] The interpretation that began with objects, with the aim of producing an understanding of cultures, had the museum as its center. But another sort of ethnography developed in the Anglophone world, with Malinowski, in particular. The long stay in a single place with the aim of showing the practical reason of life there left the study of objects behind. One can say that the witness, the person who could attest to the nature of life in faraway places, replaced the collector and the analyst. Both the study of objects and the direct study of societies were domesticating in a positive sense of the word. They showed the common humanity of the peoples studied and thus related peoples to one another. Ethnography took the route of generality to accomplish the same end—the establishing of a place for the foreign—as the ethnology museum did for Bataille through its display of singularity.

The study of objects came to seem outdated when evolutionary classification depended on the frozen identities of the peoples who made the objects, despite the work of many to counter this trend. But it was the success of both ethnological methods and the grand historical changes that came with the end of colonialism that deprived ethnography of the means to elicit interest in the unknown. It has been two generations since there has been an Anglophone anthropologist capable of speaking to those wanting a general culture, much less a figure such as Bataille, who linked peoples on the basis of incomparable (because ungeneralizable) differences.

When the place of the object could be made explicit, the document had served its purpose. Around it a view of everyday life formed. The document, as Bataille understood it, served, rather, as a peculiar form of communication between cultures—peculiar because the meaning of Quetzalcoatl as Bataille explains him can in no way be verified. It remains idiosyncratic. One learns nothing much about "Mexicans," as he anachronistically terms Aztecs, but one feels in touch with them. This view could only be eroded by ethnographers' patient explication of local context.

The difference between the two forms of document can be seen in a passage from Michel Leiris's account of his expedition to Francophone Africa collecting for the Trocadéro Museum. The following excerpt from his notes was made in the south of colonial French Sudan:

> The old man who has been teaching me the mysteries of the mask society since the day before yesterday for the second time since yesterday took out an astonishing text in a secret language. I took down the text, I read it aloud with its intonations, and the old man, delighted, got up, clapped his hands, and cried, "Pay. Pay" ("Excellent! Excellent!"). But at the moment of translation everything went wrong. The secret language is a language of formulas, made up of enigmas, of cockcrows, of puns, of cascades of phonemes and interpenetrating symbols. The old man, thinking that I really wanted to be initiated, applied his usual principals of teaching. When I asked for a translation of a word or an isolated phrase, he lost his place and had to start over from the beginning and go to the end, but he got mixed up and, naturally, gave me a different text each time. Playing the role of teacher, when I interrupted he became furious and shouted "Makou!" ("Silence!").[37]

This formula is effective only through the exactness of its repetition, not through its semantic content. But what is repeated is unclear, not only because it sounds to Leiris like "cockcrows" and "interpenetrating symbols" but because it varies with each repetition. Leiris presumes that the teacher cannot repeat any particular word of the text accurately unless he starts from the beginning. Each time he is asked to do so, the teacher gives a different text. Another example, however, indicates that Leiris misunderstands what the teacher is doing: "Enraged with a man who came to sell gris-gris. When I asked for the magic formulas one has to pronounce to use them, each time I made him repeat one of the formulas in order to take it down, he gave a different version and each time it came to a translation, more new versions."[38]

This seller of amulets, giving the text that goes with them, also gives a different version each time. The text is never an original, it seems. It is, rather, only one instance of what is said magically. The teacher of the first example, asked for a translation, understands that no movement from one language to another is possible. Instead, the magical text fulfills itself, to use a Benjaminian construction, differently each time. Magical language here is secret language, meaning that an original, authoritative version is never revealed, not that the language that it takes in practice is itself secret. The series of "cockcrows" and "interpenetrating symbols" that carries it forward never arrives. It is never understandable, it is never precisely repeatable, and its sounds cannot all be identified. Leiris therefore resorts to approximation of the sounds and to concluding that they are conflations of symbols and animal sounds. Leiris, however, thinks it can and should arrive. There should be an identifiable, authoritative version, and it should be understandable. He tries to take it down accurately—to the frustration of his teacher, who, no doubt, thought his pupil an idiot, and to the frustration of Leiris, who obviously had the same opinion of his teacher and the seller of gris-gris.

The "secret language" is revealed to Leiris, but he never knows it. The secret here is not its content—whether it actually has a content is unclear. One learns this secret language only by repeating it. But what one repeats one does not know. It is as though magic arrives from a different and un-findable source each time it is used. The old man knows the secret does not depend on a content that might be paraphrased or on matching his own recitation with whatever issued from his mouth when he last said it. It depends, rather, on seeing that it is "communicable," that it is even communicability itself, and he is delighted when Leiris seems to be affected by his, the teacher's recitation. But when Leiris interrupts the recitation to request that one of its elements be reiterated, the teacher finds serious "misunderstanding." Reiteration is impossible, and therefore no text can be constituted. Instead there is "iteration," which is at once unique and yet seems to be a repetition of something. With that, it seems that something has been said. To borrow the terms used by Samuel Weber in reading Benjamin, the sheer mediacy, or inbetweenness, of the formulas has to be taken as such.[39] Even to call these "formulas," which means the repetition of the same words, is wrong. This language has no generic title—neither formulas nor incantation accurately names it. That would mean that the words refer to ascertainable versions of themselves, and this is wrong. The magic of language depends not on lack of reference but on leaving references behind.

When something is communicable and yet does not arrive, one cannot predict the result. In the case of Leiris and the teacher, the teacher is enraged in the first instance; in the second, it is Leiris. It seems that at least one of the pair has to be. They are in communication with each other, but they have incompatible ideas of how magical language works. It is not only that Leiris does not understand "them," "the other." The teacher also misunderstands not only what Leiris wants but magical language itself. Suppose the language had worked as it was supposed to. Leiris would then have been initiated into the mask society. He would be one of them. Magical language would then be "understood" in the fashion of the place. A hierarchy would be established. One would no longer be able to speak of the mediacy of language, only of its social effectiveness, meaning its capacity, finally, in some way or other to achieve an intention and so to obscure the moment we have noticed. The mediacy of language is marked here by the fury it incites as it communicates but does not join—not linking but "adjoining," placing people mentally next to one another, as it were, across cultures only to make war.

But perhaps war is not the only possibility. There could be merely the confusion experienced exiting from the museum after seeing something with aesthetic force. "Aesthetic force" here is not exact. One does not appreciate what one sees as though there were a difference between subject and object; one loses that difference between oneself and the object. The force of magic can make one into the other through a form of communication that is never appropriated but only suffered. There is still magic within beauty—but magic, in societies where it is recognized, can consolidate new identities. The confusion of identities on exiting from the museum in a society where magic is denied inflects social intercourse only indirectly. At best the object asserts itself through the individual only surreptitiously, without his knowledge. There is, then, no understanding between cultures through the art museum, only communication. And, as has often been pointed out, this communication is rapidly put into aesthetic terms that do not correspond with its culture of origin. One sees the need for a serious weighing of the value of understanding, with all the complications of different ways of understanding, versus the value of communication. And one will not mistake the latter for cultural or political harmony if one realizes the incompatibility of modes of apprehension.

As it stands, magic, hidden in a museum such as the Quai Branly under the guise of beauty, might stimulate the radical possibilities of the age of Bataille and Sartre, but then is reduced to the contemporary understanding of aesthetics. Such a movement would form the substance of honor while permitting the fearless expulsion of those honored from the country. At the same time, it is not certain that magic has been definitively discarded or that the domestication of ethnic others marks the end of the totally other.

Exchanging Glances

The exchange of glances across boundaries opening a reflection on social order takes place differently today. We turn to the encounter of Jacques Derrida and his cat, described in *The Animal That Therefore I Am.*

Derrida asks, "can we say that the animal has been looking at us?" He expands: "I often ask myself, just to see, who I am—and who I am (following) at the moment when, caught naked, in silence, by the gaze of an animal, for example, the eyes of a cat, I have trouble, yes, a bad time overcoming my embarrassment."[40] If Derrida is embarrassed in front of the cat, then, of course, he will have exchanged glances with it. The thought of such an exchange occurs to Derrida in an instant of surprise. It brings a comparison of himself and the cat: "Before the cat that looks at me naked, would I be ashamed *like* a beast [*bête*] that no longer has the sense of its nudity? Or, on the contrary, shamed *like* a man who retains the sense of his nudity? Who am I, therefore? Who is it that I am (following)? Whom should this be asked of if not the other? And perhaps of the cat itself?"[41] Derrida asks himself in what identity he could be ashamed if he could not restrain his capacity to be ashamed in front of an animal. Is it because, like the cat, he does not feel nude, or is it because he does and therefore shamefully attributes to the cat the ability humans have to trigger shame? "It is as if I were ashamed, therefore, naked in front of this cat, but also ashamed for being ashamed."[42]

But he keeps his embarrassment in check. The encounter puts his identity into question and leaves him to think how he might find out who he is, even to asking the cat. But he does not think about what the cat must think of him; he does not ask the cat who he is. The shame he imagines is not like the awkwardness of the white confronting a black who sees that he is dressed unnaturally in his white skin and thinks that he should be like the person in front of him. "Who am I, therefore?" he asks, but the question does not lead to an answer, as it does in Sartre. There are, rather, two answers. He could be like the cat, that is, without a sense of nudity, or he could retain his sense of being naked and then attribute to the cat the possibility of triggering this shame. In one instance, he is the cat, as it were; in the other, the cat is him, that is, human. There is no resolution, and the remainder of the book does not expand the two possibilities. Instead, it leads to a reflection on what makes his confrontation potentially embarrassing and to the failure of previous philosophers to think about such an encounter.

If Derrida has difficulty restraining his embarrassment in front of the cat, if the cat triggers shame and thus opens the two possible effects of being ashamed, it is because this cat is not symbolic and is not a type. ("I must immediately make it clear, the cat I am talking about is a real cat. . . . It isn't the *figure* of a cat."[43]) If it were the figure of a cat, Derrida would not be "ashamed for being ashamed." A figure is always at a remove from whatever it figures. This cat is not like that. It is a singular being, not a figure or an example of a type "cat." Were the cat just "a cat," her look could be disregarded. But precisely this particular cat cannot be reduced to "an animal," "a cat" (hence without shame) and therefore embarrasses him. It embarrasses him precisely because it offers a look that meets his own, but the source of that look is and remains enigmatic. Why he should be embarrassed by the cat is never made clear and cannot be made so. Precisely as a singular being, a totally other, the cat at once causes shame and offers no identity with which to resolve it. Derrida is only possibly like the cat, while this singular being cannot be appropriated as himself, since the totally other offers nothing to appropriate. At least it does not do so before it is elaborated into a figure.

There is, in fact, nothing in the exchange to make it memorable. We do not see a menace, for instance. It is easy, therefore, to dismiss, and that is what philosophers before Derrida seem to have done. Philosophers before Derrida have disregarded the return look of the cat. It simply did not signify for them.

> there would be, at bottom, . . . two grand forms of theoretical or philosophical treatise concerning the animal. . . . In the first place there are texts signed by people who no doubt have seen, observed, analyzed, reflected on the animal, but who have never been *seen seen* by the animal. Their gaze has never intersected with that of an animal directed at them. . . . If, indeed, they happen to be seen seen furtively by the animal one day, they took no (thematic, theoretical, or philosophical) account of it. They neither wanted nor had the capacity to draw any systematic consequence from the fact that an animal could, facing them, look at them, clothed or naked, and, in a word, without a word, address them. They have taken no account of the fact that what they call "animal" could *look at* them, and *address* them from down there, from a wholly other origin.[44]

The cat was ignored by other philosophers. Which does not mean that it did not communicate with them and even initiate the communication. From where, that is in what capacity, they might have done so is necessarily uncertain. Treating it as "what they call an animal" they have dismissed this possibility of communication. They too might have felt shame without being able to resolve it into terms of identity. Had they done so, precisely the status of the particular animal would have to be considered. But as "what they call an animal" they could and probably did merely dismiss what they saw. Or they refused to consider that the communication with the cat implied an embarrassing form of self-consciousness, embarrassing because the animal in front of them apparently shamed them for reasons that they could not take seriously, it being only an "animal" who looked at them, as they looked at their respective "animals."

The question "Who am I?" arises "from this place of intersection between these two general singulars, the animal (*l'animot*) and the 'I,' the 'I's.'"[45] Just there Derrida asks himself, "So what happens there? How can I say 'I' and what do I do thereby? And in the first place, me, what am I (following) and who am I (following)?" When one says "I" to the cat, one can't know that the cat understands "I" as the person uttering that instance of discourse. The sign "I" belongs to language and is a "general singular," transcending the individual who uses it. But in front of the cat, this sign is not shared. Within this pair, it belongs only to Derrida (if we can call him that) and is thus "singular." In front of this cat, Derrida's language is confined to himself. Language becomes useless, and with that the sense of identity that comes through it as one speaks, saying "I," finding oneself as the speaker, makes no sense. But, nonetheless, something seems to cross between the two creatures, even if nothing is said that can be reproduced. At this point, we are not far from the situation of Leiris and his teacher. There too there was communication but no understanding.

Who is this cat? It lives in Derrida's house, but it is not exactly his, he tells us, and therefore not exactly a pet. Pets, one supposes, are the residue of the time when working animals often lived in the houses of the peasants who owned them. They were not, however, part of the family in the way that pets are. One might well, for instance, kill them for their meat. It is with the bourgeois family, separated from work, that pets appeared in the form we know them. They fill in a certain space. They are, for instance, perfect siblings, especially for children who do not have them, but also for those who do. One does not fear their rivalry, for instance. They are often said to look like their owners or their owners to look like them. Projections beginning in kinship are easy to make with them. It is in this capacity that people ordinarily speak to animals and that they imagine the animal responding, though before that the work horse or the water buffalo of the tropics was also spoken to. Can one say, then, that the cat cannot speak?

Animals cannot speak to certain people. If they speak to children, it is because children find transferential relations in them. Adults might do so as well, but, out of convention, hearing the animal's response they refuse to accept the independent being of the cat. The answer of the pet is reassuring, never seriously contentious. As, too, the domestic animals that preceded the pet, though perhaps less so. The work horse, for instance, beaten by its master who depended on it for a livelihood, no doubt repeated his owner's feelings. The cat who lives with the Derrida family was not a pet and not a domestic animal, at least not at the moment she followed Derrida into the bathroom.

The animal can be a substitute human:

Everybody agrees on this; discussion is closed in advance; one would have to be more asinine than any beast [*plus bête que les bêtes*] to think otherwise. Even animals know that (ask Abraham's ass or ram or the living beasts that Abel offered to God: they know what is about to happen to them when men say "Here I am" to God, then consent to sacrifice themselves, to sacrifice their sacrifice, or to forgive themselves).[46]

The sacrificial animal can be such because he stands for a human, sometimes a son. If he "knows" what is in store for him, it simply points to the identity given to him by transference, which allows him to speak and be spoken to. The cat who enters the bathroom with Derrida, who looks at him, has been stripped of his transferential possibilities:

> No, no, my cat, the cat that looks at me in my bedroom or bathroom, this cat that is perhaps not "my cat" or "my pussycat" [*"mon chat" ni "ma chatte"*], does not appear here to represent, like an ambassador, the immense symbolic responsibility with which our culture has always charged the feline race. . . . If I say "it [*il*, "he"] is a real cat" that sees me naked, this is in order to mark its unsubstitutable singularity. When it responds in its name . . . it doesn't do so as the exemplar of a species called "cat," even less so of an "animal" genus or kingdom. It is true that I identify it as a male or female cat [*chat ou une chatte*]. But even before that identification, it comes to me as *this* irreplaceable living being that one day enters my space, into this place where it can encounter me, see me, even see me naked.[47]

This cat of which Derrida speaks has no symbolic significance. It does not stand for anything or, for that matter, for anyone, Derrida in particular. It is possibly not even his cat. It cannot be sacrificed. If there is a sacrifice here, it is Derrida himself who is offered up. He, naked in front of the cat, is no longer Jacques Derrida. He has given up his social identity, or had it taken from him, including his name. There is only the gesture, the exchange of glances that, taken into account, tells of the impossibility of this gesture ripening into the symbolic or the semiotic. Derrida questions his own identity when he finds himself in that situation and asks who he should ask to find it. "Who am I therefore? . . . Whom should this be asked of if not of the other? And perhaps of the cat itself?"[48] But he does not ask the cat, no doubt because this cat has been deprived of its transferential associations, leaving nothing to address.

Instead, Derrida turns to other philosophers, who have never mentioned being embarrassed by the gaze of an animal. Such an event has been excluded from serious philosophical consideration. It is an ambiguous moment. To take the cat seriously is to risk being exposed by a philosophical judgment. But if one is correct and one is a philosopher oneself, one is embarrassed on philosophers' behalf. They have missed something elementary, and Derrida is embarrassed to be grouped with them.

Suppose Derrida made no reflection on the neglect of philosophers before him. What if, instead, he had spoken of the exchange of looks with the cat? Had this been the case, we would have looked for the reasons for this moment. We would have searched his biography for something like the *Pieds Nickelés* as the basis for his recognition of the cat. Very likely we would not have found it. No doubt Derrida also did not find it or did not look for it, occupying himself instead with the reasons for his predecessors' neglect of the possibility of such an exchange. If he had merely reported the exchange alone, the encounter with the cat would possibly be uncanny. The exchange might seem to be based on something other than the established relationship—master and pet, perhaps—which would have called for a search for the basis of a transferential moment. Once the cat appears as something else than the cat and we do not know what that might be, the exchange would be unsettling. But this cat has no references; there is no figure to unpack. What is left to trigger shame is simply its glance, or rather, its return glance. Something passes between them. At a moment of nakedness, Derrida notices and is embarrassed—but for no given reason other than the sense of having been seen and having noticed that he was so.

Derrida is ashamed or embarrassed, but also "ashamed for being ashamed." Seeing the cat look at him, he moves to the cat, with which philosophers have never exchanged glances. It is this absent cat, absent from Derrida's predecessors' experience or at least from their accounts, that then appears in front of him. This is what previous philosophers did not see. But once seen, it reveals nothing about itself, nor does there seem to be anything special to be revealed. It is not, for instance, the return of earlier cats, thus producing the uncanny. It is merely the cat that followed Derrida into the bathroom and that stimulated his thinking about philosophy. The cat that looks at Derrida has a reference that is plain to see once one looks (or thinks). One does not find an uncanny presence, one calling for references that need to be revealed. This cat is, indeed, "totally other." It is taken as such rather than being transformed into something to be wondered at or made into a figure—of evil, of beauty, of wisdom—in the way of the savage other whose otherness is threatening. It is not a figure, Derrida says. It is simply an other, one out of "all others" who is "totally other." Stop. Or rather, think about why this totally other has not been thought about. *Follow* this cat. Follow it to philosophers who ignored animals. Follow it further, to the totally other before the uncanny has been attributed to it. Follow it further, to the appearance of totally others—but not uncanny ones—as they manifest themselves in other forms and places.[49]

Liberty Today

> Circule en toute liberté avec Vélib'.
> —Brochure "Des milliers de Vélos à Paris c'est la . . . liberté,"
> issued by the City Hall of Paris

Bicycling on the streets of Paris, one finds oneself in a society where animals are excluded but almost everyone human has a place regardless of his or her origins or attributes. None of the questions of respect for the "other" raised in the founding of the Quai Branly are in doubt. The City of Paris has invented a society with fluid membership, almost totally inclusive, working by mutual respect. The terms that regulate this society are only secondarily fixed rules. The city does not seem to issue directives about, for instance, priorities—whether priority belongs to those on bikes or those who enter on the right and so on. One does not need to pass a test proving that one knows the traffic regulations. One has only to get on the bike to circulate freely: "Circulate absolutely freely [or in complete liberty] with the Velib'," the rental bicycles furnished by the city, the mayor's office tells you. The city agency in charge of these bicycles issued "five rules essential to taking the bicycle in Paris." These rules do not state priorities but rather tell the bike rider to keep in communication with others. "Keep in visual contact: if you can see the eyes of the driver in his rearview mirror, he can see you as well" is the first of these.[50] Indeed, traffic in France in general depends as much on mutual communication between drivers as on rules. Even on the highway one can see drivers, alone in their cars, speaking. They are not talking on a portable phone or to themselves. They are speaking to others on the road, often calling names.

When the City of Paris mandates mutual regard, it formulates practices already habitual. These are still short of legal regulations, but they give habits already in place official approval. These habits supplement the legal rules and indeed often enough supplant them—sometimes to the terror of pedestrians, as when drivers regularly go through red lights. Indeed, in two months on one corner of the Boulevard Magenta, three pedestrians were struck by cars, one of them being killed. For this American, crossing this boulevard is thrilling. But once on a bicycle, what I felt up until that point as the dangerous egotism of drivers breaking rules meant for the safety of everybody I saw was quite logical, because one knows that one is in visual contact. It is not egotism at work but its opposite. The driver ignoring the red light was attending to me, certain that I saw him and would not step in front of him, even though I had the legally mandated priority. So far, he has been right.

The second "essential rule" of taking a bike in Paris is "Never stop under rearview mirrors or level with them." In other words, always be in communication.[51] The feeling that one is so gives one confidence to continue, even when traffic is heavy and buses seem to come within inches of the handlebars. Everything depends on visual contact, and even if one cannot look back, one is sure that the practice holds sufficiently for the other that one is probably safe. Just this assumption is in question, however, as we will see.

The mutual gaze must take place. And in fact it is not hard for it to do so. Everyone, no matter what language he speaks, can see someone else looking at him. For that matter, he can quickly understand that green means "go," *aller, pergi,* etc., and red means the opposite. The identity of the person on the street, at least in regard to traffic, depends not at all on his name, origin, or language. In that sense, people are interchangeable. Traffic raises no question of identity. To become the other simply means keeping one's place. Communication, in that situation, takes place without language and without challenge to who one is. This makes a near-perfect society, almost the sort of terrestrial paradise that Kant, according to Miladus Doueihi, describes,[52] one in which reason rules as one sees the other and, so doing, respects him and adjusts one's course to him, as he does to oneself. It requires no interiorization of rules, nor even any memorization of them. In effect, there is no reason to change anything of the person, to assimilate him or her to the place. One only has to keep one's eye on the next driver, in a form of seeing that is free of almost all interpretation, limited as it is to the judgment of whether or not one has been seen by the other. Based simply on vision, bypassing languages and seemingly cultures as well, this paradise has broad social limits. The cyclist is a cosmopolitan, in no way depending on civil status, nationality, language, place of origin, his or her sex, or almost any other sort of distinction that pertains between humans today. Still, there are exceptions. One cannot be a young child or, indeed, a cat and safely insert oneself into traffic. The return gaze of such creatures cannot be elicited with certainty, nor can it be counted on to indicate subsequent behavior. But for everyone else the gaze must count. Working usually without sign of acknowledgment, one has to assume that the driver sees the cyclist and the reverse.

This assumption does not always hold. When it does not it, gives rise to much wishful thinking and even magic, as we shall see, starting with the nature of waiting on the street. Waiting has changed and with it certain behavior on the street. Before the bureaucratization of life, one waited for what one wanted or perhaps what one feared. Waiting today is not, for the most part, provoked by either of these. Now one waits in order to get to the next task. Whatever arrives when the wait is finished seldom finishes anything. It is only a step made in order to do something else. "Patientez" says the screen on the French public telephone when one picks up the receiver. "Be patient." "Wait." One waits not to have what one wants, a person one desperately wants to be connected with, but only to begin the procedure that will lead to a conventional telephone conversation.

The image associated with public waiting is, of course, the line. It is claimed, for instance, that the Soviet Union collapsed because one had to stand in line for everything. One joined a line before one knew what it was for, such was the scarcity of goods. Waiting then was the interruption of life, an indication that something was amiss. One should not have to wait, but one accepts that one must, at least up to a certain point. When that point is reached, cars sound their horns; one glares at the next person simply because he is closest and the real target is probably unknown. Or one simply remains impassive, at a distance from social life in order not to provoke conflict and to preserve one's calm. At a distance, but not far enough.

And yet one wonders if one is not sometimes at a greater distance than one realizes. When one waits for the bus, for instance, there is a tendency to look in the direction from which it should arrive, not only to spot it, but as an expression of a wish of the type one makes not for something one wants but for something one needs, where the word *need* means only a necessity that arises out of routine.

Waiting today is, then, a break in routine, but not one that takes one out of it. The real break comes with accident. When an accident occurs on the street, one is prepared for it. Everyone knows he should be careful, he should obey the traffic rules in order to avoid accident. And yet when it occurs, it provokes excitement. One of the important works of modernism, Robert Musil's *The Man Without Qualities*, begins with a driver clumsily gesturing (*mit groben gebärden*), trying to explain how his truck ended up on the sidewalk. He does so "clumsily" not because he is by nature inarticulate or because his trajectory could not be precisely described but because accident as such has no explanation. No doubt for that reason it produces talk. An accident confirms that routine is fragile. The normality of life as it exists today is shattered. One is compelled to explain that the accident was no accident; it happened like this, precisely not by accident at all. The alternative would be to accept that routine is invested with accident, that between normality and its opposite there is no difference. Accident confirms what one suspected already: that life is out of kilter. To explain the accident is, then, to deny this suspicion, and in doing so to create a narrative that, while borrowing the vocabulary of experience—"I did this. he did that"—does not begin with experience at all. It starts, rather, by attempting to explain what cannot be explained: that there was an "accident."

Waiting today, we hope that there will be nothing to explain, no accident. Waiting for the bus, looking for it, is not merely expecting its arrival with impatience. It is also a strong wish that the bus come—not because it is raining, but because if it does not come, one's faith in normality, already fragile, will be further shaken. Looking for the bus is, then, a way of making it come. It appears in view, and one is relieved. It has come not merely because it is supposed to come but because, in a certain way, one, along with others, no doubt, has made it come, as though the commonality of looking in the direction of the bus were a communal ritual, binding potential travelers together, their collective efforts producing normality, the harmony of the disparate parts of the social. The strange wish for what one does not truly want, all the purer for that, has been effective.

This wish, then, is generated out of modern necessity. It feels as if it is effective, but of course the bus did not come because I wanted it to. It has its own reasons, which have nothing to do with what I was thinking when looking in the direction of its route. Everyone knows that, all the more so since this wish is impersonal, a hope that social connections that obtained in the past will be maintained, a little like a communal prayer for peace.

Looking for the bus, one is not aware that one is expressing a wish, putting the emphasis in this sentence on the verb *express*. This wish belongs to the strange unconscious that is better termed "preconscious." But it is a "pre" that seldom appears subsequently in our awareness, one in which one's own connection with those next to one is merely banal. This banality, itself evidence of normality, is not consciously overcome. But if the bus does not come and one starts to speak with the person next to one, which "normally" one would not do, one understands that for a moment a small society has been formed.

Finally, one sees the bus. At that moment, well before one steps into the vehicle, one is relieved. One knows not only that the bus is coming but that it will stop. One sees the bus, and the bus, in turn, or at least the driver, sees oneself. The drama, if it amounts to that, is over. There is no need to reflect on one's habit. Even if the bus never came, one would surely think more about the reasons for it than about the failure of one's wish. Magic persists in our world, providing it is unacknowledged.

It seems in this little story that there is an exchange of looks. One sees the bus, and the bus sees one. But of course the bus does not see anyone. We hypostasize the bus without knowing it, and this too might amount to a sort of magic. And so far as anyone can ascertain, the driver does not see anyone in particular. But when the bus comes it feels as if, in a quite minor way, one has been acknowledged. This fiction of an exchange of glances is not vulnerable to becoming a custom. One could never vaunt it as "our way of doing things." It works only because it goes unacknowledged. Acknowledgment would instantly bring dismissal: "mere superstition." It remains, then, apart from identity. It is not built into the definition of "us" and rests in the shadowy area of habit, capable of being brought to mind sometimes but usually left to itself. It remains what it is, not because it is incapable of being explained but because explanation brings with it the refusal to continue such a practice. One would be ashamed. The gaze of others would be intolerable. One believes in something that is incapable of being conveyed to someone else with conviction. The particular singularity of this practice, its incapacity to make itself known to others or even to oneself without being rejected as meaningless, then, drives this practice out of sight and so lets it continue.

If we were to think of this act, the other, the bus that sees us, would be endowed with properties we never expected. It is subject to our power of wishfulness. A sort of magic and an other as unlikely as the cat Derrida addresses to know who he is inflects the most banal of everyday practices. We become other than who we believe ourselves to be as we hide our magical practices from ourselves and endow the bus itself with the power of recognition. And so the exchange of glances, so easily explained away, is shored up and becomes more dependable than fact would allow. Magic and the routinization of modern life are thus made compatible.

The City of Paris instituted a system of public bicycle rentals on July 15, 2007. Before the end of November of that year, there had been more than ten million rentals.[53] This represents a large number of people, no doubt, who had not previously ridden a bike on the streets of Paris. The way was prepared for them by the construction of numerous lanes either reserved exclusively for bicycles or shared with public transportation. The construction of these new lanes, however, was limited to certain streets, while the connections between lanes on different streets was not always regulated or perhaps was not always capable of being so: for instance, one descends the rue St. Martin, a one-way street, on a bicycle using the bus lane on the left side of the street. The lane on the right, open to general vehicles, is frequently crowded. Reaching rue Reaumur, most of the traffic turns left. The bus lane—used, once again, by bicyclists—is on the right side of rue Reaumur. On a bicycle, one then has to cross in front of the traffic also turning left. One cannot be sure whether the drivers of the cars, trucks, buses, and motorcycles will yield if one continues. Turning this corner, one should be in a panic. One is surrounded by cars wanting to cross in front of one, while one wants to cross in front of them. There is no rule regulating this traffic. It depends on being seen, but one cannot be sure one is seen, since one cannot see the drivers. To turn around is to risk falling. To continue to cross is to put oneself blindly in the path of an undifferentiated mass capable of crushing a cyclist with little effort. Nonetheless, one continues somehow, confident that communication has not been interrupted, even if the line of sight has gone dead. Across this deadness, one's back to the power of the oncoming vehicles, one traces a diagonal path and arrives at the other side.

If one were on foot, in this space one would feel panic. But on the bike, one continues. It is not that one is confident because one is part of the scene. One does not know what one's place is as the web of relations between drivers dissolves and reforms on that corner. Nor is it that one counts on the good will of other drivers. No one familiar with Parisian traffic would be so foolish as to count on that rather than on mutual signaling.[54] If one continues routinely to cross this intersection, it is not through fatalism. One has a sense of continued success, if not exactly full confidence. One becomes a component of a vast signaling device. One is a relay, a switch, capable of turning on and off the cars and motorcycles at one's back. But one cannot be sure the switch works.

A pedestrian—or one could imagine, a duck or a cat—unlucky enough to find himself in the same place would not feel he could influence the cars approaching him. One hopes that in such a case traffic would stop. On the bicycle one has no assured place, and yet one assumes order, though one cannot predict what shape that order will take. Will a car behind one move to the right, to the left, will it stop, will it continue straight? One continues without confidence—which could only be obtained if one had the acknowledgment of others—but with an irrational sense that one takes a risk and will win. Something outside one's ken takes shape. One has somehow or other taken the power of the other for the energy of the switch. Their power, the power of the car or truck or, paradoxically, it seems, the even greater power of the motorcycle ("greater" because motorcyclists are less predictable than drivers of cars, in my experience), is one's own. One feels a part of a system, the equal or more of any of the other parts, the way a soldier might feel on the battlefield. The more one is vulnerable, the greater the power of the other appears, the more one has managed to take that power for oneself. But there are limits. The "animal," the cat, for instance, much less the pedestrian, is not included. These creatures are not part of the system as it is constituted at that moment. The presupposition for the exchange of regards is not there. The pedestrian might come to be included, but so too might the dog, once it is felt that they are aware of the motor vehicles that bear down on them. Thus the daring jaywalkers crossing the busy boulevard.

If one follows Heidegger in the *Introduction to Metaphysics*, when overwhelmed by a force incomparably greater than one's own, one should feel "panicked fear, true anxiety"; this should be an uncanny moment.[55] This is not my own impression. There is a force that could easily overwhelm me. I fear it. But I become a part of that force and so share in it because I feel I am recognized by the drivers of the powerful machines at my back. This is an irrational feeling. It exists—and persists—nonetheless, causing me to think that I have compelled others out of sight to see me.

One might think of this as an illusion rather than magic. An illusion is an aberration. But the use of a fetish is precisely not that, even if it does not conform to ideas of normality. A thing is involved, even if it is not material, as indeed many fetishes are not. A person's mental aberration would occur in many places in his life. But the fetish, unlike the illusion, is not a property of the person; it is not a general condition of his mental life. It is used only where it is needed. It must not belong to him in his quality as a person, or it would disqualify him from everyday life. The fetish works here only when it is applied, as it were. It belongs to its user as a piece of property does. That is to say, it is alien to him, not a property of himself, merely in his possession. He throws it away when it does not work. I, for instance, while writing this piece, realizing the danger I was silly enough to put myself in, stopped riding the bicycle. But later I began again. I still sometimes stop, and then I start again.

Picking up whatever comes one's way, finding the fetish again, comes in part out of need. It seems as though Malinowski was correct in his famous characterization of magic—it is used at sea, where there is danger, and not in the lagoon, where there is not. But the Trobrianders believed in magic and had magical institutions. We do not. It is not the pressure of the social that leads us to magic. That leads, rather, to its denial. Yet it is need, need that comes not out of danger but out of the impossibility of decision, that makes us require magic. Magic works only at the moment when decision is necessary. When it is not needed, one forgets about it, that is, discards it again and then begins using it once more. For that to be the case, for magic not to be merely a symptom of a pathology, there must be something alienable—something that, picked up as needed, thrown away afterwards, retains its invisibility to those who know the person, including himself, since he does not exhibit similar signs of pathology on other occasions. This thing that works magic we call the fetish.

But how does it work? Is not Ibn Manzûr right? "It's as if the magician . . . separates the thing from its image."[56] He states a common view of magic, so common it is dismissed as a commonplace or, nowadays, as a calumny against those who practice magic but who must not be held in contempt. Nonetheless, it is useful to us here. To imagine that the other sees me may or may not be to imagine something differently from how it is. To say that on the bicycle I see the unreal in the image of the real once again is impossible to say. I trust that the other sees me. And in a certain way I think he sees me seeing him. It is too much to say that an image substitutes here for the real, and it is even too much to say that I "imagine" something. The process remains opaque. And that is another way of saying that the fetish, which by definition I do not understand and whose mechanism I cannot see, is at work.

I know of no other way to describe what happens. Accepting that this is the only available way to say how bicycle magic operates, have we not come to a description of "the magic of language"? It is "magical" in Benjamin's sense, since it never arrives, never actually materializes between me and the drivers at my back. I am in communication with those who cannot confirm that this is the case. Language does not arrive and yet, nonetheless, it is effective.

Is *language* the appropriate word here? It is as though a formula had been invoked. But if it is "the magic of language," what language is it that has become magical? It is not French and not English. It is the language of the public street, a language understandable across different languages—a language that no one has ever heard spoken but that speaks to multitudes daily. It is this silent language, avoiding logocentric appropriations of language furthering the interest of the speaker, that contains magic. No one speaks this language, but it nonetheless speaks through those on bicycles— once again, without their knowledge that it is doing so.

This language is "effective" not simply because I am able to cross in front of traffic safely but also because somehow the drivers at my back do take me into account, as though they see me seeing them. If they thought this was not the case, they probably would sound their horns to make me aware of their presence. But this happens only rarely. An exchange of regards takes place, even though it is impossible. Without this happening, there would be carnage daily. With it, a practice or habit is established.

"God thunders but is not on that account recognized as God" is the phrase Hegel uses to describe the mentality of the African fetishist, who, Hegel thinks, believes that the power of thunder is embedded in his fetish.[57] He controls this power; there is nothing greater than himself that might be in charge. This is also the mind set of the cyclist. And yet, like the magic that makes the bus appear, it becomes known only to be dismissed for what it is—childish and insignificant. It remains lodged in rationalized society nonetheless, though, following Hegel this seems not to be possible. Where the fetish is acceptable, objects have no lasting sense, since their ostensible meanings are merely wishful. In such a climate, the king himself, he thought, was easily dethroned and replaced. Given that the reference of words varies at will, authority, which depends on a stable understanding of office regardless of whoever holds it, was inherently unstable. Moreover, fetishistic beliefs were illusory, and the illusion was invulnerable to proof. A fetish might not work, but Africans exchange an old fetish for a new one rather than changing their belief. If they realized that, when God thunders, it is God or nature that does so, if they believed that there was a power greater than themselves, they would not try to take His power for themselves. They would give deference where it is due. But they do not. They are not aware of a difference between themselves and powers outside themselves.

With such a mentality, no stable and certainly no modern society is possible, Hegel thought. What is missing is universality: "The peculiarly African character is difficult to comprehend, for the very reason that in reference to it, we must quite give up the principle which naturally accompanies all our ideas—the category of Universality."[58] There is no reference beyond the wish to categories that transcend individuals and can be used by all.

The person on the bicycle, unable to see if he is seen, though his safety depends on it nonetheless, cannot appeal to what he can be sure others know. The "law" that emerges from the exchange of regards, the recourse to a system of meanings available to everyone, does not operate at that moment. Any more than the exchange of glances between Derrida and his cat yields a sense. No understanding results as the bike crosses in front of the car, only the hope that it does, a hope, moreover, that belongs to only one of the two.

When Sartre spoke of exchanging glances with blacks, he thought a change of hierarchy would result. Bataille thought that the introduction into communication of nonsense, that is, communication that fails to make sense but that nonetheless is lodged within the social, would cause hierarchy to collapse. Derrida's exchange of regards with the cat, instead of reversing the relation of master and pet, leaves "Derrida" wondering if he has a place in the social at all. But nothing, at least so far, results. Each resumes his place.

On the bicycle there is a similar but not identical result. The easily assimilable alterity that makes foreignness inconsequential according to Viatte and that allows traffic to flow at moments becomes consequential and therefore no longer mere alterity without important difference. On the street, ordinarily each sees the other, each understands the other, and each passes the other by. But at a certain moment the other disappears from sight He is there but invisible, almost a definition of a ghost, but he is not put in that category. Nonetheless, the ordinary other becomes completely other. One cannot count on return regards issuing in sense. Nonetheless, thanks to the fetish, and contrary to rational calculation, one assumes that understanding is generated and that one is safe. Normality thus is preserved as all others become completely other. "Tout autre est tout autre."

Stop. Go. Cross. Follow/Be . . .

1. GEORG SIMMEL REAPPEARS: THE AESTHETIC SIGNIFICANCE OF THE FACE

1. Michael Landmann, "Bausteine zur Biographie." In *Buch des Dankes an Georg Simmel*, ed. Kurt Gassen and Michael Landmann (Berlin: Duncker & Humblot, 1958), 17. Simmel's American translator adds this to the anecdote: "As becomes evident from our text, Simmel must have published his study without paying heed to his professors, since footnotes and textual quotations reflect the shortcomings already criticized. Where it was possible to discern Simmel's likely source, fuller biographical information was supplied. We also compiled a bibliography of the works which Simmel might have used for his study (Appendix B). Hence, chaotic as the documentation may still appear, it is already 'improved' over Simmel's original" (Georg Simmel, *The Conflict in Modern Culture and Other Essays*, trans. K. Peter Etzkorn [New York: Teacher's College Press, 1968], 127–28n1).

2. Georg Simmel, *The Philosophy of Money*, trans. Tom Bottomore and David Frisby (London: Routledge & Kegan Paul, 1978); "The Stranger," in *The Sociology of Georg Simmel*, ed. and trans. Kurt U. Wolff (Glencoe, Ill.: Free Press, 1950), 143–49.

3. Donald N. Levine, "The Structure of Simmel's Social Thought," in *Georg Simmel, 1858–1918: A Collection of Essays, with Translations and a Bibliography*, ed. Kurt H. Wolff (Columbus: Ohio State University Press, 1959), 11.

4. Japan may be an exception to my characterizations of the treatment of Simmel. Yoneda and especially Takata's systematizations of Simmel are not matched in the Anglophone world, or so I learn from reading Masamichi Shimmei, "Georg Simmel's Influence on Japanese Thought," in *Georg Simmel, 1858–1918*, ed. Wolff, 201–15, not having access myself to the Japanese texts.

5. Max Weber, quoted in Donald N. Levine, "Introduction" to Georg Simmel, *On Individuality and Social Forms*, ed. Donald N. Levine (Chicago: University of Chicago Press, 1971), xlv–xlvi.

6. Ibid., xlvi. Weber's assessment of Simmel seems validated even in some of his translations. The first translation in English is entitled "Moral Deficiencies as Determining Intellectual Functions," *International Journal of Ethics* 3, no.

4 (1893): 490–507, and is noted in the bibliography to *Georg Simmel, 1858–1918*, ed. Wolff, on whose authority I rely for the citation. Wolff includes the anonymous translator's note: "This article is part of the second volume of the author's *Einleitung in die Moralwissenschaft* [sic]. . . . The reader finds here hardly more than a general outline of the original article. From want of space it has been considerably shortened without being able to consult the author" (379). David Frisby, in *Simmel and Since: Essays on Georg Simmel's Social Theory* (London: Routledge, 1992), points out that more of Simmel's works were published in the United States at the beginning of the century than those of any other German sociologist. Yet, of course, Simmel faded from view, only to be revived several times.

Ambivalence about Simmel extended even to his appearance. Someone who attended his lectures in 1910 felt: "When he began to speak he was fascinating and repellent alike, as if surrounded by a halo of solitude and disgust." Listening to Simmel speak was like listening to someone's words without his presence, a veritable experience in the hearing of writing, at least according to Albert Salomon: "He really did not address the audience in the reciprocal give and take of a good teacher; he was talking in a monologue. His words came from somewhere, from an opaque experience like lightning, shocking and fascinating alike. He seemed to be a stranger, an adventurer in ideas and an actor whose gestures, of his hands in particular, feigned the spontaneity of his thinking in class, while he probably performed the same gestures every time he gave the course. Throughout my reading of Simmel's works and later in my teaching Simmel, I never got rid of the ambivalent reaction of fascination and repulsion" ("Georg Simmel Reconsidered," trans. Gary D. Jaworski, in *Georg Simmel and the American Prospect*, ed. Gary D. Jaworski [Albany: State University of New York Press, 1997], 93).

7. George Simmel, "The Aesthetic Significance of the Face," in *Georg Simmel, 1858–1918*, ed. Wolff, 276–81.

8. Georg Simmel, "The Conflict in Modern Culture," in *On Individuality and Social Forms*, 375–93.

9. Simmel, "The Aesthetic Significance of the Face," 279.

10. The rest of Simmel's characterization continues as follows: "by his own desire and reflection, a salvation that will come upon him readily if he fulfills conditions that are situated only within the disposition of his soul. . . . [It] requires no transcendent power, no divine mercy, and no mediator; it is not achieved by the individual but comes to pass as the logical result of the soul's renunciation of all will to live. . . . it does not contain social norms nor is it a religion. In all other cases . . . religious obligation . . . is not a personal matter but is imposed on the individual as a member of a particular group." In religions, particularly in ancient societies: "That social requirements are expressed in religious terms, and that the relationship of the individual to the group is classified as a duty to god, is simply an outward illustration or objectification of

the inner, emotional motivation already rooted in the social relationships" (Georg Simmel, "Religion," in *Essays on Religion*, ed. and trans. Horst Juergen Helle, in collaboration with Ludwig Nieder [New Haven: Yale University Press, 1997]. 160). It follows that the representations of the Buddha's face should be expressionless, encased in the perfect symmetry that was the subject of so many of Simmel's contemplations.

11. Charles Darwin, *The Expression of the Emotions in Man and Animals* (New York: Oxford University Press, 1998).

12. At this point my editor Helen Tartar, a long-time lover of cats, comments: "I'm not sure the same thing isn't true of humans—a cat swishing its tail might be rather like an athlete focusing on a task about to be begun (or, of course, a hunter focusing on prey)—the entire body is expressive, and the face isn't oriented at that time to any other, even if the athlete is on TV and may beam at the camera theatrically after the exploit is over. It's just, perhaps, that in most interactions human culture tends to put a premium on suppressing or masking the way in which the whole body expresses emotion or whatever else is going on in that human being at any given moment."

13. Tartar comments: "The central points here may be 'aesthetic object' and 'retained after.' Cats are special in this, I think—they do look at humans (at least all three of mine have) in something like the way humans look at each other (and maybe dogs or other animals don't). I've often wondered if there isn't some knowledge on both sides that cats trigger the soft spot for a face with big eyes (like that of a human baby) that humans seem to have as a sort of innate impulse. And it's always struck me that this is very different from how cats relate to other cats. I believe the sort of direct gaze cats direct to humans is considered violently aggressive by other cats—I've seen them go ballistic when confronted with another cat gazing head on at them through, say, a window or screen door. And the sight of them studiously looking aside, even when sitting next to each other, to prevent sparking conflict is familiar."

14. Robert Musil, *Young Törless*, trans. Eithne Wilkins and Ernst Kaiser (New York: Pantheon, 1955.

15. Volker Schlöndorff, director, *Der junge Törless* (Franz-Seitz-Film, 1966).

16. I want to thank Sakiko Kitagawa for our discussions of Simmel. I dedicate this piece to her.

2. ACADEMIC WORK: THE VIEW FROM CORNELL

1. "Proposal Made by Ezra Cornell to the Trustees of the Agricultural College in September, 1864," reprinted in Carl Becker, *Cornell University: Founders and the Founding* (Ithaca: Cornell University Press, 1943), 16–161.

2. Reported by Ezra Cornell's son, Alonzo B. Cornell, as quoted in Kermit Parsons, *The Cornell Campus: A History of Its Planning and Development* (Ithaca: Cornell University Press, 1968), 31–32.

3. A. D. White, as quoted in ibid., 32, and also Morris Bishop, *A History of Cornell* (Ithaca: Cornell University Press, 1962), 70; see also W. T. Hewett, *Cornell University: A History* (New York: University Publishing Society, 1905), 1:77.

4. Solomon Southwick, *Views of Ithaca and Its Environs* (Ithaca: D. D. and A. Spencer, 1835.

5. Hewett, *Cornell University*, 1:74–75.

6. Alonzo Cornell, Ms. history of Cornell, Cornell University Archives, 47/1/26, p. 41.

7. A. D. White, quoted in Becker, *Cornell University*, 66.

8. A. Cornell, Ms. history of Cornell, p. 41.

9. Morris Bishop believes the wording of the seal was actually that of A. D. White, though he does not doubt that the sentiment was Ezra Cornell's (*A History of Cornell*, 741).

10. In all, sixty such interviews were conducted in spring 1978, 1979, and 1980. Students were first introduced to methods of transcription, learning to listen to their informants and then to record what was said immediately afterward, a common practice in anthropology today. Alternatively, students were allowed to take down what was being said in the course of the interview, as in the three interviews here. Students were not told the purpose of the interviews until they had already conducted them. Students also kept notebooks in which they recorded observations, comments, and conversations. Where material is taken from these notebooks, it is so labeled. All material is used with the permission of the recorders.

11. I have taken the term *strong image* in relation to the sublime from Neil Hertz and am indebted to him for his ideas on the relation between textuality and the sublime, as will be apparent below. See Neil Hertz, "The Notion of Blockage in the Literature of the Sublime," in *Psychoanalysis and the Question of the Text*, ed. Geoffrey H. Hartman, Selected Papers from the English Institute, 1976–77, n.s. 2 (Baltimore: Johns Hopkins University Press, 1978).

12. Statistics on rates of suicide at different universities are difficult to come by. My information comes from the statement Nina Miller, director of the Suicide Prevention and Crisis Service of Tompkins County, made in the Cornell Campus Council Suicide Barrier hearings, September 27, 1979; she has informal access to such information. Statistics on suicide at Cornell were furnished me by Lt. R. H. Hausner of the Cornell Department of Public Safety. They show that eleven of the twenty-six suicides between 1966 and November 1977 were by leaps from the bridges. Statistics published in the *Cornell Daily Sun* based on data furnished by the Ithaca Police Department show that ten of twenty-one suicides between 1970 and May 3, 1979, of people affiliated with Cornell occurred from the bridges. A spokesman for the Suicide Prevention and Crisis Service of Tompkins County is quoted in the *Cornell Daily Sun* as saying, "The suicide rate at Cornell is about the same as at any other university

of approximately the same size and status. This is contrary to prevalent myths" ("Dean Examines Evidence on Student Health," November 14, 1977, p. 11).

13. See also the *Cornell Daily Sun* of November 16, 17, and 18, 1977.

14. Eldon Kenworthy of the Government Department, in a letter to the *Cornell Chronicle*, November 17, 1977.

15. *Ithaca Journal*, November 14, 1977.

16. Professor Ian R. MacNeil of the Law School, in a letter to the *Cornell Chronicle*, September 7, 1977, repeated in a memorandum to the Cornell Campus Council, September 19, 1979.

17. See the depositions of Professor Jay Orear and Larry Kasanoff read at the Cornell Campus Council hearings on the erection of suicide barriers on September 26, 1979. These depositions are on file with the Cornell Campus Council office.

18. Professor Jay Orear, in testimony before the Cornell Campus Council.

19. I. MacNeil, published in the *Cornell Chronicle*.

3. *KIBLAT* AND THE MEDIATIC JEW

Note: I wish to thank Anne Berger and Michael Meeker, as well as the members of the conference Religion and Media, convened by Samuel Weber and Hent de Vries in Château de la Bretesche in September 1998, for their comments on this essay. I am much indebted to Sam Weber for remarks that enabled me to rethink the issues above.

1. W. J. S. Poerwadarminta, *Kamus Umum Bahasa Indonesia* (General Dictionary of Indonesian) (Jakarta: Balai Pustaka, 1966).

2. Martin van Bruinessen, "Yahudi sebagai Simbol Dalam Wacana Pemikiran Islam Indonesia Masa Kini" (Jew as Symbol in the Discourse of Indonesian Islamic Thinking at the Present Time), in *Spiritualitas Baru: Agama dan Aspirasi Rakyat* (New Spirituality: Religion and the People's Aspirations), ed. Y. B. Mangunwijaya et al. (Yogyakarta: Institut Dian/Interfidei, 1994), 253–68. Van Bruinessen points out that the *Protocols of the Elders of Zion* was not republished in Indonesia from European sources but from Arabic ones. He traces the tendency to blame Jews for conspiracy in Indonesia not to Europe but to Saudi Arabia, Kuwait, and Egypt (ibid., 254–55). He notes four editions of the *Protocols* in Indonesian, the earliest of which was published in 1982.

Media Dakwah, a journal that I shall discuss shortly, published tracts attributed to Benjamin Franklin and Martin Luther King, Jr., warning against the danger of Jews. It quotes Napoleon as saying, "The Jews are the master robbers of the modern age. The evil of Jews does not stem from individuals but from the fundamental nature of this people" (speech to the Council of State, April 30 and May 7, 1806; *Media Dakwah*, Research Team, "Fakta dan Data Untuk William Liddle" [August 1993], 53). It also published translations of Roger Garaudy in the issues of March 1986, May 1986, and July 1986. For a commentary on Garaudy from a certain Indonesian Muslim viewpoint, see Daud Rasyid,

"Geraudi [*sic*] vs. Sindikat Zionisme" (Geraudi Versus the Zionist Synidicat), *Media Dakwah*, June 1997, 17–18. Garaudy was also frequently quoted by Nurcholish Madjid.

Following conventional English usage I use "anti-Semitic" to mean "anti-Jewish."

3. A description of the institutional background of this talk can be found in Douglas Ramage, *Politics in Indonesia: Democracy, Islam, and the Ideology of Tolerance* (London: Routledge, 1995), 75–122. See also Robert W. Hefner, "Islamization and Democratization in Indonesia," in *Islam in an Era of Nation-States: Politics and Renewal in Muslim Southeast Asia*, ed. Robert W. Hefner (Honolulu: University of Hawai'i Press, 1997), 75–129. Hefner speaks explicitly of Nurcholish Madjid and describes the distribution of Islamic leadership, but he minimizes that leadership's complicated relations with the Indonesian military and makes no mention of their virulent anticommunism, which renders, as we will see, the extension of tolerance quite limited. It is hard to find a Muslim leader of national stature who openly opposed the rule of General Suharto until the last years of his regime. Nurcholish Madjid was no exception. As Hefner says, his efforts were, rather, to gain influence with the regime.

4. Nurcholish Madjid, "Beberapa Renungan tentang kehidupan Keagamaan di Indonesia untuk Generasi Mendatang." Nurcholish's talk and responses to it were republished by his opponents. See H. Lukman Hakiem, ed., *Menggugat Gerakan Pembaruan Keagamaan: Debat Besar "Pembaruan Islam"* (Jakarta: Lembaga Studi Informasi Pembangunan, 1995), 47.

5. Ibid., 51.

6. Ibid., 55.

7. Ibid., 59.

8. Drs. Nabhan Husein, "Membedah Pemikiran Nurcholish Madjid," in *Menggugat Gerakan Pembaruan Keagamaan*, ed. Lukman Hakiem, 144–73; 160. This collection of articles was originally published in *Media Dakwah* in April, May, and June 1993.

9. HM Hasballah Thaib, "Mengkaji Gagasan Nurcholish," in *Menggugat Gerakan Pembaruan Keagamaan*, ed. Lukman Hakiem, 112–23; originally given as a talk in Medan on July 27, 1993.

10. Ibid., 114.

11. Ibid., 119

12. Daud Rasyid, M.A., "Meluruskan Akidah, Menangkal Mu'tazilah," in *Menggugat Gerakan Pembaruan Keagamaan*, ed. Lukman Hakiem, 240; originally published in *Media Dakwah*, June, 1993.

13. Abu Ridho, "Hikmah Lain dari Polemik Itu," in *Menggugat Gerakan Pembaruan Keagamaan*, ed. Lukman Hakiem, 195–213; 208; originally published in *Media Dakwah*, April 1993.

14. Daud Rasyid, "Kesesatan Dikemas dengan Gaya Ilmiah" (Deviation Put Right Through Knowledge), in *Menggugat Gerakan Pembaruan Keagamaan*, ed.

Lukman Hakiem, 93ff. Originally given as an address on December 13, 1992, in the mosque of TIM where Nurcholish gave his talk.

15. Ibid., 94.

16. Ibid., 95.

17. The qur'anic verse he alludes to reads:

> Some of the Jews pervert words from their meanings saying, "We have heard and we disobey"
>
> and "Hear, and be thou not given to hear"
>
> and "Observe us," twisting with their tongues and traducing religion.
>
> If they had said, "We have heard and obey"
>
> and "Hear" and "Regard us," it would have been better for them, and more upright; but God has cursed them for their unbelief, so they believe not
>
> except a few.

(*The Koran Interpreted*, trans. A. J. Arberry [New York: Collier Books, 1955], 1:107, Surah IV, "Women").

18. Daud Rasyid, "Kesesatan Dikemas dengan Gaya Ilmiah," 105.

19. Lukman Hakiem, "Nabi Gagal Menjalankan Missinya? Meuguji pemikiran Nurcholish" (Was the Prophet Defeated in Carrying Out His Mission? Analyzing the Thought of Nurcholish), *Media Dakwah*, December 1992, 4. Nurcholish is reported to have said later that Leonard Binder was never in a position to make such an offer. R. William Liddle, "*Media Dakwah* Scripturalism: One Form of Islamic Political Thought and Action in New Order Indonesia," in Mark Woodward, *Toward a New Paradigm: Recent Developments in Indonesian Political Thought* (Tempe: Arizona State University, 1996), 353n.18.

20. See Hadiyanto, "Nurcholish Itu Neo Marxis" (This Nurcholish Is a NeoMarxist), *Media Dakwah*, December 1992, 49; Muchlish Abdi, "Angap saja angin lalu" (Simply Think of Him as Wind That Has Passed By), *Media Dakwah*, December 1992, 50.

21. Some know of the Jewish community in Surabaya, which consists today of only three families, or have heard that there is a Jew who lives in a certain part of Jakarta. These people are not thought to be a threat, whereas Jews, always abroad, are.

22. The closest one comes to a political notion in this thinking is when three reporters from Jakarta newspapers, including Islamic papers, go to Israel, reportedly to prepare the way for the recognition of Israel by Indonesia. The other political event came when a Jewish diplomat was nominated as American ambassador to Indonesia, evoking much protest.

23. "Distance" can be historical. One *Media Dakwah* article claims that Nurcholish's proposals closely resemble those of Annie Besant and the Theosophical Society, which was active in Indonesia in the early part of the century.

The Research Team of *Media Dakwah* responsible for the article sees it as still operating in an important way. In their opinion, the Theosophical Society was a branch of British Freemasonry controlled in the early part of the century, at least, from Madras. They believe it is particularly dangerous as a front organization not only for Freemasonry but for Jews: "It is here that the Islamic community has to be particularly on the alert. And from now on no longer think of Nurcholish as the person who was once head of the HMI [Muslim Students Association]. Nurcholish now, whether he is aware of it or not, is Nurcholish who, directly or indirectly, is campaigning [*mengampanyekan*] for the thinking of the Theosofische Vereeniging, which very clearly forms part of the net of the Jewish International." They go on to say that the Theosofische Vereeniging in colonial times did not seek to spread its teachings. It is all the more deplorable that Nurcholish is thought to be an Islamic figure; he uses his extensive knowledge of Islam to spread Theosophical thinking: "This is most effective for the group of orientalists and Islamicists in misleading the community" (Tim Laporan Utama, "Penyerahan diri, Yes, Islam, No," *Media Dakwah*, December 1992, 44–47. See also the accompanying article by Tim Riser, "Nurcholish Madjid dan Annie Besant," *Media Dakwah*, December 1992, 44–45. The former concludes: "We have to be very careful about whatever Nurcholish launches at us. He can zigzag in the astonishing way peculiar to the character of Jews. Islamic community, beware" (47).

24. For another view, see William Liddle, who thinks of this strain of Indonesian Islam as scripturalist: "Skripturalisme *Media Dakwah*: Satu Bentuk Pemikiran dan Aksi Politik Islam Masa Orde Baru," *Ulumul al-Qur'an*, July 1993.

25. *Media Dakwah* reports various Islamic opinions as to whether the Islamic headdress, *jilbab* in Indonesian, is required dress. The periodical is most concerned with cases where, in public schools and factories, the wearing of the *jilbab* had been banned. See the issues of February 1983, April 1984, September 1985, November 1985, March 1989, January 1991, February 1995, and March 1995 for numerous articles on the subject. For a discussion of the place of the *jilbab* in Indonesia today, see Suzanne Brenner, "Reconstructing Self and Society: Javanese Muslim Women and the Veil," *American Ethnologist* 23, no. 4 (1996): 673–97. For a general discussion of the issue, see Anne Emmanuelle Berger, "The Newly Veiled Woman: Irigaray, Specularity and the Islamic Veil," *Diacritics* 28, no. 1 (Spring 1998): 93–119.

26. See the articles in *Media Dakwah* on conglomerates as an opportunity for Islamic activities, October 1991; on Chinese and on capitalism, see the collection of articles in *Media Dakwah*, August 1991 and May 1993.

27. Of course the Sukarno regime always harbored the fear that Indonesia would be dominated by foreign ideas. This, however, was an effect of Sukarno's attempt at syncretism, given that he sought a basis in the state by accepting diverse, non-Indonesian ideologies, including Marxism and "religion" (*agama*).

Today, by contrast, the idea of a model for the nation is not at issue. It is assumed that "development [*pembangunan*]" is above all economic, and the economy is that of the market. In this view, foreign influence loses its particularity of origin; capital and technology have no smell. Or at least that is true until capital becomes "Chinese" and occasionally "Jewish." Cf. Sobirin, "Sindikat Cina dan Islam dalam Dunia Bisnis" (Chinese Syndicates and Islam in the World of Business), *Media Dakwah*, May 1993, 47–48.

28. The *Media Dakwah* editorial offices are in the yard of a mosque not far from the University of Indonesia, in the same building as that of the former Islamic political party, Masjumi, headed by Mohammed Natsir, which was banned during the Sukarno period and failed to reestablish itself in the Suharto era. A good deal of *Media Dakwah*'s resentment stems from the bitterness of its political failure, in my opinion. In the post-Suharto period it hoped to make up for this failure. This was made clear to me when I, along with Henri Chambert-Loir of the École Française d'Extrême-Orient, spoke at length with a number of *Media Dakwah* writers in June 1998.

Although the Masjumi was modernist in its orientation, Mohammed Natsir was an anti-Semite of long standing. Here, for instance, is a statement from a book of his published in 1970. Describing "the characteristics of Jews," he says: "It is in their character, no matter where they are, to be like worms on the leaves of banana trees. The leaves are destroyed, riddled with the holes they made, while their bodies get fat, just like worms on leaves. For that reason, they are a people who for centuries have been hated everywhere. Thus a few decades ago, before the Second World War, they were chased from Western Europe and Eastern Europe. They became a hated people. When Hitler was in power they were put into camps where, it is said, several million were killed." He goes on to say that, nonetheless, Jews were allowed to lived in Arab countries (M. Natsir, *Masalah Palestina* [Jakarta: Penerbit Hudaya, 1970], 12–13).

29. Nurcholish, for instance, was a prominent member of ICMI, the group of Muslim intellectuals formed by Habibie when he was vice president.

30. In another example, the "management of Bank BNI in fact feels it benefits—even though [prayer] takes time away from business hours—it feels certainty in the firmer belief of its employees and that will lessen dishonesty, corruption and manipulation" (Aru Syeif Assad, "Bias Dakwah di Lingkungan Bisness," *Media Dakwah*, October 1991, 41). This is the introductory article to a series on *dakwah* in business.

31. Religious toleration is an issue in the New Order because religion itself has become more important. Its relation to fear of the underclass and, in turn, the connection between fear of the underclass and anti-Semitism is complicated. As noted, the question of religious toleration is not a question of ethnicity. Indonesia has nearly nine hundred regional languages and as many ethnic groups. Some of these are Christian, including some Chinese. But "Muslim" is not a code word for particular ethnic groups; it is a category that transcends

ethnicity as an element of national identity. In large cities, Christians too often worship in churches with congregations from diverse ethnic groups.

32. For the history of Panca Sila and particularly of the First Principle, see Ramage, *Politics in Indonesia*, 10–20, and the literature cited there.

33. B. R. O'G. Anderson, "The Language of Indonesian Politics," *Indonesia* 1 (April 1966): 89–116.

34. Until the New Order Indonesia had less need of this word because it had a way of accounting for differences taken from the templates of Javanese mythology. Though not at all part of official state formulations, that worked in practice. See B. R. O'G. Anderson, *Tolerance and the Mythology of the Javanese* (Ithaca: Cornell Modern Indonesia Project, 1965).

35. Van Bruinessen, "Yahudi sebagai Simbol."

36. The historian Claude Guillot of the CNRS tells me that in the 1980s no more than a handful of members were left in this synagogue. In February 2000 the family of the caretaker told me that only three Jewish families remained in Surabaya. The synagogue had been used mainly by Jewish traders from what is now Iraq. The old man in charge of the synagogue told Guillot that, when asked by Indonesians about his descent, he answered "Iraqi"; although they knew that he was in charge of the synagogue, he was then taken to be an Arab. A Jewish woman, born in India and married into the community, told me a similar story about herself. As soon as the Jew appears in Indonesia, he disappears.

A Jewish traveler had this to say about the condition of Jews in 1925:

> I learned that there were several hundred Jews (perhaps as many as 2,000) scattered about from Batavia to Surabaya, but as many of them concealed their Jewish origins it was impossible to form an approximate estimate of their numbers. Dutch Jews had been living in the country for a very long period and had played an important part in its commercial development. . . . There were many Jews occupying Government positions, the most prominent being the Resident of Surabaya. . . . But there was no Jewish life in the communal sense, mixed marriages were frequent, and the only form of association consisted of a few struggling Zionist societies. (Israel Cohen, *The Journal of a Jewish Traveller* [London: John Lane, The Bodley Head Limited, 1925], 211–12)

I am indebted to John Pemberton for bringing this source to my attention. Another observer, Eze Nathan, confirms Cohen's report but adds that, after the coming of Jews from India in the late nineteenth century, there was "a semblance of communal life in a few cities." Writing in 1986, he says that from the time of the Japanese occupation there has been "scarcely a single Jewish family left in Indonesia" (*The History of Jews in Singapore: 1830–1945* [Singapore: HERBILU Editorial and Marketing Services, 1986], 175–76). On the synagogue itself, see the excellent article by Gilbert Hamonic, "Note sur le communauté juive de Surabaya," *Archipel* 36 (1988): 183–86. On the history of the

Jewish community in the Indies, see the entry "De Joden in Nederlandsch-Indië," *Encyclopaedie van Nederlandsch Oost Indie*, 6:614–16.

37. On the identification of the two by Southeast Asians, see Daniel Chirot, "Conflicting Identities and the Dangers of Communalism," in *Essential Outsiders: Chinese and Jews in the Modern Transformation of Southeast Asia and Central Europe*, ed. Daniel Chirot and Anthony Reid (Seattle: University of Washington Press, 1997), 5.

38. Andreas Harsono, ed., *Huru-hara Rengasdengklok* (Uproar in Rengasdengklok) ([Jakarta]: Institut Studi Arus Informasi, 1997), 18. The same report notes that a reporter from Agence France Presse photographed an Indonesian soldier looking gleefully at the suspended statue.

39. An interview with Ustad Holid A., an ulama and head of a school in the area. Komar, Joko, Taufik, Nuh, "Mereka Membentuk Geng Tersendiri: Warga keturunan Cina selama ini bersifaat ekslusif. Hal ini memicu kerusuhan dengan kebencian yang kental" (They formed their own gang: Those of Chinese descent act without regard. This triggers unrest and deep hatred), *Media Dakwah*, March 1997, 54–55. A team of social scientists investigating the incident says that Cigue is really "Cik Gue," "Cik" being Chinese for "older sister." They say also that the woman had Indonesianized her name, taking, in fact, an Arabic name, Nurhayati (Harsono, ed., *Huru-hara Rengasdengklok*, 6).

40. Komar, Joko, Zuki, Nuh, "H. Sobarna Noor, Sekretaris MUI Rengasdengklok: Bom Waktu di Rengasdengklok. Rumah berubah menjadi gereja itulah bom waktu yang meladak di kota bersejarah itu" (H. Sobarna Noor, Secretary MUI [Council of Islamic Scholars]: Time bomb in Rengasdengklok. Houses turning into churches are a time bomb exploding in this historic city), *Media Dakwah*, March 1997, 53–54.

41. See, in particular, *Kompas* for January 27, 1997.

42. A prominent "Chinese" from the area denied the charge, saying that the permit had not yet been officially issued but that there was provisional authority to construct the church (Harsono, ed., *Huru-hara Rengasdengklok*, 81).

43. One should note that these Muslims claim to be the majority yet find themselves condemned by most Indonesians, most of whom are themselves Muslims.

44. Komar, Joko, Zuki, Nuh, "H. Sobarna Noor," 53–54.

45. Caption to photograph, Team *Media Dakwah*, "Buntut Kerusuhan: Ramai-ramai Menyudutkan Islam," *Media Dakwah*, March 1997, 42–47; 42.

46. Harsono, ed., *Huru-hara Rengasdengklok*. I have changed their spelling of "Cigue" (Cik Gue) to match that of *Media Dakwah*.

47. See James T. Siegel, *Solo in the New Order: Language and Hierarchy in an Indonesian City* (Princeton: Princeton University Press, 1986), 234ff.

48. Harsono, ed., *Huru-hara Rengasdengklok*, 11–12

49. Ibid., 90.

50. Ibid., 116.

51. Ibid., 29.

52. See Siegel, *Solo in the New Order*.

53. I have discussed these incidents and the role of speech with minimal content in ibid., 55–58.

54. Harsono, ed., *Huru-hara Rengasdengklok*, 31. Fifty-four rioters—most in their teens and twenties, and mostly students, laborers, or unemployed—got sentences of about three months.

55. Ibid., 10.

56. Ibid., 11.

57. The mob that attacked Chinese in Rengasdengklok was termed not *rakyat* but *massa*, the "masses" or "mob." The difference is the lack of a leader. The *rakyat* always needs someone to speak for it. But had someone emerged, there still would have been no *rakyat*. The emergent social formation would still have been the *massa* rather than the *rakyat* because the new entity lacked permanence and legitimacy (Aru, "Membongkar Jaringan Kristenisasi, Yahudi dan Cina Anti Islam" ["Demolishing the Network of Christianization, Jews, and Anti-Islamic Chinese"], *Media Dakwah*, March 1997, 41).

58. "The Devious Movement of Buki Sahidin: Jewish Traces in Tasikmalaya," *Media Dakwah*, March 1997, 50–52.

59. Aru, "Membongkar Jaringan Kristenisasi, Yahudi dan Cina Anti Islam," *Media Dakwah*, March 1997, 41.

60. The prominence of the word *trauma* in latter New Order discourse may be another effect of the feeling of undefined menace. The feeling, new to Indonesia, of an incurable wound, caused by a continuing menace that often has no certain origins, occurs alongside the new upsurgence of anti-Semitism. One might think of it as an attempt to place the effects of the Jew within Indonesian society. Cf. James T. Siegel, *A New Criminal Type in Jakarta* (Durham: Duke University Press, 1998), chap. 4.

61. Martin van Bruinessen rightly points out that anti-Semitism is often found in places in Europe and America where Jews are rare. The difference between such places as rural North Dakota and Indonesia, however, is that the former belong to larger societies where Jews play a part and where the terms of their recognition are widely circulated. See van Bruinessen, "Yahudi sebagai Simbol," 259. Asian anti-Semitism in Japan and China is configured quite differently from Indonesia. See the relevant articles in Frank Dikötter, *The Construction of Racial Identities in China and Japan* (Honolulu: University of Hawai'i Press, 1997), as well as David Goodman and Masanori Miyazawa, *Jews in the Japanese Mind* (New York: The Free Press, 1995).

4. THE CURSE OF THE PHOTOGRAPH: ATJEH 1901

1. I use the Dutch spelling, *Atjeh*, to refer to the sultanate. The contemporary Indonesian spelling is *Aceh*, and I use that to refer to the province of Indonesia. The followers of the Acehnese independence movement often use English orthography, spelling the name *Acheh*.

2. Liane van der Linden, "Inleiding" (Introduction) to Anneke Groeneveld, *Toekang portret: 100 jaar fotografie in Nederlands Indie 1839–1939* (Amsterdam: Fragment Uitgeverij, n.d.), 8–13.

3. Ibid., 18.

4. Ibid., 205

5. Jan Fontein, "Kassian Céphas: A Pioneer of Indonesian Photography," in *Towards Independence: A Century of Indonesia Photographed*, ed. Jane Levy Reed (San Francisco: Friends of Photography, 1991), 47.

6. For a recent development of the idea of Java defeated by the Dutch and turned into an object of Dutch study, see Tsuchiya Kenji, "Javanology and the Age of Ronggowarsita: An Introduction to Nineteenth-Century Javanese Culture," in *Reading Southeast Asia*, ed. Takashi Shiraishi (Ithaca: Cornell Southeast Asia Program, 1990). For the Javanese response to this effort, see John Pemberton, *On the Subject of "Java"* (Ithaca: Cornell University Press, 1994), chap. 2.

7. The second story is included in the Introduction to Kassian Céphas, *Yogyakarta: Photography in the Service of the Sultan* (Leiden: KITLV Press, 1999), 7. There is some dispute about whether or not Céphas was of mixed ancestry. Claude Guillot seems persuasive in arguing that he was not ("Un example d'assimilation à Java: Le photographe Kassian Céphas [1844–1912]," *Archipel* 22 [1982]: 55–73).

8. Guillot, "Un example d'assimilation à Java."

9. J. Groneman, *De Garebeg's te Ngajogyakarta met photogrammen van Céphas* (The Hague: Martinus Nijhoff, 1895), 3.

10. A selection of these pictures can be found in Louis Zweers, *Sumatra: Kolonialen, Koelies, en Krijgers: Metvele unieke foto's* (Houten: Fibula, 1988), from which I also draw information concerning the Topographical Service (see 38ff). For a description of the encirclement of the Dutch troops, see E. B. Kielstra, *Beschrijving van den Atjeh-Oorlog met gebruikmaking der officieelle Bronnern, door het Departement van Koloniën daartoe afgestaan* (The Hague: De Gebroeders van Cleef, 1883), 1–97.

11. The photograph is that on page 29, captioned "Foto Genomen in de Nog Brandende Versterkking Batéë Ilië" (Photo Taken in the Still-burning Fortification of Batéë Ilië). See C. Nieuwenhuis, *Expeditie naar Samalanga: Dagverhaal van een Fotograaf te velde* (Amsterdam: Van Holkema, n.d.).

12. See the photograph by H. M. Neeb, "Gezicht in de kampong Lahat, na de inname door de marechaussee onder leiding van Van Daalen" (View of Lahat Village after its capture by *marechaussee* [special forces] under the leadership of Van Daalen), republished in Zweers, *Sumatra*, 57, as well as another entitled "In de veroverde benteng Koeto Reh, tijdens den tocht onder van Daalen door het Gajoland, op 14 Juni 1904; er bleven 561 gesneuvlde Gajoes liggen. Bij een in leven gebleven kind staat een schildwacht. Links bove, staande, donkere figuur: Van Daalen" (In the captured fort of Koeta Reh during the expedition of Van Daalen, June 14, 1904; 561 slain Gajos lay there. A sentry stands next to a

still-living child. Above left, standing, dark figure, Van Daalen). The picture is reproduced with this caption in H. C. Zentgraaff, *Atjeh* (Batavia: Koninklijke Drukkerij de Unie, [1930], 190).

13. Nieuwenhuis, *Expeditie naar Samalanga*, 1.

14. Ibid., 17.

15. Ibid., 20.

16. Ibid., plate 12, "Atjehsche Brug door de rawa (moeras) bij den Glé Risa Boengang" (Atjehnese Bridge over the swamp near Glé Risa Boengang), p. 15.

17. Ibid., 26–27.

18. Ibid., plate 18, p. 28: "Versperringen van bamboo doeri (stekelige bamboo)" (Thorny Bamboo Obstruction).

19. Ibid., plate 19, p. 29.

20. Ibid., 29.

21. Ibid., 30.

22. Ibid., 32.

23. Immanuel Kant, *Critique of Judgment*, trans. Werner S. Pluhar (Indianapolis: Hackett, 1987), 120.

24. Neil Hertz has two essays on the sublime in his *The End of the Line* (New York: Columbia University Press, 1985). These are, to my mind, crucial for understanding the role of the sublime in the everyday life of modernity, including, of course, in understanding the place of photography.

25. Ibid., 30.

26. For an exposition of the jihad, or holy war, as it was understood in Atjeh during the anticolonial war, see James T. Siegel, *Shadow and Sound: The Historical Thought of a Sumatran People* (Chicago: University of Chicago Press, 1979), 229–65, and James T. Siegel, *The Rope of God* (1969; Ann Arbor: University of Michigan Press, 2000), 68–77. For a discussion of the continuation of the jihad by individuals, see Siegel, *The Rope of God*, 82ff.

27. The text referred to can be found in translation in Siegel, *Shadow and Sound*.

28. Rob Nieuwenhuys, *Met vreemde ogen: Tempo doeloe—een verzonken wereld; fotografische documenten uit het oude Indië 1870–1920* (Amsterdam: Querido, 1988), 149.

29. Ibid., 163.

5. THE HYPNOTIST

1. The material on which this essay is based can be found in James T. Siegel et al., "Notes on a Trip to Aceh," Indonesia 86 (October 2008), 1–54. In December and January 2010, I made a second trip to Meulaboh with Arief Djati, considerably supplementing earlier information. I want to make clear my deep debt to my two companions, through whose minds these remarks were filtered. And I want also to thank Mercedes Chavez, who generously made her experience in Aceh available to me.

I owe a great debt to Samuel Weber. I attended his seminar on the uncanny at Northwestern University, in which the necessity for there to be an uncanny was raised. I took this idea with me to Meulaboh in 2009. His paper "A Different Partition," so far unpublished, takes Derrida's remarks on the necessity of separating life and death and the means of doing so and scrutinizes them in ways that inflected the view I had formulated of the coexistence of the living and the dead, life and death, in Aceh at this moment (2010).

2. A description of the place of death in the heartland of Aceh and of domestic arrangements can be found in James T. Siegel, *The Rope of God*, 2d ed. (Ann Arbor: University of Michigan Press, 2001), 137–99

3. See my "Dreams, Curing Rites, and Domestic Politics in a Sumatran Society," *Glyph* 3 (1978), republished as an appendix to the second edition of *The Rope of God*.

4. For an interesting account of the opposite reaction after another Indonesian disaster, see Nils Bubandt, "Ghosts with Trauma: Global Imaginaries and the Politics of Post-Conflict," in *Conflict, Violence, and Displacement in Indonesia*, ed. Eva-Lotta Hedman (Ithaca: Cornell Southeast Asia Program Publications, 2008), 275–301.

5. One explanation given for the lack of ghosts is that those struck by the tsunami were innocent or pure (*suci*). They died, it is said, the deaths of martyrs. They were not resentful (*penasaran*), so no one need be afraid of them. And they had no unfilled desires (see below).

6. In fact, I have condensed the complicated sequence of the ritual almost to the point of distortion. The sick woman does not consume the offering. It is simply put out on the occasion of a ritual feast, where the ghost apparently participates. Just how remains vague to everyone, but the presence of actual bodies, consuming ritual food, seems necessary. A fuller account is given in Siegel, *The Rope of God*.

7. Ibid.

8. The spelling of Acehnese today is not standardized. I use the orthography of the major dictionary of Acehnese, Hoesein Djajadiningrat's *Atjèhsch-Nederlandsch Woordenboek* (Batavia: Landsdrukkerij, 1934), 2 vols. After independence, not only was the value of certain letters of Acehnese orthography changed, rejecting Dutch conventions, but different people began to spell differently. Short of standardization, the most convenient usage remains that of Djajadiningrat, particularly since his dictionary is excellent. However, it is not possible always to do so: for instance, in the word *Atjèh* in his spelling and in its contemporary usage, *Aceh*. I hope any confusion will be reduced, if only slightly, by this method. Indonesian, by contrast, modernized Dutch spelling and standardized it at the same time. This marks a general difference in regard to the colonial past. It is rejected nationally. Nonetheless, Dutch practice still underlies Indonesian but not Acehnese, as one sees from the difficulty of tracing present Acehnese linguistic practices back to the usage of colonial times. There has

been no effective replacement of Dutch authority by Acehnese; only rejection of the former. Acehnese does not pass through a colonial filter. It is as though the language of precolonial times still lives and changes with the times outside political authority of whatever sort. The pull of this language is less mediated as a result. But, when it is spoken today in the capital, the language has also been modified, losing the rhythms of village speech and of Acehnese literature. One has to remark also that Acehnese as a regional language is largely ignored by the national government, as are most regional languages except Javanese.

9. See Claude Guillot, "Urban Patterns and Polities in Malay Trading Cities, Fifteenth through Seventeenth Centuries," *Indonesia* 80 (October 2005): 39–51.

10. The word *trauma* became widely used during the Suharto period, probably for political reasons. See James T. Siegel, *A New Criminal Type in Jakarta: Counter-Revolution Today* (Durham, N.C.: Duke University Press, 1998). The word has remained in the Indonesian vocabulary, meaning that one has been shaken by an event. It thus has little to do with trauma as discussed here.

6. "TOUT AUTRE EST TOUT AUTRE"

1. Louis Dumont, "Non au Musée des arts premiers," *Le Monde*, October 25, 1996.

2. Ibid.

3. Jean Jamin, "Faut-il brûler les musées d'ethnographie?" *Gradhiva* 24 (1990): 65–69.

4. President Chirac's speech can be found on the French government website: Discours prononcé par M. Jacques CHIRAC Président de la République lors de l'inauguration du pavillon des Sessions au musée du Louvre (Paris) http://www.elysee.fr/elysee/elysee.fr/francais/interventions/discours_et_declarations.

5. For an English-language account of the sources of the collections in the Quai Branly, see Sally Price, *Paris Primitive: Jacques Chirac's Museum on the Quai Branly* (Chicago: University of Chicago Press, 2007), 81–110. For an account of the war between ethnographers and their opponents told from the point of view of the first, see Bernard Dupaigne, *Le scandale des arts premiers: La veritable histoire du Musée du Quai Branly* (Paris: Mille et une nuits, 2006).

6. This happened earlier in America than in France. See William Sturtevant, who decades ago complained that anthropologists (Americans) were making no use of the extensive collections stored in museums. William C. Sturtevant, "Does Anthropology Need Museums?" in *Natural History Collections: Past, Present, Future*, ed. Daniel M. Cohen and Robert F. Cheney, *Proceedings of the Biological Society of Washington* 82 (November 1969): 619–45

7. The director of the museum, in an interview, noted that ethnographic museums "often have the weakness of presenting contemporary productions indiscriminately." He continued, "They do not take into account that, by not

taking into account the universal rules, good or bad, of contemporary art, they exclude themselves from its cultural stakes." Aesthetic value takes precedence. People who objects do not count in "cultural stakes" and will not find themselves on display in museums. He gave as an example contemporary Inuit art, which is never exhibited in the same locations as Andy Warhol or Yinka Shonibare, who were celebrated at the Venice Biennial ("Un musée pas comme les autres: Entretien avec Stéphane Martin," *Le Debat*, no. 147 (November-December 2007): 5–22.

8. Benoît de Éstoile, *Le goût des autres: De l'exposition coloniale aux arts premiers* (Paris: Flammarion, 2007).

9. Ibid., 213, citing Krystoff Pomian.

10. William Sturtevant long ago pointed out that the early history of ethnography was independent of collections. The objects from the cabinets of curiosities were not the basis for it. Rather, "the development of ethnology . . . grew instead out of written collections of customs—compendia from travelers' accounts and from classical literature of such things as religious customs and marriage customs—a different kind of collecting" ("Does Anthropology Need Museums?" But, as he also points out, the development of museum collecting and the development of ethnology were simultaneous, leaving objects important. The situation in France was different from the United States. The French museum was a much more important site of ethnological research. Moreover, objects put on public display, available for direct inspection, even though accompanied by ethnographic information, allowed for a popular understanding of cultures, which could be quite different from that of ethnographers. In particular, the idea of the savage (a word less ambiguous in English than in French) remained lodged in popular mentality. Making the provenance of these objects national rather than tribal would presumably cleanse them of this association.

11. Rolande Bonnain, *L'empire des masques: Les collectionners d'arts premiers aujourd'hui* (Paris: Stock, 2001). For the history of the Trocadéro Museum, see Nélia Dias, *Le Musée d'ethnographie du Trocadéro, 1878–1908: Anthropologie et muséologie en France* (Paris: Éditions du CNRS, 1990).

12. Jean Jamin, "*Documents* et le reste . . . De l'anthropologie dans les bas-fonds, *La Revue des Revues*, no. 18:15–22.

13. According to Rivet, the Trocadéro, the ethnology museum Rivet headed, the predecessor of the Musée de l'homme, "could become a beaux-arts museum, its objects grouped together under the aegis of a single aesthetic. A poor principle, which in truth would end in upsetting the picture" that ethnography gives. The result would be a chance collection of objects ("Le Musée d'ethnographie du Trocadéro," *Documents* 1 [1929; reissued in facsimile by Jean-Michel Place, 1991], 54–58).

14. De l'Éstoile, *Le goût des autres*, 49.

15. Michel Leiris, from the essay "La crise négre dans le monde occidental," in *Afrique noire: La création plastique* (Paris: Gallimard, 1967); republished in

Leiris, *Miroir de l'Afrique*, ed. Jean Jamin (Paris: Gallimard, 1996), 1139. Jamin characterizes Leiris's approach here as introducing African objects as art not by a priori positing an equivalence of them with Western art objects as verified by their use by Western artists but by showing their own African aesthetic ("Presentation" of *Afrique noire* in *Mirror de l'Afrique*).

16. Franz Boas described Northwest Coast Indian objects in a similar way. See Boas, *Primitive Art* (Cambridge: Harvard University Press, 1927).

17. De l'Éstoile, *Le goût des autres*, 54, quoting the *Report general* of the Exposition. Rodolphe Gasché stresses in *The Idea of Form* that the idea of beauty arises for Kant primarily out of nature, that is, out of the undefined wilds (Stanford: Stanford University Press, 2003), 1–41.

18. Rivet quoted in Jamin, "*Documents* et le reste."

19. Apollinaire too was concerned about rising prices. France was being left out, as German conservators had funds available: "Fetishes sold for a louis five or six years ago are today regarded as extremely precious objects. . . . It is time for France, whose extremely varied colonies are so rich in works of art, to save the rest of exotic civilizations." He suggested a new museum, the equivalent of the Louvre—which was, finally, the idea that prevailed nearly a century later ("Exotisme et Ethnographie," *Oeuvres en prose completes*, ed. Pierre Caizergues and Michel Décadin [1912; Paris: Gallimard, 1991], 2:254–87).

20. For Kerchache and his role in placing *arts premiers* in the Louvre and the Quai Branly, see Raymond Corbey, "*Arts Premiers* in the Louvre," *Anthropology Today*, 16, no. 4 (August 2000): 3–6, and Price, *Paris Primitive*, 33–65.

21. Anthony Appiah, *Cosmopolitanism: Ethics in a World of Strangers* (New York: W. W. Norton, 2006), 119. Appiah adds that the Nok could, nonetheless, as a culture rather than a people, have descendents. Even so, "If Nok civilization came to an end and its people became something else, why should those descendants have a special claim on those objects, buried in the forest and forgotten for so long? And, even if they do have a special claim, what has that got to do with Nigeria, where, let us suppose, a majority of those descendants now live?" (120). For another extended discussion of this issue, see James Cuno, *Who Owns Antiquity? Museums and the Battle over Our Ancient Heritage* (Princeton: Princeton University Press, 2008), esp. chap. 5, "Identity Matters," 121–45. I am indebted to Magnus Fiskesjö for bringing this book to my attention.

22. In part, too, because along with this it became harder to conceive how to present cultures. According to Benoit de l'Éstoile, the last exhibits were, for instance, influenced by formats derived from popular media. The ethnography museum died in the first place from indifference—the indifference of the state, which was parsimonious in the final years, and the indifference of the public. In 2001 the Musée de l'Homme had only 110,000 visitors, half of two years earlier. Although it had been part of the avant garde when it opened, the sections remaining from that time seemed out of date, while the renewed galleries became an "anachronism," according to Benoit de l'Éstoile (204).

23. Aminata Traoré concluded her letter by apostrophizing the objects of the museum: "I would like to address once more these works of the spirit that will know [*sauront*] how to intercede with public opinion for us. We miss you terribly. Our countries, Mali and the entire African continent, have suffered upheavals. The god of money has been added to the Christian and Muslim gods who contest your place in our hearts and your functions in our societies. You must know something of the transactions that have brought certain new acquisitions to this museum. It is the driving force of the market called 'free' and competitive, which is supposed to be paradise on earth, when it has only brought the abyss to Africa. . . . Do you not hear more and more lamentations of those who have taken the terrestrial path, losing themselves in the Sahara or drowning themselves in the waters of the Mediterranean? . . . If so, do not stay silent and do not feel yourselves to be impotent. Be the voice of your peoples and witness for them. Remind those who want you so much in their museums and French and European citizens who visit them that the total and immediate annulling of the external debt of Africa is primordial" ("Musée du Quai Branly: Une lettre d'Aminata Traoré," Corinne Perron, June 29, 2006, http://www.ust ke.org/syndicat/2006/06/29/211-musee-du-quai-branly-une-lettre-d-aminata-traore). See also her "Lettre au Président des Français à propos de la Côte d'Ivoire et de l'Afrique en général," Aminata Traoré (Fayard, Paris, 2005), Traoré speaks for "our countries, Mali and the entire African continent" as the aggrieved parties rather than those of the collectivities of the time. It makes one wonder in what capacity she apostrophizes the objects. Is it in the manner of those who made them and for whom they were often religious or ritual objects, or is it as a literary figure of today?

24. Georges Bataille, "Musee," *Documents* (1930), 300.

25. Ibid.

26. Ibid. "Deep communion" with objects is much less in evidence in museums today, where ubiquitous cameras have replaced eyes. But Bataille's observation is not out of date. Taking pictures rather than looking also acknowledges the pull of the objects—for whatever reason, but not excluding the savagery within beauty even if it is now mediated by a culture of celebrity and market value.

27. Ibid.

28. Nélia Dias, "Le musée du Quai Branly: Une géneologie," *Le Debat*, no. 147 (November-December 2007): 65—79.

29. De l'Éstoile, *Le goût des autres*, 254–87; Apollinaire, "Exotisme et Ethnographie."

30. Witness the appointment of Rachida Dati, a woman of Mahgrebian descent, as minister of justice. This ministry administers deportation quotas, often enough through illegal maneuvers.

31. It is in their quality as part of a heritage rather than, with certain exceptions (such as Aminata Taoré, to a certain extent), as magical or religious objects

that the objects of the Quai Branly are reclaimed by nations where their provenance is found. Controversies over ownership mark the formulation of national identity, and in that capacity they become objects of political controversy. One of the arguments against returning the objects is that the recipient nations do not have the means to keep them. This is often euphemistic, masking the well-known fact of major theft and resale of returned objects. This is not, of course, because Africans do not value them, but because they understand their value. Their actions mirror the close relation between the market and the museum in Europe. There is, indeed, a world market. Not only was the idea of the Quai Branly conceived by an art merchant, but there were also four major auctions of art in Paris of the type displayed on the occasion of the museum's opening.

One wonders if the same sort of claims would have been made had the objects remained in the Musée de l'Homme. Perhaps. But with some exceptions the objects are not reclaimed because of religious or magical value but for their place in a "patrimony," a term much more closely tied to their value as commodities. Ethnological value remains use value. It is less vulnerable but by no means immune to being exchanged in the market. The "patrimonies" of nations have long been filled with booty turned into commodities. The very attempt of the French state to conceal the magical use of so many of these objects by substituting transcendent beauty as their important attribute raises disputes about ownership easily resolvable were it a question of religious or magical artifacts whose use is particular to certain peoples. It is an open question whether the objects of the Quai Branly have been cleansed of their magic.

32. Jean-Paul Sartre, "Orphée Noir," in Léopold Sédar-Senghor, *Anthologie de la nouvelle poésie nègre et malagache de langue française* (Paris: Presses Universitaires de France, 1948), ix.

33. Denis Hollier, "La valeur d'usage de l'impossible," in *Les dépossédés* (Paris: Minuit, 1993; republished from the introduction to the republication of *Documents* [Paris: Jean-Michel Place, 1992], vol. 1).

34. James Clifford points out that the ethnographic object could shock in the same way as the surrealists' productions. This, according to Clifford, is by abandoning the difference between high and low culture. One could show an object to be valuable (worth seeing, even unavoidable) that had until then been thought mundane. Apparently the very display was enough to achieve this effect(James Clifford, *The Predicament of Culture: Twentieth-Century Ethnography, Literature, and Art*, (Cambridge: Harvard University Press, 1988), 117–51.

35. Georges Bataille, "Les Pieds Nickelés," *Documents* 2 (1930): 215–16.

36. "At the present moment, ethnography must be nothing other than comparative. In the beginning it is useful and even indispensable to give minute and complete descriptions of collections, to draw up inventories, and to accumulate conscientiously catalogued documents" (P. Rivet, "L'étude des civilizations matérielles: Ethnographie, archéologie, préhistoire," *Documents* 1 [1929]: 130–34). The document here begins as possibly unique and ends up being one of a type. The reduction of singularity rather than its use seems to have been the aim.

37. Entry of October 31, 1931, apparently made in Upper Volta (Leiris, *Miroir d'Afrique*, 233).

38. Entry of September 27, 1931, in Leiris, *Miroir d'Afrique*, 211.

39. This is how Samuel Weber interprets the magical language posited by Walter Benjamin in "On Language as Such and on the Language of Man," in Weber, *Benjamin's –abilities* (Cambridge: Harvard University Press, 2008). Weber's interpretation of Benjamin yields a Benjamin quite different from the one on whom Anglophone readers have concentrated. Following this further would probably expand the issues discussed here in fruitful new directions.

40. Jacques Derrida, *The Animal That Therefore I Am* (New York, Fordham University Press, 2008), 3–4.

41. Ibid., 5–6.

42. Ibid., 4.

43. Ibid., 6.

44. Ibid., 13.

45. Ibid., 50.

46. Ibid., 30.

47. Ibid., 9.

48. Ibid., 5–6.

49. One has then to ask what became of the uncanny. How is it that the appearance of the totally other occurs without it? I cannot say, except that it may mark our epoch, one that differs in important ways from the time after each of the world wars. It is not that the possibility of total destruction, which occupied the minds of people then, is not present now. But its terms are different. "We," the peoples of the industrialized world, are responsible for its coming, regardless of national identity. We cannot blame this destruction on an enemy unless we turn against ourselves. The reflection of such destruction in the totally other then disappears. Uncanny moments are then not magnified into social fears.

50. These regulations were posted on Velib' bicycles in December, 2007, with the title "Be careful on the bike." They tell the cyclist who encounters a heavy vehicle how to proceed. The other regulations are "Never stop under their rear-view mirrors or at their level"; "Do not pass a truck on the right"; "Do not try to pass a maneuvering truck, neither on the left nor on the right and particularly at the approach of an intersection"; "Stay easily visible at night and when it is gray by furnishing yourself with reflecting equipment." It is worth noting that the rules apply to bicycling "in Paris." Specifying the place implies the particularities of bicycling in that city. One might do otherwise elsewhere.

The neologism *Velib'* is a compound of *velo*, short for velocipede or bicycle, and *libre* or perhaps *liberté*. The apostrophe at the end indicates the abbreviation. But the apostrophe is seldom used in French. The last time it appeared in a popular context was in the word *pin's* for the lapel pins at that time in fashion. In that case the apostrophe, suggesting the genitive in English, though it was not so used, simply marked the word as English brought into French. The apostrophe in this case, having no grammatical significance, is a sign that marks nothing, unless, as with "pin's," it shows that this is a new word, thus open to various interpretations. It thus functions like an ellipsis, suggesting that the user can fill in the word with his own understanding. The extravagance of using a sacred political term for riding the bicycle seems to multiply this function.

51. Communication from the Mayor 's Office of Paris: "Assurez-vous que vous pouvez être vus, notamment le soir, par les conducteurs." This brochure notes that 90 people sixty years of age or older were severely injured and 14 killed in 2006, while 403 were lightly injured. Of these accidents, 5 percent were with bicycles. "SENIORS be careful crossing the street!"

52. Miladus Doueihei, *Le paradise terrestre* (Paris: Seuil, 2006), 149–61

53. , "10 millions: nombre de locations de Vélib' à Paris depuis le 15 juillet." Headline of an article in Le Monde for November 22, 2007. According to the brochure quoted above, there are nearly one hundred thousand rentals a day in a city of about two million.

54. See the book of Marc Augé, *Éloge de la bicyclette* (Paris: Payot et Rivage, 2008) in which is sketched the history of the place of the bicycle in French life, from an instrument of the working class to its recrudescence today as a factor in the environment.

55. Here I am indebted to Samuel Weber for his explication of the passages on the uncanny in this book in his seminar on the uncanny at Northwestern University in Spring 2009. "[The uncanny] is the terrible in the sense of the overwhelming sway, which induces panicked fear, true anxiety, as well as collected, inwardly reverberating, reticent awe. The violent, the overwhelming is the essential character of the sway itself" (Martin Heidegger, *Introduction to Metaphysics*, trans. Gregory Fried and Richard Polt [New Haven: Yale University Press, 2000], 159–60. Heidegger goes on to say that the uncanny is not an "impression left on emotional states" but being thrown out of the familiar (161). Derrida, so far as we are told, remains in the bathroom thinking of other philosophers. It seems to me that thinking always removes one from one's surroundings. There is nothing particularly uncanny, then, about the encounter with that singular cat. Someone else, in another time, however, might have resolved the encounter by calling that cat uncanny.

56. This is apparently the famous early lexicographer; cited in Wahid "Abdulssalâm Bâli," *Le sabre tranchant: Contre les magiciens méchants*, trans. Zahia Beddek (Al-Maktaba Al-Ilmiya, n.d., n.p.)

57. G. W. F. Hegel, *Lectures on The Philosophy of History*, trans. J. W. Sibree (London: George Bell and Sons, 1902), 94. Cf. this sentence from Hegel's *Introduction to Lectures on World History*, trans. H. Nisbet (Cambridge: Cambridge University Press, 1975), 175: "But although these natural forces . . . are recognized as powers in their own right, they are not seen as forming part of a universal and permanent natural order."

58. Hegel, *Lectures on the Philosophy of History*, 97.

ACKNOWLEDGMENTS

Many people contributed to these essays. They are named in each piece but I want to reiterate my gratitude. I want to thank Michael Meeker, Rosalind Morris, and Danilyn Rutherford for their help with the book as a whole. As usual or, I dare to say, "as always," I am happily indebted to Anne Berger. Helen Tartar has excellent judgment in editorial matters. In this case, her opinions were infallibly on the mark. I much benefited.

I dedicate this collection to Saranya Sweet Siegel-Berger, the nature of whose help I cannot specify, all the while knowing it to be essential.

The Cornell Southeast Asia Program and the Andrew W. Mellon Foundation helped fund my work. I thank them very much.

ORIGINAL PUBLICATION

"The Reappearance of Georg Simmel: 'The Aesthetic Appearance of the Face.'" *Diacritics*, 29, no. 2 (Summer 1999): 100–13.

"Academic Work: The View from Cornell." *Diacritics* 11, no. 1 (Spring 1981): 68–83.

"Kiblat and the Mediatic Jew." *Indonesia*, no. 69 (April, 2000): 9–40.

"The Curse of the Photograph: Atjeh 1901." *Indonesia*, no. 80 (October 2005): 21–38.

"Tout autre est tout autre" appears here for the first time, as does "The Hypnotist."